D1723819

	10		11		12	
ce or People.	*Last Permanent Residence.		The name and complete address of nearest relative or friend in country whence alien came.		Final Destination.	
	Country.	City or Town.			State.	City or Town.
ith	Italy	Torria	Wife Maria - Torria		NY	Oswe
"	"	"	Father Antonio "		Pa	Lub
"			Wife Angela			
"	"	"	Wife Lucenza "		"	"
			Father Raymond		Nj	
"	"	Ceriano	Wife Rosa - Ceriano		NY	Nea
		Torria	Wife Carmen Torria			
"		Torria	Wife Rosier - Torria		"	Edwa
"	"	Alessandri	Father Vito Alessandri		Ill	Chica
X	"	Cogiano	Wife Antonia Cogiano		NY	
			Father Felia "		N Br...	
					NY	
"	"	"	Father Giovanni		Nj	Paus
"	"	Montemarano	Mother Rosa Montemarano		NY	
"	"	Quaglietta	Wife Carmela Quagliatta		N	
"	"	"	Father Carmine "		NY	Paus
"	"	Avellino	Wife Emilia - Avellino		"	
"	"	Montemarano	Father Giovanni Montemarano			
			Father Yousef			

WESTFIELD, MASS.
JANUARY 27, 1995

Dear Hans,

I HOPE THAT THIS BOOK WILL HELP YOU IN YOUR STUDIES. THAT IT WILL GIVE YOU AN INSIGHT INTO THE PEOPLE WHO CAME TO AMERICA FROM EUROPE AND OTHER COUNTRIES.

WHEN WE WERE WITH YOU (IRENE & GERHARDT) AT ELLIS ISLAND AND THE STATUE OF LIBERTY IN JUNE 1994, I CANNOT EXPRESS TO YOU, MY EMOTIONS, KNOWING THAT MY MOTHER & FATHER CAME FROM LITHUANIA IN 1906 AND THAT THEY PASSED THROUGH THIS PLACE.

ENJOY READING AND LEARNING ABOUT THIS PART OF AMERICAN HISTORY AND AS YOU READ THINK OF US.

SINCERELY, YOUR FRIEND
WALTER SAMNELL

THE ELLIS ISLAND SOURCE BOOK

Second Edition

August C. Bolino

The Catholic University of America

Kensington Historical Press

Box 1314   Cardinal Station

Washington, D. C. 20064

ISBN No. 0-939133-03-2

Printed in the United States of America

by
Thompson-Shore, Inc.
Dexter, Michigan

To my Parents,

Nicholas (1893-1989) and Rose Bolino (1901-1983),

who passed through

Ellis Island in 1910 and 1919

Other Books by August C. Bolino

A Century of Human Capital by Education and Training (1989)

The Watchmakers of Massachusetts (1987)

The Ellis Island Source Book (1985)

Career Education: Contributions to Economic Growth (1973)

Manpower and the City (1969)

The Development of the American Economy (1966)

The Development of the American Economy (1961)

FOREWORD

Ellis Island and the nearby Statue of Liberty are enduring symbols of freedom and opportunity for most Americans. Professor August Bolino has written a thoroughly reseached and interesting account of the Ellis Island immigration story, the decline and deterioration era, and the beginnings of the restoration process.

Since 1965, the National Park Service has been involved in the effort to halt the deterioration of the structures and buildings on Ellis Island. A companion objective has been to have the island available for public enjoyment, education and inspiration. Many individuals and organizations have assisted through the years, but one person deserving of special commendation is Mr. Philip Lax, who has devoted years of effort in this cause.

Many first and second generation descendants of families that entered a new life in the United States though Ellis Island were the catalyst for this historical preservation initiative. Congress authorized the Ellis Island National Historic Site in 1965. Now a joint effort by the National Park Service, Statue Liberty/Ellis Island Centennial Commission and Foundation, and the people of the United States appears well on the way to achieving the earlier dream of saving the historic qualities of Ellis Island. The cost is enormous but Americans are responding and contributing generously. Particular emphasis is being given to the Great Hall, a focal point of the immigrant entry experience, with its emotional impact and associated memories. The selected date for overall completion of the Ellis Island plan is 1992, the centennial year.

The interesting and intriguing story of Ellis Island by Professor Bolino is essentially a tribute to the diverse ethnic and national origins of all Americans. It is a reminder of opportunity, courage, and the will to overcome adversity, all essential ingredients in the American experience.

Russell E. Dickenson
Director, National Park Service
December 1984

PREFACE

Twenty five years before "Roots," I started compiling a family history that took me to Ellis Island and foreign places, so that by the time of the American Bicentennial I was an avid student of immigration and ethnicity. This interest led to my association with the Ellis Island Restoration Commission and my election in 1978 as Vice President for Research. In this capacity, I studied the possible uses for the Island and I became convinced that it was a natural place for a museum, ethnic rooms and a research center. I outlined a ten-year plan and I concentrated on the research aspects: I made an inventory of all leading archives, museums and libraries in the United States to locate Ellis Island documents. My belief in the need for a research center strengthened, and I began to publicize my plan to create a research facility on Ellis Island. This plan came to the attention of Congresman Edward Koch He submitted a joint resolution to the Congress which provided that the original authorization for $6 million be increased to $37 million. When Koch was elected Mayor of New York City he turned the resolution over to his friend, Congressman Jonathan Bingham, also of New York. The Koch-Bingham resolution attempted to increase the authorization to $50 million to rehabilitate Ellis Island.

Although the Congress did not pass the Koch-Bingham resolution, it did authorize an additional $24 million for restoration in October, 1978. When President Carter signed this law, the National Park Service designated a planning team to draw a master plan.

Philip Lax, President of the Ellis Island Restoration Commission, was appointed to this team. The Commission drafted a cooperative agreement with the National Park Service to designate it as the chief private consulting and advisory commission in the restoration of the Island. This agreement was signed in December 1980.

As vice president for research of the Ellis Island Restoration Commission, I assisted the National Park Service in its planning activities. Between June and September 1979, I visited several major cities, having large ethnic compositions: Pittsburgh, Cleveland, Detroit,

Ann Arbor, Minneapolis, Boston, Philadelphia, New York, Wilmington, and Baltimore. I talked to immigration historians, demographers, ethnic historians, folklorists, archivists, and museum curators.

The purpose of this travel was to locate Ellis Island materials, to learn how many oral histories involved Ellis Island survivors, and to obtain the views of historians, ethnographers and ethnic organizations on the plans for the Island. The following summer I continued this research on the sources of information about Ellis Island, and in 1981, I agreed to prepare a manuscript on this subject for the National Park Service.

This "Source Book" is an attempt to put in one place as much as is known (or as much as I have learned in seven years) about Ellis Island. It gathers all existing information pertaining to the history of the Island, and the Ellis Island experience. I have benefited greatly from the work of my predecessors at the National Park Service. Dr. Thomas Pitkin's report, "Ellis Island as an Immigration Depot," was published in 1975 by the New York University Press as *Keepers of the Gate: A History of Ellis Island.* This volume is the most comprehensive history of the Island, with emphasis on the Commissioners of the Island. Tedd McCann was leader of the planning team which produced the 1978 report "The Ellis Island Story"--a complete treatment on the current state of the Island. Finally, Harlan D. UnraupM prepared a massive document on all historical aspects of the Island's structures. This "Historic Structures Report" was published by the National Park service in May 1981.

The words of Unrau are particularly apt in describing the state of Ellis Island research: "No further research needs to be done relative to the history of the structures on Ellis Island." But he added, "Some topics deserve further amplification." These include:

"Treatment of the immigrant on Ellis Island (i.e., dormitory facilities, diet, hospital care, registration system, etc.).

Collection, summary and significance of reminiscences of Ellis

Island by immigrants (i.e., printed, published, taped, and oral reminiscences).

Ellis Island as a deportation center.

Ellis Island as a wartime military installation and hospital (i.e., World Wars I and II).

The relationship of the developments at Ellis Island to the formulation of American immigration policy--1900-1954."

This "Source Book" attempts to deal with some of these deficiencies. It has three objectives: (1) cover the history of the growth and decay of the Island itself; (2) to deal with all of the restoration efforts and (3) to present the most complete list of sources about the place and the people, including a 112 page bibliography.

During the 64 turbulent years when Ellis Island served as an immigration station, nearly 16 million persons were recorded as having passed through the great hall. Although this count is probably understated, this was the greatest migration in world history. It is a magnificent chapter in the history of the United States, and the story needs to be preserved for all generations to know and understand. While Ellis Island is considered a "portal of hope," is also known as the "isle of tears," as families were split up and the sick returned to their native countries.

This story of joy and sorrow is preserved in memories of survivors, in the documents in museums, in the official papers of the Island, and in the ethnic festivals that dot our land, mostly in the summers. This record of Ellis Island is the subject of the pages that follow.

PREFACE TO SECOND EDITION

The second *Ellis Island Source Book* is expanded and revised. There are three new chapters. The first, "Immigrant Arrivals and Departures," asks Why did they come, Where did they go, and how many returned from whence they came? The second new chapter, "Some People Who Worked There," offers brief biographical sketches of employees and volunteers. It presents some first-person accounts of life on the Island, drawn from letters and writings. The last of the new chapters, "The Ellis Island Hall of Fame," deals with the Ellis Island experience of the famous and not-so-famous. The famous include persons in art and architecture, business, entertainment, labor, law, music, religion, sports and science. The chapter concludes with four stories of plain Americans, their journeys to Ellis Island and their experiences there.

An addition, Chapter II adds a new section on "The Coast Guard on Ellis Island," based on a very scarce book of the same title, which a friend generously loaned to me. It fills in a major gap of Ellis Island history.

Part II of the original volume, "The Beginnings of Restoration," (Chapters IV and V) has been completely rewritten to reflect all the progress made by the Statue of Liberty-Ellis Island Presidential Commission and the Ellis Island Restoration since 1985.

Finally, a new section, "Additional Bibliography," is added to the Appendix.

August C. Bolino
September 1990

ACKNOWLEDGEMENTS

I have learned much from persons in many places, and I should like to acknowledge this help now. To avoid any bias, I list their names alphabetically: Professor Dan Ben Amos, University of Pennsylvania; Professor Karl Bonutti, Cleveland State University; Professor Dominic Candeloro of Governor's State University, Illinois; Judge Nicholas Cipriani, Pennsylvania Fraternal Congress; Professor Charles Cubelic, Robert Morris College, Pittsburgh; Professor Otto Feinstein, Wayne State University; Elsie Freifogel, National Archives and Records Service; Dr. Annette Fromm, Cleveland Ethnographic Museum; Professor Nathan Glazer; Harvard University; Professor Ira Glazier, Temple University; Dr. John Grabowski, Western Reserve Historical Society; Professor John Higham, Johns Hopkins University; Dr. Mary Ann Johnson, Hull House, Chicago; Professor Richard Juliani, Villanova University; Betty M. Key, Maryland Historical Society; Dr. Vitaut Kipel, New York Public Library; Dr. Kenneth Kovach, Ohio Historical Society; Dr. John Kromkowski, National Center for Urban and Ethnic Affairs, Washington, D.C.; Professor Janet Langlois, Wayne State University; Irvine M. Levine, Institute on Pluralism and Group Identity; Reid Lewis, American Council for Nationalities Service, New York City; Professor Marion Marzolf, University of Michigan, Dr. William Moss, John E. Kennedy Library, Boston; Dr. Ann Orlov; Harvard Ethnic Encyclopedia; Peter Parker, Historical Society of Pennsylvania; Rev. Gianfausto Rosoli, Centro Studi Emigrazione di Roma; David Roth, American Jewish Committee; Professor Vincenze Scarpaci, formerly of Towson State University; Dr. M. Mark Stolarik, Balch Institute, Philadelphia; Lucretia Stoica, The Nationalities Service Center, Cleveland; Deborah Stultz, Minneapolis Ethnic History Project; Rev. Lydio Tomasi, Center for Migration Studies, Staten Island; Professor Rudolph Vecoli, Immigration History Research Center; St. Paul; Dr. Robert Warner; former Director, Bentley Historical Library, now Archivist of the United States; Dr. Bernard Wax, American Jewish Historical Society; Dr. Paul Weinbaum, American Museum of Immigration; and Dr. Frank Zabrosky, Archives of Industrial Society, University of Pittsburgh.

It is appropriate also that I acknowledge the contribution of what was originally called "The Washington Group." When it first began meeting in early 1977, it included Meyer Fishbein, then of the National Archives; Professor Richard Kolm, a colleague of Catholic University of America and Edward S. Yambrusic, a Canadian who was active in local ethnic affairs. The group was expanded later to include Helaine Cohen; Elena Bradunas, of the Library of Congress, and Susan Kalcik, of the Smithsonian Institution. These persons offered excellent guidance in my pursuit of Ellis Island information.

Countless other persons helped with their letters and their phone calls. I can't list them all, but I would like to single out those few persons who made my way easier. I thank Ross Holland, former Chief of Cultural Resources Management for the National Park Service, now with the Statue of Liberty Ellis Island Foundation, and Philip Lax, President of the Ellis Island Restoration Commission for giving me this opportunity to work on this labor love. I thank also the librarians of the Catholic University of America who never tired of my constant demands for interlibrary loans, Mr. Sten Sture Nordin, of the Ellis Island Heritage Institute, who was very supportive, and I salute the entire Staff of the National Park Service, who welcomed me graciously when I intruded repeatedly into their normal affairs.

Finally, I must give special thanks to the directors of the Ellis Island Restoration Commission, who contributed much towards the publication of this book.

Professor August C. Bolino
March, 1985

Acknowledgements to Second Edition

I must, again, thank all the consultants at the Catholic University Computer Center for laboring much to make my word processing way easier, especially, Betsy Pohlhaus; Mary Mastroianni, who perfected all programs and cleaned up the manuscript for publication; Special thanks go to Richard Levenson, of D'Arcy, Masius, Benton & Bowles, and his staff who donated much time and effort; Andersen Consulting, the General Contractor for the Family

History Center;

Special thanks, also, to certain members of the Ellis Island Restoration Commission: the Technical Committee of the Ellis Island Restoration Commission, Dr. Ira Glazier, Meyer Fishbein, Elder Richard Scott, James Dent Walker; and consultants Dennis Shasha and Robert Warren; Norman Liss, Chairman of Fund Raising and Development; Set Momjian, Chairman of Ethnic Affairs.

Finally, we are grateful to Cliff Robertson for producing a public service announcement of the Family History Center.

ELLIS   ISLAND   RESTORATION   COMMISSION,   INC.
MEMBERS

President:

Philip Lax
President,Chathill Management Co., Inc.,
830 Morris Turnpike,
Short Hills, NJ 07040

Vice-Presidents:

Dr. August Bolino
Catholic University of America
Washington, D. C. 20064

Norman Liss, Esq,
200 West 57th Street,
New York, New York 10019

Set Charles Momjian
Ford Aero Space
1235 Jefferson David Highway, Suite 1300
Arlington, VA 22202

Secretary:

Dr. Francis P. McQuade
Seton Hall University Law School,
2 Burnett Street,
Maplewood, NJ 07040

1775 Grand Concourse,
Bronx, New York 10453

Maryland Historical Society,
8944 Madison Street,
Savage, MD 20763

Zachary Fisher
Fisher Brothers,
299 Park Avenue,
42nd Floor,
New York, New York 10017

Meyer Fishbein
Retired Director,
Military Archives of the
United States,
5005 Elsmere Avenue,
Bethesda, MD 20814

Hon. Louis Fusco,
Justice of Supreme Court,
851 Grand Concourse
Bronx, NY 10451

Rosemarie Gallina
Assistant to the Governor
for Ethnic Relations,
Two World Trade Center,
New York, New York 10047

Dr. Ira Glazier
Director,
Temple Balch Center
for Immigration Research,
18 South 7th Street,
Philadelphia, Pa 19196

Philip Guarascio
Executive Director,
Advertising Services
& Strategic Planning,
General Motors Corporation,
3044 West Grand Blvd,
Room 10-210,
Detroit, Michigan 48202

Dr. Alex Haley
PO Box 826
Norris, TN 37828

Henry Justus
Phillips-Van Heusen
1290 Avenue of the Americas
New York, NY

Richard Levenson,
D'Arcy, Masius,
Benton & Bowles Inc.,
909 3rd Avenue,
New York, New York 10022

Suzanne Marx,
4004 Rogen Drive,
Encino, California 91436

John Reagan McCrary (Tex)
Apt. I-C,
385 South End Avenue,
New York, New York 10280

Morris Pesin,
Commissioner,
Liberty State Park NJ,
280 Grove Street,
Jersey City, NJ 07302

Rear Admiral R.I. Ribacki
Cmdr. First Coast Guard District
Boston, MA 02210

Lynda H. Scribanti
622 N. 38th St.,
Omaha, Nebraska,

James Dent Walker,
Associate Director/Archivist,
The Charles Sumner
School Museum Archives,
1201 17th Street, N.W.
Washington, D.C. 20036

Ex-Officio:

Herbert S. Cables, Jr.
Regional Director,
U.S. Department of Interior,

Suzanne O'Neil
State of New Jersey,
Office of Governor,
Trenton, NJ 08625

Cliff Robertson
Actor

Elder Richard G. Scott
President,
The Genealogical Society,
47 East South Temple Street,
Salt Lake City, Utah 84250

Rabbi Malcolm Stern
President,
Jewish Genealogical Society,
300 East 71st Street,
Apt 5-R,
New York, New York 10021

Eunice B. Whittlesey
118 Acorn Drive,
Scotia, New York 12302

Nancy Nelson,
U.S. Department of Interior,
National Park Service,

National Park Service,
15 State Street,
Boston, Mass 02109

15 State Street,
Boston, Mass 02109

Michael Adlerstein
Chief Historical Architect,
National Park Service,
Washington D.C 20013

Kevin Buckley
Superintendent,
Statue of Liberty
National Monument,
Liberty Island,
New York 10004

Robert Warren
Courant Institute,
Immigration & Naturalization Service,
425 I Street, N.W.,
Washington, D.C. 20001

Dennis Shasha
Statistical Analysis Branch,
New York University,
251 Mercer Street,
New York, New York 10012

Gerald Patten
Regional Director

National Park Service
15 State Street
Boston, MA 02109

Steve Fenton
D'Arcy Masius Benton
& Bowles
1675 Broadway
New York NY 10019

TABLE OF CONTENTS

PART II: DECAY AND RESTORATION

PART III: SOURCES

PART V: END MATTERS

LIST OF TABLES

LIST OF FIGURES

PART I

"How will we know it is us without our past"

--John Steinbeck

CHAPTER I:

HISTORY AND GROWTH OF ELLIS ISLAND

"Only an immigrant can appreciate America."

Ellis Island has been in federal possession since 1808. Before that time, it was known by a series of names, some of which denoted its primary use. The Dutch Burghers from Amsterdam called this Island "Oyster Island," because it was there that they shucked and ate the oysters from the clear waters nearby. When the British took this region from the Dutch, they renamed it "Gull Island." Later it came to be known as "Gibbet Island," because it became the site of executions of a number of pirates in the eighteenth century. Towards the end of the eighteenth century, the Island was sold to a New York businessman named Samuel Ellis; his heirs sold the Island to New York State in 1808, and in the same year it was sold to the Federal Government for $10,000. After serving as a defensive outpost in the War of 1812, the Island resumed its position as a chief execution post. Before and during the Civil War, the Navy Department used the Island to store powder magazines and hence it became an arsenal. At the conclusion of the Civil War, New Yorkers were shocked to learn that if the munitions stockpiled on Ellis Island had exploded, they could destroy all of New York, Brooklyn, and Jersey City, as well as villages as far away as Staten Island.

The debate concerning the safety of Ellis Island went on for nearly 20 years; but it was a little-noticed bill passed by Congress in 1882 that was to have a much greater effect on the future of the Island. The law excluded from settlement in the United States, "Any convict, lunatic, idiot, or any person unable to take care of himself or herself without becoming a public charge." Prior to the passage of this law, the states had the responsibility of determining the admissibility of immigrants. However, beginning in the early 1880's, there were recurrent newspaper and magazine articles which told of European and Asian nations dumping their prisoners and insane persons into ships for destinations to the United States and other parts of the Western Hemisphere. Although it is known now that most immigrants did not become public charges, there were enough persons who did to raise an exaggerated fear.

Another development was crucial to the history of Ellis Island. As the growth of New York City moved away from the waterfront, Castle Garden, which had for years been the most popular amusement place for the city, fell into disuse. Because the big red buildings had walls that were nine feet thick and could be used for almost any purpose, the New York State Immigration Commission took over the buildings in 1855 to begin its use as an immigration processing center. From that year until 1891, approximately 7 1/2 million aliens were processed at Castle Garden.

As the immigrant flood grew, overcrowding at Castle Garden was almost impossible to correct. New York State officials had charge of immigration at the port, but it was discovered that they were using the Immigration Bureau for political purposes. For this reason, the 1891 law put the Bureau under Federal control.

The number of aliens coming in grew daily, causing a breakdown of the entire inspection process and making it impossible for the authorities to keep the white slave and the confidence men away from the incoming immigrants. It was this lack of supervision that prompted the Federal Government to alleviate the conditions of the immigrants. The Congress appointed a joint committee to recommend a location for an immigration station. Senator McPherson of New Jersey, a member of the committee, suggested that converting Ellis Island into an immigration station would solve two problems: it would remove the dangerous munitions dump, and it would provide much-needed space for an immigration station. Against the recommendations of some cabinet members, the Congressional committee chose Ellis island as the first Federal immigration center and appropriated $150,000 for this purpose in May 1890. The selection of an island had several advantages over a mainland location. The placement of immigrants at an island center would ease the fears concerning the moral character of the immigrants. It was reasoned also the it would be much easier to protect and guide immigrants if they were confined to the island. Moreover, it would be much more difficult to escape from an island where a swim of at least 1,500 feet would be necessary to reach the mainland.

During 1891, a large three-story reception center, a hospital, a laundry, a boiler house, and a generating plant were constructed-- mostly of Georgia pine. But there were several brick and stone buildings on the Island which were used as naval magazines. These were connected to vaults that stored immigration records. Other buildings were enlarged to form a two-story dormitory for detained immigrants. The hospital and immigration buildings were new wooden structures. [Figure 1]

FIGURE 1   The Original Ellis Island (National Park Service Photo)

While construction continued, the Congress expanded the immigration law of 1882. It required steamship companies to exercise greater care in handling passage to would-be immigrants, and to enforce this rule, the government required the steamship companies to return immigrants who were rejected by the authorities to their homeland free of charge. The companies were also required to pay for any meals of the aliens detained for examination on the island.

The new Ellis Island Immigration Station was officially dedicated on New Year's Day, 1892. it was designed to permit the entry of up to 10,000 immigrants per day and to handle up to 12,000 pieces of baggage. On the first day of operation, 700 immigrants passed through the Island. When it opened at 8 a.m., there were three large ships waiting to land. The first person processed was a "rosy-cheeked Irish girl," -- Annie Moore, aged 15, from County Cork. She arrived on the *Nevada* on January 2, 1892, and hers was the second name on the manifest. She was presented with a $10 gold piece by Superintendent Weber. She was accompanied by her two younger brothers, all of whom came to join their parents, living in New York City. They passed inspection and boarded the ferry boat, *Brinckerhoff*, to the barge office.[1] In the first year, nearly 450,000 persons were received and inspected. In the next three years, however, the depression of 1893 greatly reduced the number of foreigners entering the United States.

When Ellis Island opened, all railroads sold tickets at the same price, a price that was significantly higher than on the New York mainland. In January 1893, Colonel John B. Weber, the Commissioner of the Port, gave an order to break up the trunk line monopoly; he decreed that all immigrants be informed that the outside lines were selling tickets that were $10-$16 lower.[2]

The problems of administering the Island necessitated constant changes of rules, all of which caused hardships on aliens. For example, Commissioner Weber ordered that the island be closed from 3 p.m. on Saturday to 8 a.m. on Mondays during January and February, 1892. The *New York Times* reported that this rule was "harsh discrimination" because the ruling allowed officers to assist the cabin passengers to get ashore at once upon the arrival of the ship, but it kept the poorer immigrants on board ship from twelve to

---

[1] *New York Times*, January 2, 1892, p. 2.

[2] *New York Times*, January 27, 1893, p. 3.

twenty-four hours.[3] One result of the Sunday closing order can be seen in the case of the Cunard ship, *Umbria*. It arrived in port one day early, on a Saturday at 2 p.m.-- one half hour before normal closing time. Colonel Weber informed the Captain that the steerage passengers would have to remain on board until Monday. The captain obeyed the order, but he gave the command to unload the cargo, thereby making it impossible to heat the steerage section of the ship. The closing order was soon rescinded.

In June, 1897, a fire of undisclosed origin completely destroyed all the wooden structures on Ellis Island. The immigrants who were sleeping at the time were evacuated to New York City and thereafter immigrants were assigned to the Battery Barge Office, where conditions were not satisfactory. The quarters were far too small to handle the crowds of aliens, and the crowding was complicated by the widespread graft among employees of the immigration service.

Colonel Herman Stump, the Commissioner of Immigration, inspected the ruins of the old station and oversaw the operation of the new one. He also made a contract with the Long Island College Hospital for the care of sick immigrants.[4] Fortunately, few immigrants were arriving, and they were handled on the pier at New York City, where miniature immigration stationsions were built. Temporary aisles and desks were set up for use of the registry clerks, and those who were detained were quartered at the Barge Office annex. In retrospect, the greatest loss suffered in the fire was the destruction of all the immigration records of the Port of New York for the years 1855 to 1890.

When Federal officials addressed the problem of replacing the burned structure, they made a serious error. Believing that the depressed economic conditions of the time were normal, they replaced

---

[3]New York Times, January 24, 1892, p. 2.

[4]New York Times, June 17, 1897, p. 12.

the original wooden structure with a new complex that could accomodate no more than 500,000 aliens per year. This was a gross understatement of the number of persons who would be coming to the United States in the next two decades.

The temporary quarters that were being used as an immigration station produced great chaos, hence when the new structure was sufficiently advanced, it was opened before completion. The main building of French Renaissance style, was on the original site. It was fireproofed, and it was a large brick and iron structure trimmed with limestone. The dimensions were impressive. It was 338 feet long, 168 feet wide, and 100 feet high, with four turrets (See dust jacket). The first floor contained a baggage room for new arrivals, administrative offices, a large railroad room, and a new wide stairway. This led to the main Registry room on the second floor, where the actual processing of immigrants occurred. [See Figure 2]. To the north of the Great Hall stood the restaurant, laundry, bath house, and power house--all of which were added by land fill. The bath house could provide showers for up to 8,000 immigrants per day.

The Enlargement of the Island

Ellis Island consists of three parts, only one of which was the original island. It began as a total of only 3 1/2 acres, but it has been enlarged from time to time until it now totals 27 1/2 acres. This enlargement is an interesting story of engineering work. Two other islands were built to the southwest of the original one and they were created by a series of landfills. [See Figure 2]. Island number two, which is separated from Island one by a ferry slip, was filled in from 1898 to 1902, contains the hospital buildings, and island number three, which was added in 1905 to 1909, is where the contagious disease hospitals stand. The three "islands" were connected by landfills.

Between the main island and island number two, there is a ferry basin enclosed by a sea wall. This wall required considerable dredging, which was accomplished around 1919. The concrete blocks making up the wall measured 17 feet high, 12 feet wide, and 9 feet thick, and they weigh 87 tons each. They were set on concrete which was reinforced with railroad rails. The blocks were lowered into place by means of grooves formed on the adjacent blocks. This type of wall was unnecessary around islands two and three, where there was no need for deep water access. A crib foundation was utilized in those locations.

The Report of the Ellis Island Committee of 1934 resulted in a number of changes to the buildings and grounds. A new pavilion was built for housing personnel, nurses and medical doctors. It contained kitchens and dining rooms. Also, verandas were built on four pavilions (numbers 13, 1, 19 and 23) of the contagious hospital on island three). [Figure 3] The space between the hospital buildings on islands two and three was repaved with cinders and landscaped for use as a recreation area for patients. In addition, a new recreation building was located in the space between the two hospitals, replacing an older building located on island two that was determined to be a fire hazard.

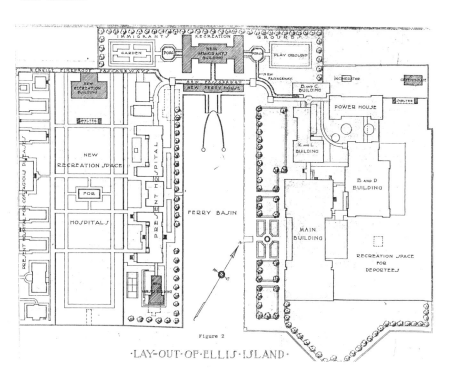

Figure 2

·LAY·OUT·OF·ELLIS·ISLAND·

A. recreation area was created east of the main building, and it was fenced in to provide space for deportees. This space was located east of the main building so as to leave the surrounding areas to the south of the main building unobstructed. The designers did not wish to destroy the beautiful view of upper New York Bay and the unparalleled skyline of the city. Much of the improvements in Ellis Island in 1935 were completed with the help of the Pubiic Works Administration.

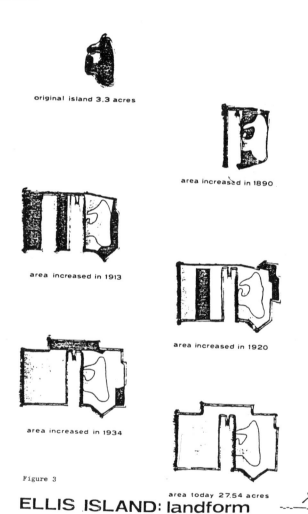

original island 3.3 acres

area increased in 1890

area increased in 1913

area increased in 1920

area increased in 1934

Figure 3

area today 27.54 acres

ELLIS ISLAND: landform development

CHAPTER II:

PASSING THROUGH THE GOLDEN DOOR

In the years between the opening of the new immigration center and the beginning of World War II, the highest rate of immigration in American history was recorded at Ellis Island, and in one year alone--1907--more than one million aliens checked through its halls. This total was more than twice the capacity of the buildings, and was one reason why the entire operation was often criticized in the American press. The lure of the "Golden America" was strong. It was also wrong. The immigrants dreamed of gold and silver in the streets, so they came by every possible conveyance to the ports to make the ocean passage. Most came in steerage.

Steerage Class

The ocean voyage by steerage was described well by an investigator who disguised herself in making the crossing.[1] She told us that a steerage berth was an iron bunk with a mattress of straw and no pillow. The floors of the compartment were made of wood, which was swept every morning and sprinkled with sand. Two washrooms were provided for the steerage class, and both were used by both sexes at the same time. There was a small basin and a dishpan plus some other cans that were used as laundry tubs. Since most of the metal cans were used for washing, there was a shortage of receptacles to use in case of seasickness. Thus, as the voyage progressed, the conditions became more filthy and more unbearable. During the twelve days across the ocean, only the salt breeze overcame the odors. And by the end of the journey everything was dirty and disagreeable. On rough passages, the conditions were far worse, because the decks were filled with vomit and there was no provision for personal cleanliness.

All passengers suffered from lack of space and privacy. There

---

[1]U.S. Immigration Commission, Steerage Conditions, 1911, p.12.

was no room for hand baggage, there was no open deck space and there was no dining room. Usually there was a scarcity of water for drinking. Anna Herkner, investigating steerage conditions for the United States Immigration Commission, reported that, "the passengers would arrive at the journey's end with a mind unfit for healthy, wholesome impressions and with a body weakened and unfit for the hardships that were involved in the beginning of life in a new land."[2] Before docking, each woman was given a piece of candy and each man a pipe and tobacco. For this experience, the travellers paid $30 to the steamship companies (the amount was raised from $20 in 1893).[3]

The Immigration Commission distinguished between the old and the new steerage. They called the old steerage a "horror." The new steerage was the same as second class accommodations. However, this type of accommodation was available only on lines from northern Europe. Despite better conditions on these lines, "the air was still foul, the floors still wet and the overall comfort still lacking."[4]

As potential immigrants learned of the discomforts of steerage, they also learned how to deal with it. When on board ship, they "greased the palm" of officials who could then exempt them from the rigid examination of ordinary steerage passengers.

Arriving in 1907

1907 was the peak year (when over one million persons came to New York and 866,660 were shunted to Ellis Island--11,747 on April 17). The entire work load was so staggering for the officials that

---

[2]New York Times, March 13, 1893, p. 3-6.

[3]Quoted in Milton Meltzer, Taking Root (New York: Farrar, Straus and Giroux, 1976), p. 38.

[4]Immigration Commission, Steerage Conditions, p. 13.

each immigrant was given only two minutes to pass or fail. What were conditions like on Ellis Island then? We can begin as the ship approached the United States. The steerage passengers arranged their bundles for the last time and counted their money for the hundreth time. They washed in their basins with cold, salt water and made their clothes as tidy as possible in preparation for the inspection. As they pushed up to the deck, it became nearly impassible with baggage.

The ship passed into the Narrows -- that piece of water between Brooklyn and Staten Island. The aliens were amazed at the view of the buildings and the many ships from nearly evey continent in the world. This was the culmination of the greatest mass migration in history. Over three million persons lived this same experience between 1905 and 1907. On April 17, 1907, the most active day in Ellis Island history, 11,745 aliens were processed.

As the ship slowed down for docking, a small cutter came alongside bringing the uniformed personnel, who would "inspect" the second cabin passengers. It was all quite perfunctory. The inspectors asked two or three questions and the medical doctor glanced at the passengers to look for obvious signs of illness. They only looked at the list of first cabin passengers -- the wealthy visitors who somehow did not fit the appellation "immigrant," though some surely were.

The inspectors asked the ship's doctor if there were any contagious diseases on board, and if the reply was positive, the entire crew and passengers would be isolated at the Quarantine Station at Staten Island or at Hoffman Island. If there was no need to quarantine the entire vessel, the passengers were separated according to those who were entering the United States for permanent residence and those who only sought to visit. Those passengers who intended to immigrate were placed on board a tender for Ellis Island. As the vessel docked, the passenger lists were examined by the inspectors. Cabin passengers could be sent to Ellis Island also, but in practice few were.

Nearly every activity stopped as the ship made its way north past the Statue of Liberty. Just ahead was a sight that every immigrant long remembers -- the skyline of Manhattan. It was taller than anything in Naples, Hamburg or Liverpool, from where most had departed. And on the left were the red brick buildings of Ellis Island where they would soon learn whether they had in fact found a new home (ninety eight percent of them did). The liner docked to discharge its second and first class passengers, and the steerage class was taken to Ellis Island by ferry. When the tender docked at the slip on the Island, the prospective citizens dragged their luggage ashore and into the vastness of the Reception Hall. Both the immigrants and their luggage were inspected. The immigrants carried a great variety of luggage representing a subtantial part of their worldly goods. They brought bags, boxes, trunks, wooden containers and wicker baskets. The oddly-assembled baggage or its metal contents often inflicted wounds on innocent bypassers. The main concern was that these meager treasures might be lost or stolen. Many aliens refused to part with their luggage even when they were guarded, and language problems made matters worse. As Figure 4 shows, they carried a motley array of sacks and bags.

From the baggage room below, the immigrants were led upstairs in the large arena of the Registry Hall. They were examined in groups of thirty at a time. Before leaving the ship, each person was given a card bearing the individual's name and the letter or number of the manifest sheet. When the aliens first entered the examination building, they passed before medical officers. At least two such officers had to be present, though at times there were three to five available. This physical examination might take an hour or several days, depending on whether or not the individual was confined to the station's hospital or not.

To describe what happened next, we have the words of an eyewitness who was an inspector on Ellis Island.[5] Here is what he recounted. The inspectors' work began at the Barge Office at the

[5]Edward Corsi, In the Shadow of Liberty (New York: Macmillan, 1925), "A Picture of Liberty."

FIGURE 4   Italian Family With Baggage. (Photo from the Terence V. Powderly Collection, The Catholic University of America.)

Battery.   From there the ferry boat took the employees to Ellis Island at nine in the morning.   Already there were hundreds of people waiting to get on the same boat.   These were the friends and relatives of immigrants who were expected during that day or who were already being detained on the Island.   Upon arriving on the Island, the employees had to plunge immediately into the work because there were boatloads of immigrants waiting to be inspected.

As the inspection process proceeded, each alien was tagged with a number corresponding to numbers on their manifest, after they had landed from the barges.   In the main building, they were lined up and doctors went through their medical inspection.   The aliens passed down a long line where they again grouped, this time according to letters.   The inspecting team of physicians looked for signs of illness, such as lumps, fatigue, shortnes of breath.   Persons were brought together according to the letters received -- either written on the lapel or shoulder or on a tag.   "H" meant heart disease, "X" indicated a possibie lunatic or one with a mental problem, "B" for back problem,

"L" for lameness. At this point the eyes were checked, particularly for a contagious disease --trachoma. If the aliens survived the physical examination, they were taken to the Registry section to be interviewed. In all, there were as many as 29 questions. Your name? How did you pay for your passage? Do you have promise of a job? Are you an anarchist? Are you going to join a relative or friend? What is your address? Occupation? Where born? Where last resided? Not all inspectors asked all 29 questions, and some inspectors by failing to ask all the questions missed certain cases of irregularities that were picked up later on in the process line.

In the process of inspection, many a future American "suffered" a name change. These instances must have perplexed the aliens, who found themselves addressed in a fashion they did not recognize. Jones discusses some typical cases. In one, a German Jew became flustered at the questions of the inspector, and when he (the alien) was asked his name, he answered, "Ich vergessen" (I forget) whereupon the man wrote his name as Fergusen. On another occasion, a Greek boy took the name of a dead friend named Hohannes Gardashian. When he pronounced it at Ellis Island, the inspector told him it was too long and that he would need a shorter name to make it in America. The man wrote Joe Arness.[6] An Italian told the man questioning him that his name was Mastroianni, and he became Mister Yanni. He had to add a first name later for official records.[7] To continue the tale of inspection, the mingling of strange tongues, children crying, guards yelling, and the smell of the crowded humanity was not a pleasant experience. Oftentimes, the guards and officials were petty and arrogant and this caused dismay amongst those who were shuttled from one post to another in the process. And for many years, immigrants were herded between barriers like cattle. [Figure 5]

---

[6]See Jones, Destination America, p. 63.

[7]The American Name Society of Ohio has a computerized record of the many name changes.

FIGURE 5   The Inspection Process (National Park
Service Photo)

Those gaining admittance to the United States were placed on
the ferryboat to Manhattan Island; those who were detained for one
reason or another were led by guards into the detention room.   The
place for the of immigrants inspection and approval or rejection is
pictured in Safford describes what happened to those who were
excluded and detained by the Boards of Special Inquiry.   He analyzed
5,362 cases of appeals to the Secretary for the year 1917.   Forty-six
percent of the cases were reversed and the aliens admitted.   Sixteen
percent of the cases were admitted by the Secretary after relatives
posted bond and another twenty-eight percent were reversed admitting
the aliens unconditionally.[8]

Women were a special problem.   The interrogation was much
more intensive if the woman travelled alone.   The precautions were
made necessary by the high number of white slave traders who

---

[8]Safford, Immigration Problems, p. 26.

operated around the docks and on board the ships. The problem became so severe the the YWCA began to assign women to act as escorts to incoming single girls. The interrogation of women began in the same way. If she was alone, she was asked how much money she had, if she was going outside of New York City, whether her passage was being paid by herself or by some charitable institution. If she came to marry, as many did, she had to give the name of the prospective husband, and often times they were married on the Island itself. If she came to join her husband in New York City or Brooklyn, the inspectors arranged for meetings. Women without escorts had to remain in the detention area, sometimes for a number of days. If no caller came for the women, the inspectors in charge then sent out telegrams to immediate relatives ordering them to come to escort the woman. Any irregularities in this process were usually referred to the Board of Special Inquiry, which would hear the case to make its ultimate decision on admittance or rejection.

The problems of single women getting through Ellis Island were illustrated in the first week of the Island's operations. When the Cunard liner *Servia,* landed on January 8, 1892, Commissioner H. J. Schulteis, who was investigating the presence of paupers amongst the steerage passengers, brought charges of immorality against Miss Ingebab Petersen, a young Swedish girl from Gottland, who was on her way to Manistee, Michigan, to join relatives. Superintendent Weber, not convinced of the charges, ordered the girl and the rest of the passengers released. When Petersen reached Michigan, she sued Schulteis for $25,000.[9]

Ernest C. Cotterill, a Philadelphian who was Secretary of the Manufacturers and Traders Association, took an interest in the plight of the steerage passengers; he made six trips across the ocean to study steerage reform. He wrote that the liners were corrupting the youth and that we should protect them from "The wiles of money sharks, the swindles of traveling gamblers, and above all...the morals of girl

---

[9] New York Times, January 9, 1892, p. 5.

travelers." He continued, "The girls, ignorant, unsuspecting, filled by the very fact of immigration -- an epochal matter to most of them -- with the excitation which amounts to an intoxication and puts them off their guard, unprovided with any harmless amusement to occupy the long, tedious days of the voyage, greet with gratitude the attractive and attentive male stranger."[10]   But this may be only one side of a difficult situation. Terence Powderly, former Commissioner General of Immigration, travelling though Europe on special assignment, met a woman who procured "girls of tender years" for prostitution. She said her firm was one of several branches in Paris, Brussels, Antwerp, Berlin, Budapest, Vienna, and Marseilles, and that they dealt with American branches in New York, Philadelphia, Boston, Chicago, Denver, Buffalo, and Columbus.[11]

Accommodations at Ellis Island were inadequate when immigration was at a peak. This was particularly true in the detention room, where as many as 2,400 persons were put into a space with only 1,800 beds. This situation persisted for periods of up to two weeks at a time. As the number of women and children who were detained increased, the problems of sanitation multiplied. At one point in 1907, there were 1700 women and chiidren detained in a room which had a normal capacity of 600 persons. It was so crowded that the inspectors were unable to reach persons in the center of the room to discuss the reasons for their detention. And with so many persons packed into such a small area, it was impossible to keep those with infections isolated.

The sleeping quarters were very crude and inadequate. The bedsteads were of iron and were of the folding type. They were placed in the rooms in triple tiers. For those persons who could not be assigned beds, sleep usually meant benches, chairs, or the floor.

---

[10]New York Times, November 30, 1913, Part VI, p.10.

[11]Reel 80, Powderly Papers, Catholic University of America, p. 6.

In 1907, the overcrowding was "an endless affair."[12] The number of persons detained generally averaged about 2,000 per day -- considerably more than the facilities were prepared to handle.

The process of feeding the immigrant was complicated and was made much more difficult by the shortage of interpreters. The aliens were herded together and were ordered to move with their cards in their hands down the steps to a little hut where they were served some most uncommon fare. For example, for several days in 1907 they were fed only prune sandwiches. An investigation of the food provisions showed that the person in charge had been making exorbitant profits by providing cheap food and pocketing the balance of the per capita allowance. This condition was rectified by the Immigration Commissioner, Mr. William Williams. The Ellis Island dining room is pictured in Figure 6.

Commissioner Henry Curran pinpointed the general problems of serving satisfactory food. "If I added spaghetti, the detained Italians sent me an engrossed testimonial and everybody else objected. If I put pierogi and mazovian noodles on the table, the Poles were happy and the rest disconsolate. Irish stew was no good for the English and English marmalade was gunpowder to the Irish. The Scotch mistrusted both. The Welsh took what they could get:"[13]

Anyone having symptoms that attracted the medical examiners' attention was sent to the Island's hospital. A person who could perform manual labor was considered recovered. Those who were seriously sick were usually kept until their strength returned.

Twice a day the inmates were lined up at the foot of their beds to discuss their ailments and progress with medical officers. At other times the inmates could lounge about in the verandas, where they

---

[12]Corsi, In the Shadow of Liberty, Part III, Chapter 1.

[13]Henry H. Curran, From Pillar to Post (New York: Charles Scribner's, 1941), p. 291.

FIGURE 6   Ellis Island Dining Room (1901)
Photo from the Terence V. Powderly Collection)

brought welcome news from abroad.   Children used the playground in
the rear of the hospital.   These activities were paid for with the head
tax on immigrants.[14]   The conditions detailed above did not apply to
those who passed inspection.   For them, the entire process took only
forty-five minutes and they received a card stamped "admitted." They
were eligible to take the ferry to the mainland [Figure 7]

      But they were required to pay a head tax of two dollars until
July 1, 1907, when the tax was increased to four dollars.   Proceeds
from the tax went to support the Immigration Branch of the

---

[14]Safford, Immigration Problems, p. 53.

Figure 7   Immigrants Arriving at New York City
(Photo from the Terence V. Powderly Collection)

Department of Commerce and Labor. In 1907, the fund exceeded two
and a half million dollars.

The next stop was the currency exchange and the railroad ticket
office.   The money changers usually paid in gold, but there were
many complaints of short-changing.   About one-third of the aliens
stayed in New York City and about two-thirds left.

The railroads also took advantage of the new arrivals, either
ovecharging them or putting them on very slow trains. Commissioner
Robert Watchorn filed an official complaint with the Interstate
Commerce Commission, asking Inspector Philip Cowen to investigate.
Cowen posed as an alien and went to the railroad room on Ellis
Island at 10:00 a.m. to buy a $2.50 ticket to Philadelphia.   He waited

Figure 8   Currency Exchange and Railroad Ticket
Office (National Park Service Photo)

until 4:30 p.m. before a barge took him to Pennsylvania Station.
After boarding a train with filthy water and no beds, he arrived in
Philadelphia at 1:10 a.m. Cowen reported making the same trip other
times in two hours.[15] This was an extreme case, but it occurred
often enough to cause Watchorn to file a complaint.

Some persons were detained on Ellis Island because they were
awaiting relatives or money for a continuation of their voyages.
Others were detained because the inspector doubted their admissibility.
These persons were required to appear before the Board of Special
Inquiry. The alien who had been denied admission and his or her
relatives and friends were allowed to testify before the Board. If two
of the three members of the Board voted for admission, that was
sufficient. The entire process of inspection is depicted in Figure 9. If
an alien was denied admission and subject to deportation, that person

---

[15]Philip Cowen, Memories of an American Jew (New York: International Press,
1932), pp. 151 -2.

22

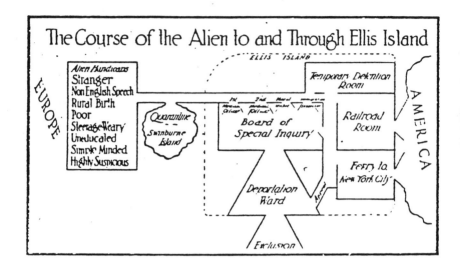

Figure 9   Source: R. L. Breed, *The Immigrant Gateway*
(New York: Missionary Education Movement, 1913,) p. 16.

could appeal to the Secretary in Washington. The U. S. Supreme
Court ruled in 1892 that, under the March 3, 1891 Act, appeals from
decisions of immigrant inspectors must be made to the U. S. Circuit
Courts not to the Superintendent of Immigration and the Secretary of
the Treasury (later Secretary of Labor).

The entire process of Special Inquiry was criticized endlessly.
One immigrant brought suit before Judge Learned Hand of the
U. S. District Court in 1909 charging that Commissioner William
Williams had "terrorized" Ellis Island officials so that aliens could not
get a fair hearing before the Board. Discussions of the trial indicated
that aliens were not always allowed counsel at the hearings.

Writing much later the Ellis Island Committee stated that when
aliens were brought before the Board they were not advised as to the
reason for their detention. It also pointed out that many inspectors
refused to make a determination in controversial cases, preferring to
pass the responsibility on to the Board of Special Inquiry, thus

creating a bottleneck and unnecessary delays for aliens.[16]

The issue of who shall be inspected was a recurrent one. On October 14, 1915, Commissioner-General Howe ruled that second-class passengers must pass through Ellis Island. One reason he gave was that a number of Greeks and Italians arrived in second class who should be in steerage(!) Once again the steamship companies complained about the order. They forecast that passengers would bypass New York City and go instead to Boston, Philadelphia, Baltimore, San Francisco or Canada, where everyone landed on the pier. At the crux of the matter, however was the $1 daily fee that the companies would have to pay for the upkeep of any persons who were detained at Ellis Island. The problem would be particularly acute for them if a liner arrived after 2 p.m., which would mean keeping all passengers overnight.[17]

There was strong feeling that the entire inspection process at Ellis Island was degrading. The *New York Times* described this process as follows:[18]

The immigrant is a patient, stolid animal as he appears at the handling station. With bags and bundles and cheap gripsacks, packed in Continental Europe, and half dazed with the new experience, this horde of human beings found themselves, the instant they set foot beneath the stars and stripes, prisoners, as effectively as if they had met at a prison station in Russia, bound for Siberia. They might walk in but one path from the gangplank -- the one leading to the easterly end of the long, low building. In this they might enter but a single room. This room was bound by an

---

[16]Report of the Ellis Island Committee, 1934, p. 32.

[17]New York Times, October 13, 1915, p. 8.

[18]New York Times, December 11, 1893, p. 1.

iron fence, and once within, the immigrant on a search for the land of freedom became deprived of all personal liberty for the moment.

Degrading, perhaps; but like a Russian prison, no. The key phrase is "for the moment." The end of this temporary indignity was freedom. Actually, four out of five persons were processed and made the mainland on the same day, although some were confined for weeks, usually awaiting records or relatives or spouses.

In percentage terms, a relatively small share of those who attempted to enter the United States were refused entry, but as one person stated, "Statistics are a bloodless thing." To find the human side of immigration, you had to climb the steps of the Great Hall to talk to one of the "undesirables." Many had saved a few pennies a day and gone without meals to pay the steerage ticket. One such story involved a 16 year old Russian boy. The *New York Times* described him as a cripple, who could not earn a living in the fields at home. He was sent to the United States by an uncle with a letter attached explaining his situation. When he was interviewed, he made the following statement:[19]

> I stood on the front of the ship with several of my fellow countrymen who like me were bound for America. As we came closer to the shore my joy knew no bounds. I was soon to be in a land where my race is not persecuted. I heard of this gold that could be had for the asking, and I longed to gather some of it and return it to my old parents in Russia. Now they tell me I must return home, for they cannðt find my uncle, and furthermore, cripples like me are not wanted here.

On hearing this, the inspector said, "Hunchy is clean loco."

---

[19]*New York Times*, August 12, 1906, Part 3, p. 6.

Conditions on the Other Side

At various times, there were outbreaks of cholera (1893), trachoma (1910), and typhus (1921) in Europe. This was a matter of great concern for U. S. health authorities and, occasionally, they would halt steerage traffic entirely (for example, from January 1 to March 12, 1893). Usually, however, steerage passengers were examined by Consular physicians; their baggage disinfected and a certificate of approval given. In the United States, ships were stopped outside the harbor, some awaiting the end of the incubation period of the disease (21 days for typhus).

But the chief problem was still laxity in handling cases at foreign ports, so we need to consider how some of the ports dealt with the problem. At Liverpool, where steerage passengers often came from Russia and Scandinavia, inspection procedures were thorough. For example, on the *Cedric* of the White Star Line, three doctors lined the gangplank. The inspection included examination of head, wrist, eyes, and general appearance. Of Course, some did not pass. One was a Jewish woman, who had sold all her things, severed all ties and who made a long tedious journey by rail and sea to arrive in Liverpool. She found herself penniless, separated from family and in a strange land, where she could not communicate.

All steerage passengers going to Rotterdam were met at the trains and transferred to the NASM--a hotel built by the Netherlands-American Company. It could handle 600-800 persons at a time.[20] The hotel was "fitted up" in the shape of a third-class cabin. All the appliances were placed in such a manner that the emigrants could familiarize themselves with them prior to sailing.

The largest number of immigrants entering the United States came from Hamburg, Germany, the finest Station in Europe. Called "Passagierin Halls," it could accommodate 5,000 people. Trains came

---

[20]*New York Times*, March 13, 1893, p. 3.

to Hamburg from Tiflis, Damascus, Kurdestan and Greece. In 1914, they took up to twelve days to arrive, since they were often sidetracked when other trains (such as freight trains) had to pass. At the depot in Hamburg (where over twenty-five languages were spoken at any one time), each immigrant took a hot bath and the men shaved and hair trimmed. The children were separated, given identification tags and put into play areas. A scramble usually ensued to find the right child when the parents were ready to leave. Karl Bilsen, the play area attendant, claimed that many parents carried the wrong children with them to the United States "and [the children] lived happily ever afterwards without ever knowing who their parents were." [21] Those who passed inspection at the depot were given a "registered certificate," which was punched daily until the immigrant's departure. Significantly, the Hamburg depot kept records of the person's name, nationality, age, sex, and physical condition. [22]

The depot at Bremen did not compare to Hamburg. Emigrants boarded in houses costing two marks and fifty pfennig a day while waiting to board the North German Lloyd Line ships. According to Powderly, a careful physical was given to each immigrant in the building next to the railroad station. [23]

Most of the southern Italians left from Naples. It was but an hour or two from all major points by train, or a bit longer by wagon. The Sicilians could take a ferry up the straits of Messina. When the emigrants reached Naples, they had the benefit of the *Opera Assistenza Emigranti*, the immigrant aid society [See Figure 11]. But, the Italians did not provide the accommodations or the thorough inspections of the Germans or the English. The Italian provinces

---

[21] New York Times, September 28, 1932, p. 14.

[22] Immigration slowed in the 1930's and the depot was renamed Uber Seeheim -- a hotel for people of small means.

[23] Powderly Papers, Reel 80, p. 29.

Figure 10   Arrival of Immigrants at Hamburg, 1909

functioned at or near minimum-level budgets. The laws of inheritance resulted in smaller and smaller subdivisions of what arable land there was, and farming methods did not change much from Roman times. The primitive agrarian society, in which farmers used hand hoes (zappi) to cultivate was the essential cause of the massive drain of population and the lack of facilities with which to assist them in reaching the United States.[24]

America in World War I and After

The war in Europe disrupted the normal process at Ellis Island. Not only did the flow of immigrants nearly cease, but many persons who were scheduled to be deported were kept on the Island for the duration of the war. For example, in November, 1915, there were 500 hundred aliens who were under sentence to be deported; they were kept at the expense of the steamship companies because it was

[24]Maldwyn A. Jones, Destination America (London Weidenfeld and Nicholson, 1976).

Figure 11 Italian Immigrant Aid Society (Photo from Jones, *Destination America.*)

unsafe to send them to Europe.[25]

The effect of the war can be seen in the statistics of immigration. In 1914, over a million persons came to the United States, but this figure dwindled to two hundred thousand by 1916. The largest group came from Liverpool (59,797); next in order was the Holland-American Line (16,686), the National Steam Navigation Line of Greece (14,940), and the Scandinavian -American Line (10,265).[26]

The war came to Ellis Island on the morning of July 30, 1916, when 14 barges and railroad cars, which were loaded with ammunition off the New Jersey coast, were exploded by German

---

[25] New York Times, November 27, 1915, p. 9.

[26] New York Times, January 15, 1916, p. 4:5. These figures were given by landing agent W. C. Moore and they differ somewhat from the official statistics.

saboteurs. Windows were smashed all over Manhattan Island, and the shocks were felt as far south as Philadelphia. The initial blast blew out many of the windows and doors on Ellis Island, but none of the brick structures collapsed. At the time of the explosion, there were several hundred persons detained on Ellis Island, as well as all of the employees. They were taken immediately to the eastern side of the Island, away from the blast, and later placed on barges where they were moved to Manhattan. On the following day, when an inspection could be made, it was determined that the Island had suffered nearly $400,000 in damage. There were no deaths or serious injuries, however.[27]

When the United States entered World War I in the spring of 1917, it rounded up the crews of all the ships of enemy countries and sent them to Ellis Island for internment. These persons were joined by other persons who were of German origin and were considered "suspicious." The government decided that this location was not desirable and all these persons were moved to other camps in the American South.

The Bureau of Immigration reported in April, 1918, that Ellis Island was being devoted to military and naval uses. The Navy was in complete occupancy of the Baggage and Dormitory Building, including the railroad ticket office and waiting rooms, and the War Department occupied the hospitals, main inspection halls and special inquiry rooms.[28]

The Bureau retained sufficient quarters to house aliens held for special inquiry and those waiting to be released to relatives. Because of the space limitations, any persons who were to be detained for long periods were sent to the Philadelphia Immigration Station, Gloucester, New York. It was fortunate that, because of wartime restrictions, few

---

[27]Pitkin, Ellis Island as an Immigrant Depot, p. 133.

[28]U. S. Bureau of Immigration, Service Bulletin, April 1, 1918.

immigrants came.

Before the United States Congress imposed an immigration quota system, an incident occurred which marred the reputation of Ellis Island and the United States. During World War I, immigration slowed considerably, but after the war when it grew again rapidly, Americans began to doubt their ability to assimilate such a mass of people. Further, the Communist Revolution of 1917 created doubts as to the type of people entering the country. "America First" groups, such as the American Protective League, fanned the flames of dissention within the United States by noting that southern and eastern European immigrants tend to come from anarchic areas emphasizing syndicalism.

The Immigration Act of 1918 required that anarchist and other classes be excluded or expelled. The following spring, America went through a "red scare" wherein Attorney General A. Mitchell Palmer led a series of raids to round up labor agitators, whom he labeled as Bolsheviks. Several thousand were arrested in 1919 and held for questioning. Many were deported, including Emma Goldman and Alexander Berkman. This hysteria reached a peak by the middle of 1920. The Communist promise to export revolution to the capitalist nations created a frenzy in the United States leading to a wave of alien deportations, many of which were completed at Ellis Island. Americans multiplied the crimes attributed to aliens and combined this with their own prejudices. The Department of Justice fed these fears by practicing know-nothingism. Detectives raided homes and meetings, arresting immigrants in their beds and made unlawful searches of private property. The most famous of these deportations was the "Soviet Ark" or the *Buford*, which sailed from New York to Finland with 249 Russian Americans. They were banished by "administrative process" and given only a few hours to depart, thereby preventing them from contacting relatives, friends or lawyers. Since the United States did not communicate with Russia at the time, the deportees could not be sent "back to the country whence they came," as the law specified. When the *Buford* sailed for Finland, the deportees' wives and children were left behind.

This celebrated deportation case, wherein anarchists Emma Goldman and Alexander Berkman were sent to Finland, was the beginning of what Assistant Secretary of Labor Post called the "deportations delirium."[29]

The rounding up of these members of the "Federation of Unions of Russian Workers" was the culmination of months of agitation between anarchists and government officials. The workers raided and bombed several cities on "May Day" in 1919 and in June of the same year, they bombed a Catholic church and the homes of a judge, a mayor and a Congressman while attempting to kill Henry Frick and other "Capitalists." The Federal government's response was a "red" crusade initiated by Attorney General Palmer, an aspiring presidential nominee, whom many claimed was using the crusade for political ends.

The 1918 Act of Congress made membership in the Communist Party of America a justifiable reason for deportation. Membership was determined by the signature on the membership application or that of someone appointed to sign for an individual.[30] The crusade started in January 1920. The Department of Justice ordered raids in more than thirty cities and towns, during which 2,500 Communists and members of Communist parties were arrested.[31] Although raids took place everywhere, the majority occurred in New England; fourteen cities and towns in Massachusetts were hit, most of them industrial areas such as Boston, Worcester, Springfield, Lowell and Lawrence.

As a result of the New England raids, immigrants were confined

---

[29]Louis E Post, The Deportations Delirium of Nineteen-Twenty (Chicago Charles H. Kerr, 1923).

[30]For complete information on methods used to review cases and the Advisory Committee work in determinations, see Annual Report of the Secretary of Labor (1920), pp. 73-76.

[31]Post, The Deportations Delirium, p. 91.

at Deer Island. The New York raids are more relevant since immigrants were deported from Ellis Island. In New York, on the evening of January 2, 1920, three thousand were arrested and six hundred taken to the Island. From New Jersey and Philadelphia came an additional five hundred, with only three hundred deportable cases. The rest were classified as "hopelessly non-deportable." Between July 1, 1919, and January 1, 1921, 6,328 arrest warrants were issued. O these, 2,919 were cancelled while 1,119 were sustained and the individuals deported.

Movement to Restrict Immigration

Almost as soon as Ellis Island began as an immigration station, American policy towards European immigration became more restrictive. Those who favored restriction can be grouped into one of the following categories: those who feared competition for jobs, those who feared a "mongrelization of the races"; those who feared an increase of crime; and those who believed that many aliens would become a public charge. The movement to restrict immigration encountered substantial opposition from a variety of groups. The Jews saw the movement as anti-Semitic and as a threat to their economic and social status in the United States. Others saw restriction as a negation of the American tradition of asylum and refuge from oppression abroad. When the literacy test was first proposed in 1896, many Americans joined in opposition. They used the results of the 1900 census to buttress their case. It showed that immigrants were very desirous of having their children attend school and that their record was superior to that of native Americans. In 1900, 71 percent of the children of foreign born were attending school, compared with 65 percent for children of native parents. Moreover, only 1.6 percent of the children of foreigners were illiterate against the 5.7 percent for native children.

The *New York Times* presented an interesting case as an answer to those who claimed that the literacy test was the only sure way of controlling the entry of undesirables into the United States. It cited a speech of Gaetano d'Amato, of the New York City Bureau of

Licenses, who stated that the southern Italians love of home, family, and loyalty to employers, his honesty, his natural genius and joy for work, and his splendid health make him the raw material out of which the best citizens are made. The Times editor countered this hyperbole by stating that the Italians live in "little Italies" where the "criminal padrone" offers protection, and he declared that the Italian deserves a better fate, because "he digs our tunnels and ditches, cleans our streets and peforms the menial tasks which forty years ago were done by the Irish."[32]

The first restrictive immigration laws were aimed against Asians, especially the Chinese and Japanese. [See Table 1] Although this legislation was based on cultural and racial aspects, it was passed for economic reasons as well, with strong support from the new American Federation of Labor. The Contract Labor Law of 1885 excluded many alien laborers, mechanics or artisans who, prior to embarkation, had entered into "a contract or agreement... to perform labor or service in the United States." Through the Act of 1891, the Federal government assumed control over immigration regulation as part of its power to regulate interstate commerce. Administrative changes were made in 1893, and the Act was amended in 1903, 1907 and 1912. Safford, an Ellis Island medical officer called these laws "remarkable, homogeneous, constant, definite and concise."[33]

---

[32] New York Times, April 22, 1907, p. 8.

[33] Safford, Immigration Problems, p. 185.

Table 1

LEGISLATION AFFECTING STEERAGE PASSENGERS

1819-1908	Regulated the number of passengers. Two passengers for every five tons.
1875	Restricted the number of Chinese and Japanese, and those brought here "for lewd and immoral purposes."
1882	Chinese Exclusion Act (repealed in 1943). Exempted teachers, students, merchants, and pleasure travelers.
1885	Contract Labor Law. Excluded alien laborers and artisans who prior to embarkation had entered into a contract or agreement to perform labor or service in the United States.
1903	Barred anarchists (after the assassination of President McKinley).
1903	Applied $2 head tax.
1917	Required literary test.
1921	First quota law. Total immigration restricted to 350,000 and individual quotas limited to 3 percent of persons from each nation based on Census of 1910.
1924	Revised quota law. Reduced quota for each nation to 2 percent and changed base to 1890 Census and total to 150,000. Not more than 10 percent of any nation's quota could be admitted in any one month.
1940	Alien Registration Act.
1948	The Displaced persons Act authorized the entry of 400,744 persons (mainly from Poland, Germany, Latvia, Yugoslavia and the USSR)-gave priority to

persons in agriculture, educated persons and relatives of U. S. citizens.

1950 The McCarran-Walter Act provided for the exclusion and deportation of persons who were considered a danger to the security of the United States.

1952 Retained the quota system but provided that the first 50 percent of the quota was reserved for the first preference status (highly skilled or educated persons); 30 percent was reserved for alien parents of U. S. citizens; and 20 percent was reserved for spouses and children of aliens who have been lawfully admitted.

SOURCE: U. S. Senate, *The Immigration and Naturalization Systems of the United States,* Report No.1515, 81st Congress, 1st Session, March 29, 1950. (revised to 1952)

During World War I, nationalistic sentiments gave added impetus to the movement to restrict immigration. Consequently, the literacy test was enacted over a presidential veto in 1917. The Act of February 5, 1917 compiled the restrictive provisions of earlier acts, added the literacy test and prohibited immigration from certain "barred" Asian countries. Among the most important exclusions were the insane, those who were mentally defective, had tuberculosis or had committed a crime involving moral terpitude. Prostitutes, white slavers, polygamists, anarchists, dangerous radicals, paupers, professional beggars, vagrants, anyone likely to be a public charge, contract laborers and illiterates were also excluded. The law of 1917 specified that any alien who had been in the United States less than three years and could prove he was destitute could return to his native country at government expense.

Despite the restrictions of the 1917 Act, it did not establish quotas. The act of 1921 did. It limited the number of immigrants entering the United States to 357,000 per year, and it specified that the quota for each nation would be restricted to three percent of the number of each nationality residing in the United States in 1910.

The 1921 Act was superceded by the Act of July 1,1924, which became known as the "National Origins" Act . The annual quota was limited to two percent of the number in the 1890 Census. The annual quota from any nation was to 150,000 as the number of inhabitants in the United States in 1920 from the national origin was to the total population in 1920. The minimum quota for any nation was set at 100 persons. This act meant that the place of birth, not citizenship, determined under which quota a person would belong. The Act also exempted immigration from Canada, Cuba, Mexico and other independent countries in the Western Hemisphere. Wives and minor children of citizens could also enter the United States on a non-quota basis.

The Immigration Act of 1924 altered the entire processing system whereby aliens entered the country. The visas from this time were issued by American consuls abroad. A system of intensive examinations was established in twelve European countries, which at that time were the principle sources of U. S. immigration. At the same time, officials of the United States Public Health Service and certain immigration inspectors were assigned to advise the consuls in dealing with applications for visas. In addition, many immigrant aid societies offered assistance to immigrants on board ship [See Figure 12].

The 1924 immigration law required that "immigrants obtain visas based on examination from American consuls" and it specified that not more than 10 percent of a yearly quota's visas could be issued in any one month.[34] The overseas examinations were meant to eliminate rejection of aliens in the United States. Thus, Ellis Island lost one of its primary functions--the inspection of immigrants, although it

---

[34]Pitkin, Ellis Isand as an Immigrant Depot, p. 154.

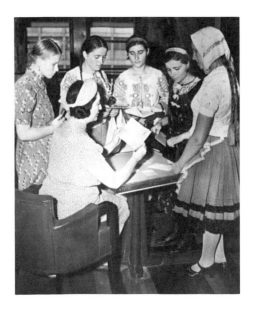

Figure 12 Caseworkers Completing Papers Aboard Ship, 1923 (National Catholic Welfare Conference Photo)

continued to serve as a primary inspection location in places where inspection teams had not been installed in consulates.

Immigration quotas under The 1924 Act (Amended by the 1929 law) were set at 153,774 for all countries, not counting non-quota immigrants. As Table 2 shows, this system was particularly damaging to Southern and Eastern Europeans, whose numbers in 1890 were relatively small. For example, the Italian quota was restricted to 5,802 per year under the new system, and the Czechoslovakian quota was 2,874, while the first three categories (Great Britain, Ireland, Germany and Austria accounted for 72 percent of the total.

The Italian Government protested loudly because it had adopted a policy encouraging the export of what it considered to be its surplus population in the Mezzogiorno. Before the restrictions, Italian immigration was as much as 250,000 persons per year.[35]

---

[35]See Monte S. Finkelstein, "The Johnson Act, Mussolini and Fascist Emigrant Policy: 1921-1930," Journal of American Ethnic History, VIII (Fall 1988), 38-55.

Table 2

IMMIGRATION QUOTAS UNDER 1924 LAW

```
Great Britain
   (and N. Ireland) .................................... 65,721

Germany (and Austria) ................................. 25,957

Eire .................................................. 17,853

Poland ................................................ 6,524

Italy ................................................. 5,802

Netherlands ........................................... 3,153

France ................................................ 3,086

Czechoslovakia ........................................ 2,874

Belgium ............................................... 1,304

Hungary ............................................... 869

Yugoslavia ............................................ 845

Portugal .............................................. 440

Lithuavia ............................................. 386

Greece ................................................ 307

Spain ................................................. 252

China ................................................. 105
```

SOURCE: Frances Kalnay and Richard Collins (eds.), *The New Immigration* (New York: Greenberg Publications, 1941), pp. 3-4.

Depression and More Deportations

The number of immigrants who entered the United States in the 1930's was the smallest in more than a century. The factors are easily pinpointed. The strict enforcement of the immigration laws, the worldwide depression, the unsettled political conditions in Europe, and the difficulty of travelling to port cities. In 1930, conditions for entering were tightened when President Hoover, because of high unemployment and stagnant economic conditions, required the Department of State to reduce the number of aliens to a bare minimum. Thus, consular officers overseas were advised to give visas to no person who did not have sufficient resources to maintain himself or herself for a considerable length of time. In 1932, only 35,567 aliens were admitted (about one-fifth of the quota) and this was the smallest number since 1831.[36] It was also the first time in American history when the number of aliens leaving exceeded the arrivals.[37]

Of the one million who came to New York in 1932 on some four thousand ships, less than five percent were sent to Ellis Island. One was referred to the Island if: (1) papers were not in order; (2) the alien intended to overstay the six-month limit; (3) the alien might become a public charge; (4) relatives failed to claim the alien; or (5) the alien was sick.

During the depression, the reasons for deportation changed. There were three kinds of deportees: volunteers (those who proved their destitution), criminal aliens (those who were in the United States less than five years and who were convicted; or those who were convicted twice, regardless of the length of residence) and illegal aliens.

The Act of 1929 gave amnesty to illegal aliens who entered the country before 1921 and who legalized their status by obtaining a certificate from the Bureau of Immigration. Those who entered between 1921 and 1924 were not subject to deportation under this act, but if they left the country they could not return.

In 1931, with the support of President Hoover, Secretary of Labor Doak promised to rid the nation of "everyone who cannot prove

---

[36]New York Times, October 8, 1933, IX, 12.

[37]Corsi, In the Shadow of Liberty, p. 95.

he is lawfully resident here."[38] In a matter of weeks, Ellis Island
was crowded with people awaiting deportation and 18,142 were actually
deported, "the greatest number of deportions in the history of the
bureau."[39] Tugs left Ellis Island two or three times a month carrying
deportees; mostly men who had been in the country for anywhere
from two to thirty years.

On any given day a barge from Jersey City tied up at Ellis
Island bringing those who were labeled "undesirable." They came
from every part of the country by train to New Jersey. Cases were
settled in the area in which the deportation proceedings were held.
Thus, Ellis Island officials had nothing to do with case histories, and
the Island began to resemble a prison with its armed guards, locked
doors and barred windows. The regular immigrants were separated
from the deportees. Each group had its own waiting rooms, dining
halls and dormitory playgrounds.[40]

By 1933, despite the hard conditions of the place, more than
two hundred persons per month applied for deportation due to
destitution. Frequently husbands who were unable to support their
families asked the U. S. government to deport them to their native
land. Some who wanted to leave were unable to find a country which
would take them, for example, "a Turk with a Syrian wife whose
child was born in France."[41] Steamship companies cooperated with
the government and the voluntary deportees by alloting up to ten
spaces per journey for destitute aliens. Some illegal aliens were
discovered by accident or through anonymous letters involving spite or
grudges In one case, a woman who was jilted by an alien turned him

---

[38]New York Times, February 16, 1931.

[39]Annual Report of the Commissioner General of Immigration, (1931), p. 35.

[40]New York Times, October 8, 1933, IX, p.12.

[41]New York Times, November 12, 1933, VIII, p. 2.

in because he had entered illegally through Canada.

The League of Abandoned Wives

Another unusual aspect of Ellis Island history arose in in the 1930's, when complaints about aliens alleged to be illegally residing in the United States were referred to the Law Division of the Island. Complaints came from the League of Abandoned Wives, an organization of women who had married abroad and whose husbands had been admitted to the United States as non-quota aliens. The background of the complaint in most cases followed a similar pattern:[42] In many ethnic groups an unmarried daughter presented a problem that had to be corrected. When all efforts failed, the naturalized immigrant parents would take their American citizen, unattached daughter on a trip to Europe back to their native village, where getting a visa to emigrate to the United States involved long years of waiting. In their native village the visitors from America would receive a warm welcome, with their daughter receiving particular attention. It must have been a heady experience for a hitherto neglected young female to find herself desirable, and sought after by eligible suitors. In no time her hand would be won--not improbably by the village Romeo--and the happy newlyweds would depart for America, where the quota would pose no problem for the groom since he would be admitted as the spouse of an American citizen; but where, alas, in many cases they did not live happily ever after, because after a little while, when the groom had had time to catch his breath and look around, so to speak, he would realize that the bride definitely was no dreamboat-- and he would take off. After another liitle while, when the bride could no longer deny to herself the horrid truth, she would join the League, and eventually appear at Ellis island. There the Chief of the Law Division would strongly counsel careful, thoughtful consideration before taking any step toward

---

[42]This account is taken verbatim from a letter to the author by Alice M. Galvin, who was a Hearing Stenographer and Secretary to Edward Barnes, Chief Inspector at Ellis Island. As she said," This is an accurate recollection."

seeking her husband's deportation. To no avail, however, since this was a determined infuriated woman. She simply would not leave until her complaint was taken-- and it would be on the ground that by abandoning her her spouse had compromised his status as the husband of an American citizen, and could be subject to deportion.

What ensued, usually, was that the husband would be apprehended under a Warrant of Arrest, and brought to Ellis Island. Almost simultaneously with this would be the appearance at Ellis Island of the tearful complainant wife protesting it was all a mistake and demanding that the matter be dropped at once with the release of her husband. No way. Instead, she would be advised that the alien would be accorded a hearing under the warrant; that he had the right to representation by cousel; that she could testify in his behalf; and that he could be released on bond pending disposition of the case; and further, she was referred to the social service agency of her choice, if she wished to avail herself of the service (there were over 20 represented on the Island). Usually, at the conclusion of the proceedings, final disposition was held in abeyance, and the alien would remain on bond. Seldom, if ever, was deportation effected.

War Comes Again: The Coast Guard on Ellis Island

The slow pace of activity on Ellis Island changed abruptly with the war in Europe. Between September 3, when the war began and September 16, 1939, ninety thousand applications were received for certificates of arrival or first papers. Fourteen additional clerks were hired to process the requests. Since the clerks could process only two hundred and fifty per day, it would have taken three hundled fifty days to complete the task, if no additional requests came in.[43]

The war in Europe also brought the Coast Guard to Ellis island. It was activated as a Receiving Station in October 1939, and it was

---

[43]New York Times, September 16, 1939.

decommissioned on August 15, 1946.[44] It was obliged to enforce the Neutrality Act, and for this it needed a training facility with housing. For this purpose, it was assigned the immigration baggage and dormitory buildings, which earlier had been assigned to the Treasury Department.

In its seven years on Ellis Island, the Coast Guard had six commanding officers:

Lt. Comdr. A. W. Davis	Comdr. H. F. Walsh
Oct. 1939 to Oct. 1940	June 1944 to July 1945
Cmdr. R. R. Ridgely, 3rd	Comdr. R. R. Curry
Oct. 1940 to Dec. 1942	July 1945 to Sept. 1945
Comdr. R. M. Hoyle	Cmdr. J. M. Mazzotta
Dec. 1942 to 1944	Sept. 1945 to Aug. 1946

The Coast Guard was given the job of training 60,000 inexperienced men for sea duty. Crews were needed to man the large number of ships that the Navy assigned to the Coast Guard. Training commenced in the pre-war, but the largest complements began training in June 1942. Crews were assembled and trained at Ellis Island for special duty assignments; the first of these was a transport crew of 303 men for the U.S.S. *Bayfield*, which later served in both the European and the Pacific invasions. Other crews that trained on Ellis Island included those of the U.S.S. *Cepheus*, the U.S.S. *Cavalier*, the U.S.S. *General William Mitchell*, the U.S.S. *General Randall*, the U.S.S *General Meigs*, the U.S.S. *General Gordon*, the U.S.S. *General Richardson*, the U.S.S. *General Weigel*, the U.S.S. *Sheliaok*, the U.S.S. *Theenim*, the U.S.S. General Brechenridge,] and the U.S.S.

---

[44]This section is based on The Coast Guard on Ellis Island, which was published to commemorate the "Second Annual Reunion of Ellis Islanders (the Coast Guard), on August 28, 1948. I am grateful to former Coastguardsman Joseph Gregory for loaning me this very scarce book.

Monticello. In addition, the Coast Guard trained replacements for large transports, DE's, LST's, LCI's, minesweepers, patrol boats and tankers. When the Receiving Station was decommissioned in 1946, all the equipment was transferred to the base at St. George, Staten Island.

Figure 13   Guardsmen Leave Ellis Island for Sea Duty
(Photo from *The Coast Guard on Ellis Island, 1948*)

One highlight of the Coast Guard years on Ellis Island was the celebration of the fiftieth anniversary as an immigrant station. Commissioner Rudolph Reimer sponsored a luncheon to commemorate the occasion.   An eleven-gun salute was fired from nearby Governors Island and the Coast Guard joined in with its own cannon.[45]

The war in Europe brought some policy changes.   Since aliens were considered a potential threat to the nation's safety, the Immigration and Naturalization Service was transferred to the Justice

---

[45] New York Times, April 12, 1940, p. 48.

Department. In June 1940, the Alien Registration Act required aliens to register and be fingerprinted.[46] After the United States entered the war Ellis Island again became a detention camp for enemy aliens. German, Japanese, and Italian nationals and their families were "temporariiy detained." By May 1942, one thousand aliens were confined.[47] To alleviate crowded conditions, the Island's administrative work was transferred to the old WPA building at 70 Columbus Avenue, since the WPA was being phased out and was in the midst of completing its final report. By 1946, most of the aliens had been released from Ellis Island and the Coast Guard Station disbanded. Since many of the buildings were vacant and the Federal government was anxious to reduce its expenses, the administrative work of the National Park Service returned to the Island in 1949. *The New York Times* reported that German prisoners of war left their dormitory walls covered with nostalgic murals of their homeland, however enquiries at the National Park Service show that neither the murals nor records about them exist.[48]

On one occasion a G.I. widow was held on Ellis Island "due to a freak omission in the law." Public Law 271 admitted wives and children of servicemen, but failed to mention widows. Two wives were involved in this case, but for unknown reasons, one was admitted as a six-month visitor and the other was detained.[49] Additional legislation removed the discrepancy.

---

[46]Marion T. Bennett, American Immigration Policies (Washington, D. C.: Public Affairs Press, 1963), p. 66.

[47]Pitkin, Ellis Island as an Immigrant Depot, p. 218.

[48]New York Times, April 8, 1949, p.27.

[49]New York Times, October 12, 1946, p. 8.

The Last Days of Ellis Island

When World War II ended, Europe was in a devastated state and this created an unprecedented number of refugees. Religious and immigrant aid groups approached the Congress to alleviate the hardship and suffering. Congress responded by passing the Displaced Persons Act of 1948, under which 205,000 refugees could enter each year. Few were satisfied with this number, and in 1949 the limit was raised to 400,000. But only about one percent of these refugees were taken to Ellis Island, usually to have passports and papers re-examined. As the "Cold War" became hotter, the United States Congress took sterner measures against aliens. They passed the Internal Security Act of 1950, the McCarran Act, which excluded members of communist and fascist organizations. All screening under the Act was done at Ellis Island and all suspects were held there. Many persons were taken off ocean liners at New York ports and removed to Ellis Island. Individuals formerly affiliated with Nazis, Fascists or Communists in their youth had to retell endlessly their war a activities to authorities. These abuses ended when the McCarran Act was amended in 1951.

Figure 14   A Post World War II Refugee at Ellis Island
(U. S. Catholic Conference Photo)

By 1950 the number of detainees reached fifteen hundred, straining the capacity of an island which processed five thousand in one day in 1920. The delays embittered and frustrated aliens who expected to enter the United States without difficulty. An amendment to the Act in 1951 resolved this confusion. The U. S. Public Health Service, managers of the Island's hospitals, closed its doors in March 1951. For thirty years, ailing merchant seamen, members of the U. S. Coast Guard and sick immigrants had received treatment there. The Special Survey Board of the Immigration and Naturalization Service declared the hospital obsolete and its equipment outmoded.[50]

In the Island's last year of operation, 1954, the chief inhabitants were seamen who ovestayed their shore leaves, sick immigrants and deportees. The Coast Guard retained a small part of the Island as a base for security forces. The last person to be processed at the Island was a Norwegian seaman who had ovestayed his shore leave. He was parolled.[51]

Tragedies of Our Inexorable Immigration Laws

The above title, taken from the *New York Times*, serves to show that, in an operation involving so many persons, there are bound to be human tragedies that "sunder families" and "wreck hard-saved fortunes."[52] The following involve several such cases. A wealthy Englishman was advised by his physician to go to Arizona for his health. When he landed at Ellis Island, the medical doctor informed him that he had TB. Not so, cried the Englishman, but he was not admitted until he told the inspectors that he was the son of Professor

---

Romanes--a great scholar. A mother and her children arrived at Ellis Island to join her husband, who was doing well in the garment trade in Philadelphia. One child was found to have a ringworm. The government decided that he should stay on the Island until cured and that the father should pay 75 cents per week for the child's maintenance. In April, 1909, the father's business declined and he did not send the required money. The child, aged three, was deported. A Jewish Association located him and returned him to the United States with a certificate from a German physician that he was well. A young man and woman, about to be married, decided to take their life's savings to the United States, where he could establish himself as a butcher and she as a dressmaker. On Ellis Island, the inspector sensed a kind of dark plot and refused to admit them until they were married there. A Turk was asked by the immigrant inspector. Do you believe in Polygamy?" The Turk replied, "I do not have even one wife." The inspector persisted, "Don't dodge the issue. The Koran permits polgamy. Do you believe in it?" The Turk responded that he would not take two wives in the United States, but that he did not believe that polygamy was sinful. He was deported. The next case involved a Greek, who immigrated and settled in San Francisco. He worked hard and saved enough money to bring his girlfriend to the United States. He returned to Greece in triumph, where he married his childhood sweethead. But she was stopped on Ellis Island for a minor eye problem. He protested that he was an American citizen, but he was unable to prove citizenship, because his papers were burned in the San Francisco fire.

In one case, justice prevailed via the back door. An Irish girl married a man from New Jersey. After a few years, he died so the woman returned with her two children to Ireland to visit relatives. When she attempted to reenter the United States she was stopped because the inspector said she was a poor widow and she might become a public charge. But, she pointed out, her two children were born on the United States and they were entitled to enter. Rightly so, the inspector responded, but she was not. Justice was victorious, however, because the children had to have a guardian to enter and their mother was so appointed.

The Isle of Tears

Of all the "Inexorable Immigration Laws" the one that caused the most tears on and off Ellis Island was the quota system established by the law of 1921. When the 1921 law was pending, there was a mad rush of thousands of ships to cross the Atlantic to beat the quotas. They raced into New York's harbor and actually collided in several cases in order not to be subject to the national quotas. The steamship companies were particularly concerned about the loss of profits in the steerage trade. Several ships did not beat the deadline, and many persons who sold their homes and expected to start a new life in the United States were forced to return. Riots often occurred when these immigrants were so informed. They broke windows and furniture in waiting rooms and attacked attendants.

Each year the situation got worse. The quota year ended June 30; the new quota started July 1. Commissioner Curran described the scene on June 30, 1923. There were twenty ships in the bay, one loaded with ten thousand immigrants. At midnight, they all dashed across the entry line (an imaginary line between Fort Wadsworth and Fort Hamilton on either side of the Narrows). It was first come, first served for the racing ships. As a result, the quota was filled in excess of two thousand for the month only seconds after midnight![53] Those who failed to make the quota were required to return to the country "from whence they came" and to reapply in a month or a year.

It would be difficult to find a better statement than this one from Curran about the mess Congress created by the quota law, irrespective of the inequities and the racism of the legislation.[54]

---

[53]The law required no more than twenty percent of a nation's quota be filled In any one month.

[54]Curran, Pillar to Post, pp. 290-91.

In a week or two they all went back. I was powerless. I could only watch them go. Day by day the barges took them from Ellis Island back to the ships again, back to the ocean, back to-- what? As they trooped aboard the big barges under my window, carrying their heavy bundles, some in their quaint, colorful native costumes worn to celebrate their first glad day in free America, some carrying little American flags, most of them quietly weeping, they twisted something in my heart which hurts to this day.

One case was pure comedy. It involved some Finnish carpenters on the Swedish ship *Drotningholm*. As the ship steamed towards port, she had to swerve to avoid hitting still another ship. At exactly midnight the *Drotningholm* was on the line spanning the Narrows. Thus, for quota purposes, the stern was subject to September's quota, but the bow, which came across the line seconds before midnight was subject to August's quota, which was long filled. The inspector asked each carpenter, "Were you on the bow or the stern?" Since they did not understand, they chose the most American position, "We were hurrying to come in." They were deported, but in a few days returned and explained they had transferred to another ship using the lifeboats on board. They were again rejected because they had not returned to the country "from whence they came." In a month, they returned a third time with photographs to prove they had returned to Finland. They were admitted. Within a week they were happily building houses in downtown New York.[55]

Who Shall Apologize?

In his *In the Shadow of Liberty,* former Commissioner of Immigration Edward Corsi described the exploitation of thousands who came to America with high hopes of becoming citizens. He catalogued the stories of abuse and fraud that pervaded the human

---

[55]Curran, Pillar to Post, pp. 297-98.

history of Ellis Island. Quoting a study by Professor Steiner of Grinnell College, Corsi disclosed the following, based on a sample of returned immigrants: "80 percent were cheated by employment agencies, 60 percent were cheated by Austrian boarding-house keepers, 72 percent received rough treatment by their bosses, 80 percent were robbed by railroad crews in Montana, 40 percent were robbed of money and tickets before leaving for home, 36 percent lost their money by giving bribes to Irish-American bosses, and 15 percent were Shanghaid--they were made drunk and were railroaded from St. Louis to southern Kansas." (p. 283) At various times it was charged that immigrants were forced to pay for haircuts they did not need, to overpay for food served in the dining halls, to pay for protection, and to pay for some form of favoritism on the Island. These abuses are chronicled in investigation after investigation by the United States Congress, and many nations protested vigorously against treatment of their citizens coming to the United States. The British Parliament debated the cessation of immigration, the Irish declared that it was time to stop immigration from Ireland to the States, the King of Italy protested the treatment of Italians on ships in the steerage class. But the defrauding of immigrants was not confined to the United States. There are ample stories of persons who paid for second-class passage and who were assigned crowded space in the hold of the ship. There were 250 immigrants stranded in France who had purchased worthless tickets.

The pathetic story of the exploitation of immigrants pales next to the callous disregard for human dignity that was often exhibited by those who administered our immigration laws. These headlines from the *New York Times* tell their own story "Bonci, A. and wife detained because he forgot to have passport signed"; "French persons -- 35 who were detained because of lack of proper passports ordered released by State Department"; "Genoese -- 35 held at Ellis Island"; "Uhl admits the examinations of aliens at Ellis Island is a farce"; "73 radicals held at Ellis Island go on hunger strike to compel removal of screen barrier separating them from visitors"; "Madeline Pagut deported, came to U. S. to wed A. Wright"; "Polish Government begins investigation and results of Commissioner Wallis' report on robbery of immigrants"; J. Olestic, 14 years old, comes to NYC from Massachusetts to get sister who was sent back to Poland ten years earlier."

We are brought back to Corsi's question, "Who Shall Apologize?" or to another question, "Should We Apologize?" While it is true that many of the human sensibilities were blunted and that the total experience on Ellis Island was for many a form of torture, this view of the conditions did not see the other side. A letter from a French woman to Commissioner Curran offers another evaluation:[56]

> The ladies and gentlemen in charge of the emigrants have inexhaustible patience and kindness. The large admission hall is (in the evening) used as a concert room (once a week) and a cinema also. Sundays a Catholic, a Protestant and Jewish services are held so any creed can be followed. All this is free. Above, all around the hall, is a balcony. This has white tile walls and floors, porcelain lavabos and baths. There are two hospitals, a kindergarden, medical attendance, all free as well as board lodging, entertainment, etc., etc. Interrogation rooms, etc., are on the ground floor. Besides breakfast (coffee, eggs, bread, butter) lunch -- meat, vegetables, cheese, tea) (dinner -- soup, meat, etc.) there are (morning, afternoon, evening) three distributions of the best of sweet fresh milk and crackers. Many days thirty of those enormous cans are needed (they contain fifty gallons each, I was told). Six hundred and fifty employees are daily in attendance. Eighteen languages are interpreted. From morning till night colored men and women clean incessantly. Towels are changed daily. Sheets three times a week. I leave to a competent man the estimate of the daily expense of such an establishment, and I should thank heavily an expert to compare Ellis Island to anything of the same sort, any

---

[56]New York Times, February 17, 1924.

other nation in the wide world has to offer.

And then there is the hope and the promise of immigration; it is the other half of the description of Ellis Island; isle of hope, isle of tears. Many of the claims in all the presses of the world of inhuman treatment of immigrants were political charges directed at governments or at a political party in power. Many foreigners who came here from the middle and upper classes expected to receive a form of royal welcome, but instead were dealt out a dose of American democracy. They were not given private rooms, they were compelled to go in the same lines as the rest of the masses, and they were unprepared to deal with the petty annoyances that the peasants had dealt with for centuries. In spite of all the problems, Ellis Island was a marvel, one of the wonders of the world. It was too small and too poorly equipped for the work that was cast upon it. But at no other time in world history has any social institution been called upon to process ten thousand persons in one day. The miracle is not that a few were abused but that most were not. The Americans, as is their custom, dealt with the problems of Eliis Island pragmatically. As problems arose, they found solutions. They cleaned up the Island, they built a new records building, they built a beautiful plaza and covered it with flower beds. They built playgrounds for the children and recreational rooms for the adults. The legacy of Ellis Island is one of accommodation, of consideration, and of practical application of American democracy. This is what history should record.

Figure 15   Some Native Attire on Ellis Island (Photo from National Park Service)

Chapter III:

IMMIGRANT ARRIVALS AND DEPARTURES

Introduction

It has become a cliche to speak of the United States as a nation of immigrants. A central feature of America's pluralist democracy is the broad cultural diversity that is the product of immigration. The history of the United States is a history of varied racial, religious and national backgrounds.

These immigrants came in waves. We can identify four such movements: the first were the Irish and Germans, 1840-1860 (the old immigrant); the second were Jews, Italians, Slavs and Scandinavians, 1882-1930 (the new immigrants); the third group was the refugees, displaced and dispossessed persons before and following World War II (Jews, Hungarians, Cubans) and the last wave continues to the present. It is composed of Vietnamese, Koreans, Filipinos, Chinese and Latin Americans who came after the passage of the Immigration Act of 1965.

While immigrants retained some aspects of their culture, other traditions were discarded in the adjustment to the new society. But very little of the immigrants' heritage was left untouched by the American experience. Assimilation reflected the interaction of traditional cultures with the rapidly-changing conditions of an emerging urban and industrial nation. The immigrant experience of migration and resettlement encouraged them to regenerate their culture through the development of new forms here.

Immigrant Arrivals

Immigration statistics were recorded by the Department of State for the period 1820-1870, and by the Treasury Department from 1867 to 1895. It was not until 1892 that the first coordinated statistics of arrivals were published in the *Annual Reports* of the Bureau of Immigration. These continued until 1933, When the data were incorporated in the *Annual Report* of the Secretary of Labor. In 1941, immigration statistics were included in the *Annual Report* of the Attorney General, and since 1943, these data were published by the Immigration and Naturalization Service. (No report was issued in 1942)[1]

In the century after 1820, it estimated that 33,224,800 immigrants were admitted to the United States. 1907 was the peak year when 1,285,349 entered. In 1905, 1906, 1907, 1910, 1913 and 1914, total admissions were over one million per year.[2] it has been estimated that approximately eighty percent of all those who entered in the first two decades of the twentieth century came through Ellis Island.

It is impossible to state accurately how many were processed at Ellis Island. According to an early National Park Service report, between 1890 and 1932, 15,890.973 were received at the port of New York.[3] Using essentially the same printed sources, Pitkin obtained a slightly larger total. 16,000,000. Pitkin states, however, that, the port of New York and Ellis Island "were never synonymous."[4] At various times and for several reasons, immigrants by-passed Ellis Island, From June 1897 to the end of 1900, immigrants were received at Castle Garden, because a fire destroyed the original Ellis Island buildings. Further, cabin passengers were not classified as immigrants until 1904. They landed directly at the piers throughout most of the

---

[1]Jerry C. White, "A Statistical History of Immigration, I and N Reporter, (Summer 1976, page 1.

[2]Historical Statistics of the United States, Colonial Times to 1970, p. 56.

[3]Sidney Berengarten, Ellis Island (Washington, D. C.: Civil Works Administration, 1934).

[4]Pitkin, Ellis Island as an Immigrant Depot, p. 232.

history of Ellis Island.[5] Only aliens in steerage were so classified.

Using the 1905 Annual Report of the Commissioner-General of Immigration as a point oI reference, Pitkin estimated 11.6 percent of all arrivals in New York that year did not go through Ellis Island. On this basis, he extrapolated a ten percent figure for all the years from 1830 to 1932 and estimated there were 11,660,000 "bona fide Ellis Island immigrants,"[6] Unrau perpetuates this estimate: "All told, over twelve million immigrants entered the U. S. through Ellis Island, representing more than half the total number of " immigrants entering the country between 1892 and 1954.[7] However, in another place in the same report we learn that there were 18,018,759 immigrant arrivals at the port of New York (Table 3). If we accept Pitkin's own estimate that 88 percent of those landing at New York were sent to Ellis Island, then nearly 16 million persons were processed there. But even this figure is probably an undercount, as the *New York Times* recognized when it stated, "Over 20 million were processed in 62 years."[8]

There are other irregularities in the twelve million estimate (besides The ten percent extrapolation). Many ship manifests were lost, incorrectly completed or in some cases, fraudulently reported. For example, when the Immigration and Naturalization Service became part of the Justice Department in 1940, frauds were discovered which had been going on for several years involving alterations and insertions in five thousand passenger lists filed at Ellis Island.

---

[5]The exceptions were those occasions when second class passengers were ordered to Ellis Island by the Conmissioners of the Port of New York.

[6]Pitkin, Ellis Island, p. 233.

[7]Harlan D. Unrau, Historic Structures Report--Statue of Liberty-Ellis Island (National Park Service, May 1981, p. 1.

[8]November 13, 1954, p. 20 and November 14, p. 2.

Table 3

IMMIGRANT ARRIVALS AT PORT OF NEW YORK

Fiscal years 1890-1928

Fiscal Year	No. of Immigrants
1890	364,086
1891	448,403
1892	445,987
1893	343,422
1894	219,046
1895	190,928
1896	263,709
1897	180,556
1898	178,748
1899	242,573
1900	341,712
1901	388,931
1902	565,983
1903	631,885
1904	606,019
1905	809,847
1906	925,011
1907	1,123,842
1908	689,474
1909	733,267
1910	912,026
1911	749,642
1912	726,040
1913	1,040,457
1914	1,008,750
1915	200,000
1916	176,611
1917	160,105
1918	50,000
1919	62,306
1920	334,310
1921	652,909
1922	279,598
1923	391,316
1924	421,785
1925	241,319
1926	271,371
1927	300,136
1928	294,088
TOTAL	18,018,759

SOURCE: *Annual Report, Commissioner-General of Immigration* (Washington, 1928), pp. 27-28.

To put the statistics of immigration in proper perspective, consider the following facts. Between 1900 and 1920, approximately 15 million persons immigrated to the United States. This number exceeded the population of all states west of the Mississippi, except Iowa, California, Missouri, and Texas. More Italians entered than were found in Genoa, Florence, Milan, Palermo, Rome, and Turin. The more than one million Poles exceeded the population of the largest city in Poland; the number of Germans was greater than the population of Hamburg; and the number of Irish exceeded the total population of Connaught.[9]

Table 4 gives the passenger arrivals for 1895 by steamship lines. It Can be seen that the Northern European lines dominated the passenger traffic, and that the numher of steerage passengers was many times that of cabin occupants. In 1895, the ships of the Bremen service of the North German Lloyd's Line made the largest number of trips--130 voyages in that year.

The Hamburg Line was second with 93 voyages, followed by Cunard, 56; the French Line, 54; the Red Star, 53; the White Star, 51; and the American Line, 52.[10]

Some liners held as many as 2,000 passengers in steerage and realized enormous profits on these Atlantic trips. One gauge of the profitability can be seen by the fact that it cost a line only $.60 per day to feed an immigrant. The lucrative nature of the steerage carriage brought on a rate war between the steamship companies. It began in 1905 when the Cunard Line signed an agreement with the Austro-Hungarian government and made Fiume and Trieste ports of call. By undercutting prevailing rates, Cunard was able to take business away from German lines, particularly the Hamburg-American Line. The competition became even more intense when Cunard put the *Lusitania* and the *Mauretania* into service.

The number of aliens checking into Ellis Island peaked in 1907, In one period, between the closing on Saturday March 16, 1907 and the opening on March 18, 11,200 immigrants arrived at the Island. In this time, the following vessels arrived with the designated number of steerage passengers-- all of whom were required to be processed at Ellis Island: the *Chemnitz* from Bremen, 1527; the *Saint Louis* from

---

[9]Joseph I. Breen, "Our Immigrants--Who Are They, Whence They Came," The National Catholic Welfare Council, Bulletin, Nov. 1922.

[10]These numbers show how difficult it is to locate a single person from a ship list if one does not know the date of arrival.

Table 4

PASSENGER ARRIVALS BY STEAMSHIP LINES

1895

	Cabin	Steerage
North German Lloyd, Bremen	10,805	44,326
White Star, Liverpool	11,805	30,725
Hamburg American, Hamburg	10,543	30,141
Cunard, Liverpool	18,844	21,724
American, South Hampton	16,146	19,580
Generale Transatlantique, Havre	7,587	16,469
Red Star, Antwerp	4,890	12,554
North German Lloyd, Mediterranean	2,065	11,691
Netherlands-American Steam Navigation Co., Rotterdam	2,855	11,416
Anchor, Glasgow	6,604	10,011
Anchor, Mediterranean	41	9,837
Fabre, Mediterranean	20	7,477
Thingvalla, Copenhagen	747	6,889
Union, Hamburg	--	6,404
Scandia, Gothenburg	47	6,398
Hamburg-American, Mediterranean	535	3,972
Allan State, Glasgow	2,509	3,512
Netherlands-American Steam Navigation Co., Amsterdam	291	2,286
Cunard, Mediterranean	12	929
Baltic, Stettin	--	347
Floro, Mediterranean	--	44
Miscellaneous	212	1,837

SOURCE: W. C. Moore, Landing Agent, Ellis Island, *New York Times,* Jan. 7, 1896 p. 10:5.

Birmingham, 777; the *Perugia* from Italy, 1285; the *Amerika,* 1809; the *La Touraine,* 856; the *Cedric,* 1990; and the *Caledonia* from Glasgow, 800.[11]

Two weeks later, the *Kaiserin Auguste Victoria* from Hamburg brought a total of 2,386 passengers--the largest number ever to land. It was the last ship to dock that day and it brought the total for the day to 7,799 passengers of all classes-- 551 first class, 290 second

---

[11]*The New York Times,* July 19, 1907, p. 5:5.

class, 23 third class, and 1,322 steerage. "The force of inspectors was taxed to the limit to pass the incoming flood of trunks, valises, boxes, shawl straps and what not. . ."[12] Because of the shortage of Custom inspectors, the steerage passengers were required to remain on on board ship until they could be processed,

The most popular ships making the Atlantic voyage before World War I are listed in Table 5. The dominance of Naples, Hamburg, Liverpool, Bremen, Genoa and Southampton as ports of departure is evident. The passage of the Chinese Exclusion Act marked a major turning point in the history of United States immigration. The "old" immigration from Northern and Western Europe began to decline, and the "new immigration" began to rise rapidly. It is significant that 49.5 percent of the total of all U. S. immigration occurred in the years 1881-1920.

The shift in Immigration had economic roots. When western Europe industrialized, those nations (Great Britain, Germany, Belgium, Sweden, and France) could provide jobs at home for the laborers from the rural districts. These had constituted the bulk of the old emigrants. Germany is a good example. In the decade of the 1880's, She provided almost 1.5 million immigrants, but the number declined to 505,152 in the next decade, when Germany stood atop of the industrial world of Europe.

---

[12]The New York Times, August 4, 1907, Pt 2, p. 12:5.

Table 5

POPULAR PASSENGER STEAMERS

(1900-1914)

Name of Steamer	Steamship Line	Port of Departure	Stopped at	Duration of Voyage Days
ADRIATIC	White Star Line	Liverpool ...	Queenstown	8
ALGERIA	Anchor Line	Napoli		16–17
ALICE	Austro-American Line	Trieste	Patras	20–21
AMERICA	Hamburg-American Line	Hamburg		8
ANCONA	Italia Line	Napoli		13–14
ANDALUSIA	Hamburg-American Line	Hamburg		14
ANTONIO LOPEZ	Compania Transatlantica	Genova	Napoli, Barcelona	18
ARCADIA	Hamburg-American Line	Hamburg		15
ARGENTINA	Austro-American Line	Trieste	Palermo	20–21
ARMENIA	Hamburg-American Line	Hamburg		12
ASTORIA	Anchor Line	Glasgow		10
ATHINAI	Greek Line	Pireus		19–20
BALTIC	White Star Line	Liverpool ...	Queenstown	8
BARBAROSSA	North German Lloyd	Bremen		12–13
BATAVIA	Hamburg-American Line	Hamburg .....Boulogne		11–13
BELVEDERE	Austro-American Line	Trieste		20
BERLIN	North German Lloyd	Bremen		10
BIRMA	Russian East Asiatic Line	Libau		13–15
BLUECHER	Hamburg-American Line	Hamburg		10
BOSNIA	Hamburg-American Line	Hamburg		14–15
BRANDENBURG	North German Lloyd	Bremen		13
BRASILE	La Veloce	Napoli		14–16
BREMEN	North German Lloyd	Bremen		11
BULGARIA	Hamburg-American Line	Genova	Napoli	18
CALEDONIA	Anchor Line	Glasgow		8
CALIFORNIA	Cunard, Anchor Line	Glasgow		8
CALIFORNIE	French Line	Havre		14–15
CAMPANIA	Anchor Line	Liverpool ...	Queenstown	7
CARMANIA	Cunard Line	Liverpool ...	Queenstown	8
CARONIA	Cunard Line	Liverpool ...	Queenstown	8
CARPATHIA	Cunard Line	Fiume	Napoli	18–20
CASSEL	North German Lloyd	Bremen		14–15
CEDRIC	White Star Line	Liverpool ...	Queenstown	9
CELTIC	White Star Line	Southampton.	Cherbourg	9
CHEMNITZ	North German Lloyd	Bremen		12
CITTA' DI NAPOLI	La Veloce	Genova	Palermo, Napoli	19
CITTA' DI TORINO	La Veloce	Napoli		16
CLEVELAND	Hamburg-American Line	Hamburg		9–10
COLUMBIA	Anchor Line	Glasgow		8
CRETIC	White Star Line	Napoli		12–14
DEUTSCHLAND	Hamburg-American Line	Hamburg ...	Southampton, Cherbourg.	7
DUCA D'AOSTA	Navigazione Generale Ital.	Genova	Napoli	14
DUCA DEGLI ABRUZZI	Navigazione Generale Ital.	Genova		13–14
ERNY	Austro-American Line	Trieste	Patras	21–22
ETRURIA	Cunard Line	Liverpool ...	Queenstown	8
EUGENIA	Austro-American Line	Trieste ....Palermo		20
EUROPA	La Veloce	Napoli		12
FINLAND	Red Star Line	Antwerp ......Dover		9
FLORIDA	Lloyd Italiano	Genova	Napoli	14
FRANCE	French Line	Havre		7
FRANCESCA	Austro-American Line	Trieste	Patras	21–22
FRIEDRICH DER GROSSE	North German Lloyd	Genova	Napoli	10–14
FURNESSIA	Anchor Line	Glasgow		12
GEORGE WASHINGTON	North German Lloyd	Bremen		9
GNEISENAU	North German Lloyd	Bremen		9
GOTHLAND	Red Star Line	Antwerp		10–11
GRAF WALDERSEE	Hamburg-American Line	Hamburg ...	Plymouth	11
GROSSER KURFUERST	North German Lloyd	Bremen	Boulogne	10
GUILA	Austro-American Line	Trieste	Patras	21
HAMBURG	Hamburg-American Line	Genova	Napoli	13
HANOVER	North German Lloyd	Bremen		14
HELLIG OLAF	Scandinavian-American Line	Copenhagen .	Christiania	12
HUDSON	French Line	Havre		13

PISA	Hamburg-American Line	Hamburg	12
POTSDAM	Holland-America Line	Rotterdam ., Boulogne	10
PRETORIA	Hamburg-American Line	Hamburg	10–12
PRESIDENT GRANT	Hamburg-American Line	Hamburg	11
PRESIDENT LINCOLN	Hamburg-American Line	Hamburg	11
PRINCIPE DI PIEMONTE	Lloyd Sabaudo	Genova ..... Napoli, Palermo	16
PRINZ ADALBERT	Hamburg-American Line	Genova ..... Napoli	14–15
PRINZ OSCAR	Hamburg-American Line	Genova ..... Napoli	14–15
PRINZESS ALICE	North German Lloyd	Bremen	10
PRINZESS IRENE	North German Lloyd	Genova ..... Napoli, Palermo	13
RE D'ITALIA	Lloyd Sabaudo	Genova ..... Napoli, Palermo	16–17
REGINA D'ITALIA	Lloyd Sabaudo	Genova ..... Napoli, Palermo	15
REPUBLIC	White Star Line	Napoli	13
RHEIN	North German Lloyd	Bremen	14
ROCHAMBEAU	French Line	Havre	9
ROMA	Fabre Line	Napoli	12
ROTTERDAM	Holland-America Line	Amsterdam	14
RYNDAM	Holland-America Line	Rotterdam ....Boulogne	10
SAN GIORGIO	Sicula-Americana Line	Messina ..... Napoli, Palermo	15
SAN GIOVANNI	Sicula-Americana Line	Napoli	14
SANT'ANNA	Fabre Line	Marseilles ... Palermo	16
SAMLAND	Red Star Line	Antwerp	12
SAXONIA	Cunard Line		
SICILIA	Hamburg-American Line	Hamburg	17
SILVIA	Hamburg-American Line	Hamburg ... Boulogne	14
SLAVONIA	Cunard Line	Fiume ...... Trieste, Napoli	18–19
SMOLENSK	Russian Volunteer Fleet	Libau ...... Rotterdam	17–18
SOFIA HOHENBURG	Austro-American Line	Trieste ...... Patras	20
ST. LAURENT	French Line	Havre	15
ST. LOUIS	American Line	Southampton. Cherbourg	7
TAORMINA	Italian Line	Genova ..... Palermo, Napoli	14
TEUTONIC	White Star Line	Liverpool ... Queenstown	7
THEMISTOCLES	Greek Line	Pireus ...... Patras	21–22
TRAVE	North German Lloyd	Bremen	10
ULTONIA	Cunard Line	Trieste ...... Fiume, Palermo	20
UMBRIA	Cunard Line	Liverpool ... Queenstown	8
UNITED STATES	Scandinavian American Line	Copenhagen . Christiania	11
URANIUM	Uranium Line	Rotterdam .. Halifax	13
VADERLAND	Red Star Line	Antwerp .... Dover	9
VICTORIA LUISE	Hamburg-American Line	Hamburg	10–11
WEIMAR	North German Lloyd	Bremen	15
WITTEKIND	North German Lloyd	Bremen	14–15
WUERZBERG	North German Lloyd	Bremen	15–16
ZEELAND	Red Star Line	Antwerp .... Dover	10

SOURCE:Kalnay and Collins, *The New Americans*, pp. 276-282.

The new immigration involved persons from Austria-Hungary, Bulgaria, Greece, Italy, Poland, Portugal, Roumania, Russia, Spain and Turkey. They were characterized by great poverty, surplus population, lack of economic development, illiteracy and poor health. It was these very conditions which caused the U. S. Congress to begin debating limitations on entry of aliens.

Table 6 gives the statistics of immigration by country. The shift to Southern and Eastern Europe between 1900 and 1914 is very marked. In this time, Italy, Russia, and Austria-Hungary became the three chief contributors to the immigration total. (Italians, Jews and Slavs) Italy, suffering from high rents, low wages, over population, and high unemployment, sought relief by emigration. It became official policy to encourage emigration to the Western hemisphere. Italians left mainly for Argentina and the United States. There are cases of entire villages leaving Italy in steerage. Whereas the early Italian immigrants were from the industrial north and were importers, musicians, and artisans, the new horde were illiterate laborers.

Austria-Hungary found itself in similar circumstances. It had a large peasant population with little means of support and it too found escape in emigration. Ordinarily, one person was sent to the United States to earn passage money for others who would follow. These Austro-Hungarians included a very diverse number of peoples, including Czechs, Poles, Magyars, Ukranians, Yugoslavs, Roumanians, and Jews. Clearly, no single pattern can describe the migration of such a group.

Russian emigration was different. It stemmed largely, from a desire for escape from political and religious persecution under czarist rule. Poverty simply added to the Russian problem. It is notable, also that many who fled Russia were from ethnic minorities, especially Jews, Poles, Lithuanians, Finns, and Germans.

Some of the problems of counting the immigrants by country can be seen in the German, Russian or Austria-Hungarian totals. This immigration totalled only 419,957. But there were 993,497 foreign-born Poles in the United States in 1940. Obviously, the immigration statistics understate Polish entrants.[13] .

Table 7 confirms that the largest segment of immigrants entering

---

[13]U. S. Congress, Senate, "The Immigration and Naturalization Systems of the United States," Report 1515, 81st Cong., March 29, 1950

the United States between 1880 and 1920 were classified in the domestic service and general labor categories. These accounted for nearly 8 million of the total. In addition, agriculture contributed nearly 3 million. In the time period 1901-1920, 67.3 percent of all immigrants were male and most of them were in the 16-44 age bracket. By 1960, however, the percentage of families had risen to 55.7 percent.

Why did They Come?

The popular press of the post-1890 period had much to say on why immigrants were willing to tear up roots, leave families and friends and start out on a difficult journey to the United States. A layman's answer was provided by Terence V. Powderly, Commissioner-General of Immigration, who travelled to Europe in the Summer of 1906 under instructions from Frank P. Sargent--the Commissioner-General of that year.[14] Powderly offered eleven reasons for the sustained emigration from Europe:

1. The natural desire of man to improve his condition in life.

2. The political status which the industrialist occupies in his home country.

3. The economic condition in which he is obliged to live and which, through lack of political freedom, he finds it difficult to improve or change.

4. The lack of educational facilities, in some countries, to instruct him in his political rights and through which he might be enabled to change his economic condition.

---

[14]See the 75 page report of Powderly's travels, Reel 80, of the Powderly Papers at the Catholic University of America Archives.

5. The constant stream of letters which go from those in the United States, who were formerly immigrants, to their relatives and friends in Europe.

6. The accounts of conditions, political and industrial, in the United States, given by those who return to Europe to remain either temporarily or permanently.

7. The activity of agents, sub-agents and their agents of steamship lines in selling tickets and in stimulating the business of their principals.

8. The example set by Americans who travel abroad and their advice to European industrialists to emigrate to the United States.

9. The freedom and prosperity enjoyed by the people of the United States and the remarkable, and rapid, facilities for making known conditions, and changes in conditions, in the United States.

10. The desire on the part of those having relatives, or friends, dependent on them who are mentally, or physically deficient to evade responsibility, or expense or both by sending the deficient ones to the United States or somewhere.

11. The cheap fares charged by competing steamship lines, the rapidity with which an ocean voyage may be made and the comfort enjoyed while en route.

Table 6

IMMIGRATION BY COUNTRY

1892-1954

Year	Total	Central Europe	Italy	USSR	Germany	Ireland	Scandinavia
1954	208,177	2,873	13,145	475	33,098	4,655	5,459
1953	170,434	2,885	8,432	609	27,329	4,304	5,537
1952	265,520	23,529	11,342	548	104,236	3,526	5,416
1951	205,717	10,365	8,958	555	87,755	3,144	5,502
1950	249,187	17,792	12,454	526	128,592	5,842	5,661
1949	188,317	7,411	11,695	694	55,284	8,678	6,665
1948	170,570	6,006	16,075	897	19,368	7,534	6,127
1947	147,292	4,622	13,866	761	13,900	2,574	4,918
1946	108,721	511	2,636	153	2,598	1,816	1,278
1945	38,119	206	213	98	172	427	224
1944	28,551	316	120	157	238	112	281
1943	23,725	206	49	159	248	165	239
1942	28,781	396	103	197	2,150	83	371
1941	51,776	786	450	665	4,028	272	1,137
1940	70,756	3,628	5,302	898	21,520	839	1,260
1939	82,998	5,334	6,570	1,021	33,515	1,189	1,178
1938	67,895	5,195	7,712	960	17,199	1,085	1,393
1937	50,244	3,763	7,192	629	10,895	531	971
1936	36,329	2,723	6,774	378	6,346	444	646
1935	34,956	2,357	6,566	418	5,201	454	688
1934	29,470	1,422	4,374	607	4,392	443	557
1933	23,068	981	3,477	458	1,919	338	511
1932	35,576	1,749	6,662	636	2,670	539	938
1931	97,139	4,500	13,399	1,396	10,401	7,305	3,144
1930	241,700	9,184	22,327	2,772	26,569	23,445	6,919
1929	279,678	8,081	18,008	2,450	46,751	19,921	17,379
1928	307,255	7,091	17,728	2,662	45,778	25,268	16,184
1927	335,175	6,559	17,297	2,933	48,513	28,545	16,860
1926	304,488	6,020	8,253	3,323	50,421	24,897	16,818
1925	294,314	4,701	6,203	3,121	46,068	26,650	16,810
1924	706,896	32,700	56,246	20,918	75,091	17,111	35,577
1923	522,919	34,088	46,674	21,151	48,277	15,740	34,184
1922	509,556	29,363	40,319	19,910	17,931	10,579	14,625
1921	805,228	77,069	222,260	10,193	6,803	28,435	22,854
1920	430,001	5,666	95,145	1,751	1,001	9,591	13,444
1919	141,132	53	1,884	1,403	52	474	5,590
1918	110,618	61	5,250	4,242	447	331	6,506
1917	295,403	1,258	34,596	12,716	1,857	5,406	13,771
1916	298,826	5,191	33,665	7,842	2,877	8,639	14,761

1915	326,700	18,511	49,688	26,187	7,799	14,185	17,883
1914	1,218,480	278,152	283,738	255,660	35,734	24,688	29,391
1913	1,197,892	254,825	265,542	291,040	34,329	27,876	32,267
1912	838,172	178,882	157,134	162,395	27,788	25,879	27,554
1911	878,587	159,057	182,882	158,721	32,061	29,112	42,285
1910	1,041,570	258,737	215,537	186,792	31,283	29,855	48,267
1909	751,786	170,191	183,218	120,460	25,540	25,033	32,496
1908	782,870	168,509	128,503	156,711	32,309	30,556	30,175
1907	1,285,349	338,452	285,731	258,943	37,807	34,530	49,965
1906	1,100,735	265,138	273,120	215,665	37,564	34,995	52,781
1905	1,026,499	275,693	221,479	184,897	40,574	52,945	60,625
1904	812,870	177,156	193,296	145,141	46,380	36,142	60,096
1903	857,046	206,011	230,622	136,093	40,086	35,310	77,647
1902	648,743	107,989	178,375	107,347	28,304	29,138	54,038
1901	487,918	113,390	135,996	85,257	21,651	30,561	39,234
1900	448,572	114,847	100,135	90,787	18,507	35,730	31,151
1899	311,715	62,491	77,419	60,982	17,476	31,673	22,192
1898	229,299	39,797	58,613	29,828	17,111	25,128	19,282
1897	230,832	33,031	59,431	25,816	22,533	28,421	21,089
1896	343,267	65,103	68,060	51,445	31,885	40,262	33,199
1895	258,536	33,401	35,427	35,907	32,173	46,304	26,852
1894	285,631	38,638	42,977	39,278	53,989	30,231	32,400
1893	439,730	57,420	72,145	42,310	78,756	43,578	58,945
1892	579,663	76,937	61,631	81,511	119,168	51,383	66,295

*Includes Poland, Czechoslovakia, Yugoslavia, Hungary, and Austria (except 1938-1945).

SOURCE: *Historical Statistics of the United States, Colonial Times to 1970*, pp. 105-106.

One person made a much more emotionally-charged, imagination-filled statement of the reasons for coming to the United States:[15]

To begin with, the country itself, a land flowing with milk and honey. People make plenty of money; you dig into money with both hands, you pick up gold by the shovelful! And as for 'business,' as they call it in America, there is so much of it that it just makes your head spin! You can do

[15]Meltzer, Taking Root, p. 26.

Table 7

DISTRIBUTION OF IMMIGRANTS BY OCCUPATION

1881-1960

	Total	Agriculture	Industry and Mining	Transport and Commerce
1881-1900	8,934,177	633,794	850,779	766,600
1901-1920	14,531,197	2,893,022	1,872,028	566,376
1921-1940	4,635,640	357,173	727,476	--
1941-1960	3,550,518	138,806	507,071	365,295

	Domestic Service and General Labor	Professional and Public Services	Other
1881-1900	2,949,086	49,151	4,184,767
1901-1920	4,869,108	200,913	4,129,750
1921-1940	1,078,488	193,644	2,278,859
1941-1960	385,251	765,543	1,888,552

SOURCE: White, "A Statistical History of Immigration, p.4.

anything you like. You want a factory--so you have a factory; you want to, you push a pushcart; and if you don't, you peddle or go to work in a shop--it's a free country! You may starve or drop dead of hunger in the street--there is nothing to prevent you, nobody will object.

Then, the size of the cities! The width of the streets! The height of the buildings! They have a building there, they call it the Woolworth--so the top of its chimneypot reaches into the clouds and even higher; it is said that this house has several hundred floors. You want to know, how do they climb up to the attic? By a ladder which they call an elevator. If you want somebody on the top floor, you sit down in the elevator early in the morning, so you get towards sunset, just in time for your evening prayers.

In the journal articles, scholars debated the strength of the "push" and "pull" factors in explaining the great Atlantic migrations. A push factor involved some event or problem in the home (losing) country (for example a famine); a pull factor was a stimulant to settle in the receiving country (for example, higher employment or wages).

The push-pull controversy stressed relative economic contributions in explaining decisions to stay or emigrate. The early research involved relating migration flows to business cvcles. Harry Jerome found that cyclical fluctuations is European migration were related to economic conditions in the United States.[16] Kuznets and Rubin found that before 1914, the 20-year swing in immigration (the Kuznets cycle) tended to follow the pattern of the gross national product per worker. They were not sure whether immigration was caused by improvements in levels of living in the United States or whether immigration had an effect on economic activity. When they compared net immigration with housing construction, it was found that a slackening in immigration brought a similar reduction in housing demand. Thus, they concluded that changes in immigration preceded changes in housing construction.[17]

Brinley Thomas saw emigration as a result of Malthusian pressures; those countries which experienced high population growth

---

[16]Harry Jerome, Migration and Business Cycles (New York: National Bureau of Economic Research, 1926).

[17]Simon Kuznets and Ernest Rubin, Immigration and the Foreign Born, (New York: National Bureau of Economic Research, 1954), p. 5.

and the inability to feed that population saw heavy emigration as a solution to overpopulation (Perhaps Southern Italy best exemplified this notion). In addition to this "push" effect, Thomas also found a strong positive correlation between immigration and per-capita income in the United States (those states which had the highest number of immigrants also had the highest per-capita imcomes).[18]

Gould believes that, "Economic motives do not exhaust the list reasons why so many million left their homeland in the course of the nineteenth century to try their fortunes in another continent.[19] The Jews provide the single best example of a non-economic factor influencing emigratlon. While they hoped to improve themselves economically, their primary motive in leaving was to escape persecution and to gain political and legal rights in a new land. During the 19th century, Russia passed more than 600 anti-Jewish laws, culminating in the pogroms of the 1880's and 1890's. But Jews were not the only persecuted people. In Germany, Chancellor Bismarck tried to eradicate the Polish culture, and the Magyars (Hungarians), who are of Finno-ugric stock, forbade the Slavs from using their native languages.[20] In fact, the United States has always been a haven for religious dissenters, starting with the Pilgrims, continuing to the Scandinavians in the mid-nineteenth century and to the Jews.

Political freedom also was a factor. Many immigrants who wrote letters home stressed the degree of political freedom and the absence of constraints in the United States. The non-Jewish emigration from

---

[18] Brinley Thomas, Migration and Economic Growth (Cambridge: The University Press, 1954).

[19] J. D. Gould, "European Intercontinental Emigration: The Role of 'Diffusion' and 'Feedback'," The Journal of European Economic History, IX (Fall 1980), p. 208.

[20] See Leslie Allen, Liberty: The Statue and the American Dream (Statue of Liberty/Ellis Island Foundation, 1986), p. 154.

Russia was heavily influenced by political aspects, particularly of the Poles, Latvians, and Lithuanians.

Terence V. Powderly, former Commissioner-General of Immigration, tells of one Italian from Rifredi, in whose home he slept one night, who informed him that: "A great many of our friends are in the United States, they are doing well there, better than they could do here, they write to me ahout the work there, about what wages they get, about how they live there. They tell me that in America no one meddles with your business or religion, no one comes to look through your house to see if any deserter is there or to make you pay tribute."[21]

Gould mentions another factor that became more important during World War I: the desire to escape from the obligation of military service, but he is not totally convinced that this is a major cause of emigration. The problem with this factor is that there is insufficient bunching of emigration at age 20, when men became eligible for military service.

Runblom and Norman emphasize the "friends and relatives" effect.[22] They found that there was a "remarkable stability" in the distribution of emigrants by regional origin in the successive waves of emigration (1868-73, 1879-93, 1900-13, 1920-29). Areas of Sweden that had sent out emigrants in early waves, continued to do so in the later periods of emigration. This resulted in a self-perpetuating system of immigration that was based on tradition and social factors. During a Swedish immigration period more non-heirs were likely to emigrate and, therefore, Swedish immigrants changed from those seeking land to those seeking jobs.

Some people were able to come to the United States because

---

[21]Powderly Papers, Reel 80, p. 59.

[22]H. Runblom and H. Norman (eds.), From Sweden to America (Minneapolis: University of Minnesota Press, 1976).

they received help. An example of this is the Italian *padrone* system whereby the labor contracter met his men on the dock through pre-arrangement. One young man described the experience:[23]

> We were all landed on an island, and the bosses there said that Francesco and I must go back because we had not enough money, but a man named Bartolo came up and told them that we were brothers and he was our uncle. I had never seen any of them before, but even then Bartolo might be my uncle so I did not say anything. The bosses of the island let us go off with Bartolo after he had made the oath. We came to Brooklyn, New York, to a wooden house in Adams Street that was full of Italians from Naples. Bartolo had a room on the third floor and there were beds all around the sides, one bed above another. . .The next morning early Bartolo told us to go out and pick rags and get bottles.

The efforts of the Italians pale beside those of the Jews who were aided by the Baron de Hirsch Fund. By 1892, it had donated over forty million dollars to the Jewish Colonization Association, which was used to transport the Jewish population from Russia to the United States. When the last de Hirsch died in 1899, over ten million dollars more was made available for Jewish settlement.[24]

In concluding this section on "Why Did They Come?," we need to confront Handlin's notion that immigrants were *The Uprooted* who lost all links with their past. If you accept his view that immigration was a very disruptive experience, then you may ask why did they come to the United States? Vecoli began a great debate on this

---

[23]Quoted in Alberta Eisenman, From Many Lands (New York: Atheneum, 1970), p. 116.

[24]Victor Safford, Immigration Problems (New York: Dodd, Mead, 1925), p. 38.

subject when he found that not only did the immigrant culture survive the ocean crossing, but it significantly altered how Americans lived. There was a "cultural continuity."[25]

Immigrant Destinations

Immigrants tended to be concentrated in a few states, in urban areas, and they avoided the South (except Florida and Texas). The U. S. Immigration Commission studied inmigrant destinations for the years 1899-1910 (See Table 8). It shows that just under 50 percent of all immigrants were destined for two states (New York and Pennsylvania). Since well over one-half of all immigrants landed at New York City, it is easy to understand why New York State has such a commanding spot; the reasons for Pennsylvania's popularity are not certain, but it is probably connected to the propensity of immigrants to go where others from their regions had already settled (i.e. the mining towns).

The 1910 Census showed that there were 13,345,543 foreign born in the United States--of whom nearly 5 million entered the country in that decade. Of the total of newly-entered, 2,155,772 went to the Middle Atlantic states (New York, Pennsylvania, and New Jersey), making up 43.2 percent of the total; 1,012,417 settled in the East North Central region (Ohio, Indiana, Illinois, Michigan, and Wisconsin)--20.2 percent; and 684,473 made New England their destination, 13.7 percent. These statistics indicate that 77.1 percent of the immigrants stayed in the region bounded by the area north of the Ohio River and east of the Mississippi. More important, the statistics are comparable to those of older immigrants -- 70.2 percent settling in the same region.

These statistics make it clear that immigrants avoided the American South, which was particularly bothersome to officials there, who saw immigrants as a good supply of cheap labor. For this

---

[25]Rudolph Vecoli, "Contadini in Chicago: A Critique of The Uprooted, Journal of American History, LI (December 1964), 404-417.

Table 8

DESTINATIONS OF IMMIGRANTS

(1899-1910)

States	Admissions	Percentage
New York	2,994,358	31.4%
Pennsylvania	1,737,059	18.2%
Illinois	722,059	7.6%
Massachusetts	719,887	7.5%
New Jersey	489,533	5.1%
Ohio	407,285	4.3%
Connecticut	245,636	2.6%
California	237,795	2.5%
Michigan	233,824	2.4%
Minnesota	182,558	1.9%
Wisconsin	150,162	1.6%
Missouri	123,045	1.3%
Washington	111,814	1.2%
Rhode Island	98,635	1.0%
Hawaii	98,102	1.0%
Florida	66,612	*
Texas	75,807	*
Arizona	13,414	*
Maryland	71,265	*
All others	987,974	10.4%
TOTALS	9,539,726	100.0%

* Less than one percent

SOURCE: *Abstracts of Reports of the Immigration Commission,* 1911, p. 105.

reason the Southern States Immigration Commission was formed in June 1906 to help immigrants settle in the South. Conmissioner of Immigration Robert Watchorn told the *New York Times* that if the South wanted immigration that it would have to raise wages to the levels of the West and the North.[26]

---

[26] New York Times, June 6, 1906, p. 9:5.

Several southern representatives made attempts on Ellis Island to persuade Italians and Greeks to settle in their states (Louisiana and Mississippi) without success. Commissioner of Licenses for New York City, John N. Bogart, charged cruelty and oppression against Italians and others who were sent to the South, and he stated that they were "shamefully treated." One problem was the apparent collusion between the padrones and a few unscrupulous employment agencies. The padrones employed immigrants by the thousands and used the "commissionary principle"--that is, they furnished food and lodging and deducted them from wages. In this calculation, the padrone was the "sole arbiter of these costs." Hundreds of immigrants were told they were going to Philadelphia or Pittsburgh and wound up in a Florida swamp or in the wilds of North Carolina, where they were kept on construction work by an armed guard.[27] Given these conditions, few immigrants chose the American South. They were turned away by lower wages, by the climate, by the agricultural society, and by an unmentionable--the large percentage of blacks there.

But in at least one case, the South was an attractive destination. The North German Lloyd Line found that its voyages from northern Europe to the Gulf of Mexico (Galveston) were very sucessful. It decided to divide its traffic between Galveston and New York City. This decision was very welcome in New York City, where the ports were clogged and where aliens had imposed burdens of all kinds on the citizen of the city.[28]

The Return Migrants

Many immigrants did not come to stay. Rather, they came to earn money to purchase land or property in the old country. But many who intended to return never did, while others made several voyages to the United States, some annually. These persons were

---

[27] New York Times, June 17, 1906, p. 16:1.

[28] New York Times, May 8, 1906, p. 8: 3.

known, somewhat derisively, as "Birds of Passage."

The Italians had one of the highest rates of repatriation of all ethnic groups. Robert Foerster was one of the first to note this temporary nature of Italian immigration.[29] He estimated that 300,000 to 400,000 nationals returned to Italy each year between 1902 and 1914. Cerase found two peaks of return immigration for Italians: the first after 6-10 years of residence and the other after 30 years.[30] This finding is at odds with other research that tends to show a much shorter average stay. According to Caroli, return emigration was typical of the less-educated workers who could not find work in Italy. Temporary migration was their only solution. The number of emigrants returning to Italy from North and South America was substantually higher than from the United States.

The Kuznets-Rubin estimates for total departures are shown in Table 9. The relationship to business conditions is obvious: the peak exodus was in 1908, the time of he Money Panic of 1907-08. Other peak years for departures were 1894 (210,000), 1914 (634,000) and 1920 (428,000)--all times of business downturns. The Great Depression destroyed the connection between departures and bad times, but this undoubtedly had more to do with political than economic instability.

Sizable amounts of money were sent by immigrants to their relatives through banks and post offices. In 1909, the figure was $74,931,843 ; this escalated to $165,234,813 in 1913 and to more than $247 million by 1929."[31] Austria-Hungary and Italy claimed more than one-half of the remittances, with Russia, Scandinavia and

---

[29]See Robert F. Foerster. The Italian Immigration of Our Times (Cambridge: Harvard University Press, 1919) p. 42.

[30]Francesco P. Cerase, "A Study of Italian Migrants Returning From the U.S.A," International Migration Review, I (Summer 1967), 67-74.

[31]Cowens, Memories of an American Jew, p. 185.

Table 9

IMMIGRANT DEPARTURES

1890-1945

(000)

Year	Departures	Year	Departures	Year	Departures
1890	148	1910	380	1930	272
91	153	11	518	31	291
92	164	12	615	32	288
93	163	13	612	33	244
94	210	14	634	34	177
1895	206	1915	384	1935	189
96	158	16	241	36	193
97	139	17	146	37	224
98	129	18	193	38	223
99	134	19	216	39	202
1900	134	1920	428	1940	166
01	275	21	426	41	88
02	345	22	345	42	75
03	389	23	201	43	59
04	311	24	217	44	84
1905	398	1925	226	1945	93
06	469	26	228		
07	671	27	254		
08	715	28	274		
1909	400	1929	252		

SOURCE: Simon Kuznets and Ernest Rubin, *Immigration and the Foreign Born* (New York: National Bureau of Economic Research, 1954), p. 95-96.

Germany accounting for another twenty-five percent. These amounts exclude money sent by businesses or by immigrant banks.

Breen, writing in 1922 claimed that "about 40 percent of them [immigrants] stay for a few years and then go home."[32] According to him, for the 10 years prior to 1921, more than 5,600,000 arrived and 2,200,000 "sailed away." He states, correctly, that the Southeastern Europeans have the highest out-migration, but some industrial countries had rates greatly exceeding those. He cites an 86 percent rate of return for Finns, 65 percent for Hungarians, 56 percent for Russians, 55 percent for Slovaks, 52 percent for Greeks, 50 percent for Italians, 38 percent for Poles, and 30 percent for Scandinavians.

Many Swedes returned after a stay in the United States. Runblom and Norman estimate that between 1880 and 1930, these returning migrants represented 19 percent of all migrants.[33] These migrants looked at emigration as a means of accumulating income, and they considereed the whole process reversible.

T. V. Powderly, former Commissioner General of Inmigration, found that although the Hungarian government did not favor emigration of its able-bodied people, it did not object to citizens going to America and sending remittances back to Hungary. As he said, "Go where you will through Hungary and there will you find men who speak the English language. Inquiry will show that they had lived in America, had learned the English language there and returned to Hungary either to remain permanently or to prepare friends and relatives to emigrate."[34] On another part of the same voyage, while journeying to Antwerp on the *Kroonland* of the Red Star Line, he found that of 450 in steerage, "over a fourth of them intended returning to the United States in a short time."[35].

---

[32] Breen, "Our Immigrants - Who Are They, Whence Do They Come," p. 7.

[33] Rumblom and Norman, From Sweden to America.

[34] Powderly Papers, Reel 80, p.53.   [35] Powderly Papers, Reel 80, p.3

Figure 16 Immigrants on Deck of Kroonland (Photo from Terence V. Powderly Collection)

Aliens Deported

The Immigration Act of 1893 required that shipowners prepare manifests of incoming passengers to aid immigration officials in reducing the number of inadmissible aliens. The manifests provided detailed information on individual immigrants; these forms became important references involving both naturalization and deportation cases.

Deportation of aliens was an administrative determination of the Board of Special Inquiry and of the Secretaries of the Treasury, Commerce and Labor Departments (depending on under whom the Bureau of Immigration was organized). Aliens were deported because they were undesirable, for whatever reason. In the Special Inquiry, the immigrant was not allowed counsel; but such was permitted in the appeal process. All appeals were decided by the Secretary, who often sustained the appeal and allowed the immigrant to land.[36]

In 1909, Commissioner of Immigration William Williams ruled that no one should be admitted at Ellis Island who did not have $25 in his or her possession. Following the order, 215 second class cabin passengers of 301 on the Holland-America line were detained. Many of these persons were met by relatives who assured immigration officials that these persons would not become a public charge.[37]. But William's order served to increase deportations 35 percent in 1909 over 1908.

The case of Giovanni Marte illustrates the inhumanity of applying rigid rules to personal cases. Marte, 22 years old and quite healthy, had only 19 dollars in his possession. He was offered employment in Minnesota by Inspector Green of the Employment

---

[36]According to Pitkin, on a single day in 1903, 19 telegrams were sent to Ellis Island by the Secretary sustaining appeals. See Keepers of the Gate, p. 51.

[37]New York Times, June 30, 1909, p.3:3

Bureau. Marte refused to go west, so he was deported.[38] Williams was relentless in pursuing his policy of increasing deportations. When persons arrived with little money, he blamed the steamship companies. In the first week in July 1909, he surveyed several ships. On the *Volturno* he found that "out of 251 aliens, thirty-nine had no money at all, two had less that $1, eleven " had $1 each, sixteen had $8, four had $9, fifteen had $10, and sixty-two had more than $10."[39] On the *Ragian Castle,* out of 305 immigrants in steerage, 20 had no money at all.[40] That William's fears of a large number of immigrants becoming public charges are greatly exaggerated is shown by the statistics. In 1912, the 1,ll4,989 aliens who arrived brought $46,712,697 (an average of $38 per person); this may be compared with $3,050,948 for 167,665 immigrants in 1894--an average of $18. In 1913, only 1.6 percent of all aliens were denied admittance.[41]

One deportee was detained for a record period of time. Miji Cogic, an Austrian, was deported in 1920, after being detained for five years. He arrived August 8, 1914 and was ordered deported for defective sight, but World War I intervened. He lived on Ellis Island and saved $495 by serving as a barber and tailor, He cost the United States $2,046, but the government was unable to collect since the Austro-American Line, which brought him from Trieste went out of

---

[38] New York Times, July 10, 1909, p.14:3.

[39] New York Times, July 10, 1909, p.14:3.

[40] On a personal note, I wonder how my father passed inspection, since, according to the ship manifest, he came in 1910 with $18 in his possession.

[41] New York Times, Sept. 28, 1912, p.1:5; Annual Report of the Commissioner of Immigration, 1894.

business.[42]

In the frantic activities of determining who would be admitted and who would be debarred, no one seemed to give much consideration to what happened to those who were deported. In many cases, instead of carrying aliens to the "Country from whence they came," they landed at Southampton or Dover and were stranded at these ports without passage money or means of support. To alleviate this situation, the British passed the Alien Act of 1905, which prohibited the landing of undesirable aliens on English soil. This simply shifted the problem elsewhere.

The number of aliens deported, required to depart, or excluded is shown in Table 10. It can be seen that the two peaks of deportations were 1926-1933 and 1946-1954. By 1932, more aliens were leaving the United States than were entering (for the first time in U.S. history). To protect American jobs in the Great Depression, President Hoover ordered that immigration be kept at a minimum. He declared that, "There is no longer a necessity for the United States to provide an asylum." The policy was carried out by a strict interpretation of the phrase "public charge. "Secretary of Labor Doak began to round up the 400,000 deportable aliens, In a short time, Ellis Island was crowded with persons awaiting deportation. The dining room was enlarged, a new school was opened for children of detainees, and the chapel was re-equipped. The Immigration Service predicted (wrongly) that, "Present indications are that it will be necessary for us to continue to

---

[42]New York Times, Jan. 14, 1920, p. 19:2. A reader of this chapter asked, "How could he be a barber or a tailor with defective sight? Good question.

Table 10

ALIENS DEPORTED

1892–1954*

Year	Aliens expelled			Aliens excluded	Year	Aliens expelled			Aliens excluded
	Total	Deported	Required to depart			Total	Deported	Required to depart	
1892	637	2,164			1925 ...	9,495	9,495	....	25,390
1893	577	1,053			1926 ...	10,904	10,904	....	20,550
1894	417	1,389			1927 ...	26,674	11,662	15,012	19,755
					1928 ...	31,571	11,625	19,946	18,839
1895	177	2,419			1929 ...	38,796	12,908	25,888	18,127
1896	238	2,799							
1897	263	1,617			1930 ...	28,018	16,631	11,387	8,233
1898	199	3,030			1931 ...	29,861	18,142	11,719	9,744
1899	263	3,798			1932 ...	30,201	19,426	10,775	7,064
					1933 ...	30,212	19,865	10,347	5,527
1900	356	4,246			1934 ...	16,889	8,879	8,010	5,384
1901	363	3,516							
1902	465	4,974			1935 ...	16,297	8,319	7,978	5,558
1903	547	8,769			1936 ...	17,446	9,195	8,251	7,000
1904	779	7,994			1937 ...	17,617	8,829	8,788	8,076
					1938 ...	18,553	9,275	9,278	8,066
1905	845	11,879			1939 ...	17,792	8,202	9,590	6,498
1906	676	12,432							
1907	995	13,064			1940 ...	15,548	6,954	8,594	5,300
1908	2,069	10,902			1941 ...	10,938	4,407	6,531	2,929
1909	2,124	10,411			1942 ...	10,613	3,709	6,904	1,833
					1943 ...	16,154	4,207	11,947	1,495
1910	2,695	24,270			1944 ...	39,449	7,179	32,270	1,642
1911	2,788	22,349							
1912	2,456	16,057			1945 ...	80,760	11,270	69,490	2,341
1913	3,461	19,938			1946 ...	116,320	14,375	101,945	2,942
1914	4,610	33,041			1947 ...	214,543	18,663	195,880	4,771
					1948 ...	217,555	20,371	197,184	4,905
1915	2,564	24,111			1949 ...	296,337	20,040	276,297	3,834
1916	2,781	18,867							
1917	1,853	16,028			1950 ...	579,105	6,628	572,477	3,571
1918	1,569	1,569	....	7,297	1951 ...	686,713	13,544	673,169	3,784
1919	3,068	3,068	....	8,626	1952 ...	723,959	20,181	703,778	2,944
					1953 ...	905,236	19,845	885,391	2,637
1920	2,762	2,762	....	11,795	1954 ...	1,101,228	26,951	1,074,277	3,313
1921	4,517	4,517	....	13,779					
1922	4,345	4,345	....	13,731					
1923	3,661	3,661	....	20,619					
1924	6,409	6,409	....	30,284					

*Fiscal years ending June 30.

SOURCE: *Historical Statistics of the United States,*
Colonial Times to 1970, p. 114.

occupy Ellis Island indefinitely."[43]   In November 1954, when a
new detention policy went into effect, the Immigration and
Naturalization Service was able to report, "Ellis Island and the other
large facilities were closed."[44]

But the number of deportations should not be exaggerated. In
an average week, during the peak of activities, 27,000 applied to enter
the United States through Ellis Island, and only 400 to 500 were
denied entry from all causes. In addition, 1000 to 1500 aliens were
detained on the Island at all times, mostly awaiting a decision of the
Special Board of Enquiry or recovering from illness of a non-
contagious kind. Most of these were admitted.

---

[43]Letter of the Commissioner, quoted in Thomas M. Pitkin. "A Report on Ellis
Island as an Immigration Depot, 1890 - 1954," National Park Service, June 1966,
p.224.

[44]Annual Report, 1955, p.6.

CHAPTER IV:

SOME PEOPLE WHO WORKED THERE

A great variety of persons labored on Ellis Island as Federal employees, workers in the private sector and volunteers. In this chapter, we review the history and performance of those who administered the Island, those who served there and those whose work was a labor of love. At the peak of Ellis Island immigration (1907), there were 350 persons working for pay on the Island. The major operating divisions are given in Table 11. In addition to the ones shown in the table, there were divisions for dealing with the watchman, matron, engineering, ferryboat and craft functions. In the reorganization that followed the *Report of the Ellis Island Committee* (1934), the number of divisions was reduced from 16 to 12, but the chief functions were left undisturbed.

KEEPERS OF THE GATE

The Immigration Act of 1891 created the office of Superintendent of Immigration in the Treasury Department, The Bureau of Immigration and the post of Commissioner of Immigration at the Port of New York. The position of Superintendent was superceded in 1895 by that of Commissioner-General who served in Washington, D. C.[1] (See Table 12 for names of those who held high-level positions in Washington and New York). The division of power created friction between the head of the Washington Bureau, the Commissioner-General, and the head of the immigration port, the Commissioner at New York. The feuds which developed were exacerbated by the political actions of appointees. For example, Commissioner-General Powderly, as a former head of the Knights of

---

[1]This section is based on Thomas Pitkin's book <u>Keepers of the Gate</u> (New York University Press, 1975), which is the best treatment of those who administered Ellis Island.

Table 11

MAJOR OPERATING DIVISIONS, ELLIS ISLAND

(1905)

Name of Division	Duties
Executive	Commissioner of Port and staff administration
Boarding	Medical officers made shipboard inspections, accompanied steerage passangers to Island
Medical	U.S. Public Health Services handled medical examinations and operated hospitals.
Special Inquiry	Made final determination of case of detained aliens (subject to appeal to Secratary)
Information	Provided information on aliens to friends and relatives
Deportation	Guarded detained aliens, escorted them to ships on deportation
Treasuries	Handled all financial matters

Table 12

ELLIS ISLAND OFFICIALS *

(1892-1940)

	Commissioner General Washington, D.C.	Assistant Commissioner General, Washington, D.C.	Commissioner-Port of New York
1892	John B. Weber		John B. Weber
1893	Herman Stump		John H. Senner
1896			
1897	Terence V. Powderly		Thomas Fitchie
1902	Frank P. Sargent		William Williams
1903		Joseph Murray	
1905			Robert Watchorn
1909	Daniel J. Keefe	Frank H. Larned	William Williams
1913	Anthony Caminetti		
1914			Frederic C. Howe
		Alfred Hampton	
		Alfred Hampton	
1919			Byron H. Uhi
1920			Frederic A. Wallis
1921	Walter W. Husband	Irving F. Wixon	Robert E. Tod
1922			Henry H. Curran
1924	Harry E. Hull	George E. Tolman	
1926			Benjamin M. Day
1928		George E. Harris	
1932		E. J. Shaughnessy	Edward Corsi
1933	D. W. MacCormack		
1934			Rudolph Reimer
1937	Edward J. Shaughnessay		
1938	James J. Houghteling	Edward J. Shaughnessy	

*Weber was Superintendent of Immigration; the name was changed to Commissioner-General in 1895.

Labor, was a leading force behind the passage of the Contract Labor Law. But his Commissioner, Fitchie, who actually administered the law, was not in favor of it.

The difficulties of the Washington-New York division of power were a long-standing problem. The situation was most acute in matters of detention and appeal. The commissioners at New York usually wanted to handle cases expeditiously, but Washington officials guarded their prerogatives carefully, thereby delaying the final results at the expense of the detainees who were the pawns of this political game. Commissioner John H. Senner saw the folly of this procedure. He urged that the Immigration Service be made a part of the Civil Service System; this recommendation was approved later in his administration.[2] When Theodore Roosevelt succeeded McKinley as President, he made a "clean sweep" of the Immigration Bureau by appointing Frank P. Sargent as Commissioner-General and William Williams as Commissioner of the Port of New York. (Figure 17) Williams, a young lawyer with previous government service, set out to eliminate the scandals on Ellis Island. He had served in the Spanish American War, and he turned out to be a tough and controversial commissioner. On investigation, he learned that inspectors were selling fake citizenship papers to immigrants, and this meant that diseased and undesirable persons were passing through Ellis Island. He eliminated this abuse and plunged into his program of reform. He demanded that steamships companies keep proper manifests; he cleaned up the filth in the kitchen and he ordered that aliens be given silverware with dinner. He also attacked corruption in the snack restaurants and at the moneychangers.[3] Although Williams won the support of reformers of all types, he antagonized important Republicans in his party. But more to the point, Williams was accused of mistreating immigrants.

Two other Commissioners merit special consideration: Frederic C. Howe and Edward Corsi. Howe became Commissioner of the Port of New York during World War I; he followed Williams in that post. Howe wanted to "humanize" Ellis Island by making the place a little more comfortable for those detained. He was most impressed by the idleness on the Island, so he opened two empty buildings to 750 unemployed men and he used the ferry boat to take them to the

---

[2]Thomas Pitkin, Ellis Island as an Immigration Station (National Park Service), p. 47

[3]William Severn, Ellis Island: The Immigrant Years (New York: Messner, 1971), p. 76.

Figure 17 Some "Keepers of the Gate" Top:Anthony Caminetti, Commissioner-General; Secretary of Labor William B. Wilson; Terence V. Powderly, Commissioner- General. Bottom: Daniel J. Keefe, Commissioner-General, Frank P. Sargent, Commissioner-General (Photos from the Terence V. Powderly Collection)

Battery each day to look for jobs.[4]

For detainees, Howe took benches out of storage, built playgrounds, added a kindergarten, gramaphone and band concerts. He obtained some used sewing machines, toys for the children and a small library. He beautified the area with plants, pictures and flags, and for recreation he installed swings, handball courts, and ball fields. These changes cost very little and few objected, but other policies were vigorously resisted. Howe fought the unscrupulous business elements and the railroad companies that wasted the immigrant's time. The controversy surrounding Howe became intense over his reaction to the "Red Scare," when the mass deportations commenced. Commissioner-General Caminetti wanted the aliens deported quickly, but Howe believed that every person should have a right to be heard on appeal. (Figure 18)

THEY ALSO SERVED

In addition to the Commissioners and Assistant Commissioners of the Port of New York, there were several persons who labored on Ellis Island. They can be classified in five main headings: the medical officers, the Boards of Special Enquiry, the transportation agents and baggage men and those who built the Island.

The Medical Officers

The Immigration Act of March 13, 1891 specified that there should be a mandatory health inspection of immigrants, and these should be conducted by the surgeons of the Marine Hospital Service at Ellis Island. The law excluded "all idiots, insane persons, paupers, or persons likely to be become public charges, persons suffering from a loathsome or dangerous disease." During the first year, Surgeon-General Walter Wyman posted inspectors to serve at only four ports--

---

[4]Ann Novotny, Strangers at the Door (Riverside : Chatam, 1971).

Figure 18 The Board of Enquiry Room (Photo from the
Terence V. Powderly Collection)

Baltimore, Boston, New York and Philadelphia.[5] In his second year
(1892), cholera showed up amongst steerage immigrants in New York
Bay, including one death. Wyman reacted by banning the importation
of rags from Europe, which were used to make paper, and by

---

[5]Bess Furman, A Profile of the United States Public Health Service, 1798-1948
(Washington:Department of Health, Education and Welfare, 1950), p. 206.

ordering the disinfection of all baggage bound for the United States from Asia and Europe.

But this did not satisfy Americans. They wanted an outright ban on all immigration. Since no law provided for such a ban, Wyman turned to existing laws on quarantine. The State Department informed Wyman that all States could enforce a ban of at least 20 days. An order was given by Wyman on September 1, 1892 temporarily suspending immigration, which was approved by President Benjamin Harrison.

When the order was given to medical inspectors, ships crammed with immigrants were already in New York harbor and others were on their way. To deal with this medical emergency, former Surgeon-General John B. Hamilton was brought to New York from Chicago. His solution was to build Camp Low on Sandy Hook, which could accomodate 1,000 persons under quarantine. Other ships were held at other ports, and the border patrols were increased.

These measures did not alleviate another concern: the Columbian Exposition, which was scheduled to open in May 1893. Congress responded quickly by passing a National Quarantine Act on February 15, 1893. This law required all ship masters bound for the United States to obtain a bill of health from a U. S. Consul.

We are fortunate to have in published form the "personal experiences" of a medical official in 1895 and after. At first, the medical division was made up partly of the Marine Hospital Bureau and partly of the Immigration Bureau, but subsequently all medical work was performed by the U. S. Public Health Service. These included medical doctors, stewards, clerks, nurses, orderlies, mechanics, cooks attendants and laborers.[6]

The duties and qualifications of the medical officer were not established until the Act of 1917, which required that "the physicians

---

[6]Victor Safford, Immigration Problems (New York: Dodd, Mead, 1925).

shall have had at least two years experience in the practice of their profession." In addition, it specified that medics who had special training in the diagnosis of insanity be employed. This was necessary because of the number of illnesses which could exclude an alien. These included: idiot, imbecile, feeble-minded, epileptic, insane, constitutional psychopath, chronic alcoholism, tuberculosis, loathsome or dangerous disease, and mentally defective. Most of these were spelled out in the Immigration Act of 1917.[7]

According to Safford, "It is a no more difficult task to detect poorly built, defective or broken down human beings than to recognize a cheap or defective automobile. His plan was to compel all aliens to carry their own baggage upstairs to judge the efficiency of the heart. He believed that the trained observer could detect any deformity or impairment of function, defects of posture, or continued rest stops. These would suggest hernias or lameness.

This plan was made necessary because many aliens came from steerage in very poor physical condition, Some "arrived at the island in a dying condition or so sick that their transfer to the island otherwise than on a stretcher was a outrageous cruelty."[8] For this, Safford blamed the ships doctors who were required to report cases of sickness, but who rarely did. He proposed that all ships' medical doctors be compelled to bring the aliens to the Ellis Island hospital, but the request was denied by the Commissioner. (Figure 19)

Writing a few years later, Doctor L. made these comments about the medical practice on Ellis Island:[9]

On July 1, 1929 after graduating from Tufts Medical

---

[7]Safford, Immigration Problems, p. 82.

[8]Safford, Immigration Problems, p. 77.

[9]Letter to author.

School, I entered the U. S. Public Health Service as an intern. A year later I became an acting assistant surgeon on the surgical staff where I remained until October 1, 1932.

Part of my duties as an intern was to check people on the immigration side who might need medical attention. Usually I did this at 9 p.m. daily. One night I got a call from the senior guard that a prisoner was making trouble and asked me to check it out. As you probably know aliens (undesirables) and criminals (who were released from prisons) were sent to Ellis Island and then sent back to their original country.

Prince Romanoff who really was an American citizen from Brooklyn did actually go to Europe then returned to U. S. as a Prince. When he outstayed his welcome among society he called immigration and turned himself in as an undesirable alien then he was returned to Europe at U. S. expense.

On that night it was the "Prince" who was exciting the other prisoners to start a riot and refuse the food. In order, keep out of this situation and get the Prince out of this area, I had him removed to the hospital mental ward. I felt that anyone who refused to eat must be insane. He was placed in a padded cell where he remained until the senior officer (Psychiatrist) found him sane and returned him to the immigration alien prison quarters. He was sent to Europe and later returned to Los Angeles and opened the famous Prince Romanoff Restaurant.

The marine hospital took care of Coast Guard personnel, the custom service and merchant marine. Occasionally Immigrants were kept at the hospital for treatment and then OK'D and released. There were many children who had trichinosis and never treated for this eye disease. After treatment and cure, they were allowed to join their families in America.

The pharmacist on the island adds these observations and conments:[10]

After graduating from College of Pharmacy (Mass.) I started to work in 1928 at the U. S. Marine Hospital as a pharmacist. Every morning I boarded the ferry from the Battery in New York to make the trip to the Island. I saw many interesting people while crossing. An actress who came to pick up a child she was adopting from Europe. If I remember correctly she was one of the Bennett Sisters movie actresses. I saw the strange ladies of Africa who came here to join the Bailey circus. . . My job as a pharmacist was to keep supplies for the hospital wards. I made up solutions, ointments, cough syrups, stomach powder that were divided into doses and wrapped in squares of paper. Everything was made up even suppositories. I was also in charge of the pure alcohol which I kept constantly locked up. . .

There were tennis courts on the island between the hospital buildings and during lunch periods we played or watched the active ones. Some of the men often swam in the water around the Island but we felt all kinds of garbage floated by and it was too much for us to plunge into.

And the wife of the last Medical Director of the U. S. Public Health Service on Ellis Island wrote from California as follows:[11]

And don't ever believe that Immigrants were ill treated there. Or course couldn't come and go but they would have company, families were together, special food was prepared if

---

[10]Letter to author.

[11]letter to author

nationalities required and hospital care if necessary. When the powers that be in Washington decided to close the hospital Doctor A. arranged for a "Sick Bay" on Island 1 with one of his staff, Werner B. himself a Jewish immigrant from Germany in charge, with hospitalization if necessary on Staten.

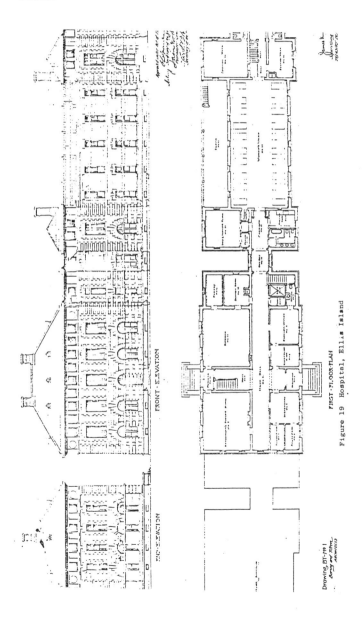

Figure 19 Hospital, Ellis Island

The Inspectors and Interpreters

The inspector examined the alien concerning his or her right to enter the United States. The law allowed only those to land "who have an undoubted right to enter." This meant that the inmigrant had to prove against the arguments of the inspector that there was a right to enter. The inspector used the 29 questions shown on the manifest sheet as a basis of the inspection. But this information was provided by the immigrant upon purchase of a steamship ticket.

Whenever possible, the inspector made use of an interpreter, who stood next to the immigrant facing the inspector. When the inspector made his determination about the right to enter, he communicated this to the alien and ordered the guard, who stood next to the inspector, to carry out the order (admittance, detention or deportation),

Thomas P. Galvin spent 34 years with the Bureau of Immigration and the Immigration and Naturalization Service. (Figure 20) He began as an inspector at Detroit, where he served on the new Ambassador Bridge. In 1932, he was transferred (at his own request) to Ellis Island, and he was assigned to the Law Division. In this capacity, he investigated the immigrant's status and conducted hearings under warrants of arrest. These sometimes led to deportation. Two years later, he was assigned to the Board of Special Inquiry and subsequently became chairman. He served in this post until 1948, when he requested and was granted a transfer to Tampa, Florida. There he was Inspector in Charge of Arrivals and Departures, a post he held until he was subject to mandatory retirement regulations in 1960. He died on January 29, 1978. Galvins wife, Alice, also worked on Ellis Island as a secretary to the chief of the legal division. As she stated, "the happiest days of my life were spent on Ellis Island. They had radio shows and Christmas parties that were wonderful."[12]

---

[12]Phone call July 11, 1980.

Figure 20   Thomas P. Galvin, Immigrant Inspector
Photographed by Twentieth Century Fox for the motion
picture, "Gateway" (Photo donated by Alice Galvin)

Fiorello LaGuardia was probably the most famous interpreter who worked on Ellis Island. He was hired because he spoke Croatian, Italian and German, and this job enabled him to pay for evening Law School at New York University. He worked 7 days per week for two years, at a time when immigration was at an all-time peak (1906-1907). His strenuous schedule called for more stamina than most people possessed; the grind was constant from the moment he put on his uniform until he took the boat back to the mainland to go to evening classes.

The interpreter's duties were many. He worked with the sane and insane, with the sick and the well. He often accompanied couples to New York City Hall who were about to be married. Many men came first to the United States and then sent for their fiances. LaGuardia would accompany bride and groom, witness the ceremony, and then give the bride clearance to enter the country. This practice continued until the last wedding took place in 1946. (See Figure 21)

It was in this role that he first learned that the aldermen, who at that time could perform weddings, were overcharging and taking bribes. As Mayor LaGuardia, he later fought "this contemptible petty thievery."[13]

LaGuardia put his work in proper perspective: "At best, the work was an ordeal. Our compensation, besides the salaries, the heartbraking scenes we witnessed, was the realization that a large percentage of these people pouring into Ellis Island would probably make good and enjoy a better life than they had been accustomed to where they came from."[14]

---

[13]Fiorello H. LaGuardia, The Making of an Insurgent (Philadelphia: Lippincott, 1948), p. 69.

[14]LaGuardia, Making of an Insurgent, p. 69.

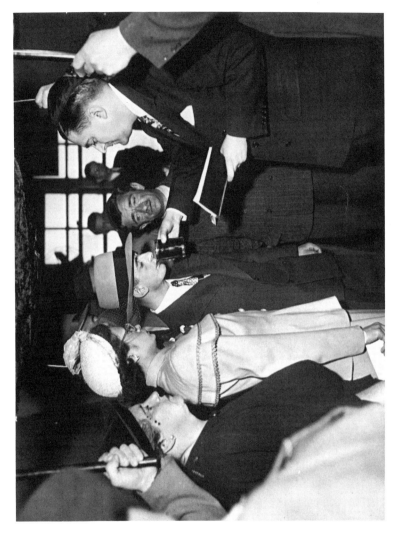

Figure 21 The Last Wedding on Ellis Island (Photo donated by the groom, Harry W. Methner (wearing hat)

Transportation Agents and Baggagemen

Up to one-half of the persons employed on Ellis Island were not employees of the Federal government. Various firms held privileges at the Island under contract. The largest part of these non-Federal workers was in the transportation and baggage department. All passenger transportation companies that carried immigrants from New York City were allowed to have a representative on the Island.

Under the "Railroad Pool," passenger companies maintained a complete organization for ticketing and forwarding passengers and baggage; this came to be known as the "clearing house." It was responsible for dealing with persons in twenty five languages. The Immigrant Clearing House Lines, sorted out immigrants and tagged them with placecards. In terms of dealing with approxmately 1,500 to 2,000 persons per day who were leaving New York City, the number of mistakes was surprisingly small.[15]

Thomas F. Murphy was a ticket agent from the time Ellis Island opened until 1931, and he became very adept at sending people to the right places, even if their tags were misplaced or misstated. He became by practice an expert in ethnology. He knew that many Portuguese went to Massachucetts, and he knew that a German asking for Amsterdam, New York really didn't want the city but rather Amsterdam Avenue in New York City, where many Germans settled.

The six ticket agents in the department were surprised one day to receive two little Italian boys, who had been shipped by American Express. Their uncle had contracted with the company to send them alone to San Diego California to join their parents. The boys were properly tagged, and after much solicitation they joined their parents.
[16] Peter McDonald (Mac) was a very colorful baggageman in the heyday of Ellis Island. Working his way up from a helper, he became chief of the department, a post he held for over 35 years. In an interview, he made some interesting observations about national characteristics. The Scandinavians all brought more things with them, including mattresses belonging to their parents or grandparents; the Irish, English and French brought "better baggage," and the Greeks

---

[15] Safford, Immigrant Problems, p. 93.

[16] New York Post, 1931.

and Arabs brought the biggest bundles. According to McDonald, the Polish immigrants carry the least baggage of all."[17]

Augustus F. Sherman, Clerk/Photographer

Augustus F. Sherman came from Pennmsylvania to work for the Bureau of Immigration in New York. He began as a private secretary to the Commissioner of the Port of New York, but he became clerk and chief clerk of the Bureau in the late 1890's. In 1921, he again became private secretary--this time to the Commissioner Robert Tod. He died in 1925. He would have remained an obscure clerk were he not an outstanding photographer. He became so expert that he was designated the official photographer of thwe Immigration Service, and his photographs were used in the Annual Reports of the Service.

Sherman had a keen interest in unusual things, persons and places, and he reflected this in his photos. His niece, Mary S. Peters, donated Sherman's collection to the National Park Service, where they are now part of the Statue of Liberty National Monument.

The collection tends to emphasize national costumes, but he also photographed midgets, giants, soldiers in uniform, and children at play and in stern poses that showed their concern for inspection process, of which they were a part.

They Built the Island

There were literally hundreds of companies and thousands of persons who built and maintained Ellis Island. These are the subject of an excellent report by Harlan D. Unrau, of the National Park Service.[18] The main construction contracts that were awarded are

---

[17]The (New York) Evening Telegram, Dec. 29, 1912.

[18]Harlan D. Unrau, Historic Structure Report--Ellis Island (National Park Service, May 1981.

given in Table 13.

Dr. Anthony Zito, Archivist of the Catholic University of America, in poring over letters in the Terence V. Powderly Collection found a current link with the past. In one letter, Powderly wrote, "In 1882, a young Italian came to Scranton, Pennsylvania. I was mayor of the city at that time and was instrumental in getting employment for him, at his trade, stone cutter, with the Lackawanna R.R. Co. He couldn't speak a word of English. In 1898 I as Commissioner General of Immigration, passed on the contracts for the erection of the Ellis Island Immigrant station. The contract for the stone work in the foundation of the building was let to Frank Carlucci, the Italian immigrant boy of 1882. Just take another trip to Ellis Island and note how well the work was done." That Frank Carlucci was the grandfather of the Secretary of Defense in the Reagan Administration.

IMMIGRANT AID SOCIETIES

To meet the many needs of immigrants, Protestant, Catholic and Jewish agencies organized themselves into the Committee on Immigrant Aid on Ellis Island, as well as an Immigration Division of the National Conference of Social Work. There was a growing partnership between the Federal government and volunteer agencies. Under the American system of voluntarism, the agencies performed tasks that were the responsibility of government in other places. In the United States, the volunteers supplemented or complemented the government's role.

An agency did not automatically win the right to help on Ellis Island. Several were refused space there, and others were ordered off for infringement of what some called petty rules. Assistant Secretary of Labor Post refused a request of the American Legion to start an Americanization Bureau on Ellis Island. He based the refusal on two grounds: the crowded conditions and the fact that he had earlier denied a request by the American Federation of Labor to use Ellis Island as a base of operations (supposedly to enroll union member

Table 13

CONSTRUCTION CONTRACTS AWARDED

Ellis Island

Name of Firm	Name of Building	Contract Date	Amount
R. H. Hood	Main Building(New)	August 1898	419,298
Louis Wechsler	Kitchen and Laundry	May 1900	135,400
Louis Wechsler	Powerhouse	April 1900	47,500
New York State Construction	Baggage and Dormitory Building	January 1908	
Daniel A. Garber	Main Hospital Building	February 1900	116,867
Attilio Pasquini	Surgeon's House and Hospital Outbuilding	August 1900	35,551
Northeastern Construction	Contagious Disease Hospital	October 1906	201,590
Attilio Pasquini	Ferry House	September 1900	53,292
George F. Driscoll	Ferry House (New), Immigrant Building Recreation Building	October 1934	1,151,800

SOURCE: Harlan D. Unrau, Historic Structure Report-Ellis Island (Washington: National Park Service, 1981)

there).   Post said he was denying all organizational requests for space.[19]

Earlier, several charities were ousted from Ellis Island for a variety of reasons.   In 1909, Commissioner Williams went on a campaign to rid the Island of what he called "bogus charities." He

[19]New York Times, Oct. 5, 1920, p. 2:4.

claims they were used to lure girls. The Swedish Inmigrant Home at 5 Water Street and the St. Joseph's Home for the Protection of Polish Immigrants at 117 Broad Street were barred from working on the Island. Congressman Bennet claimed that hundreds of girls dropped out of sight after leaving a home and that call women were using the aid society homes for illicit purposes. Father Joseph L'Etauche of the Polish home denied claims that he used the home for profit, that he beat immigrants with a hose and that he catered to drunk employers.[20]

The Austrian Immigrant Society Home on 170 E. 80th Street was also ousted from the Island. Commissioner Williams said it "was not a fit place to go."[21] Its predecessor, the Austro-Hungarian Home was put off the Island in 1904.

These groups were unusual. By 1921, when the quota law was enacted, there were several aid societies performing admirably on Ellis Island, including the National Catholic Welfare Conference, the Hebrew Immigrant Aid Sociery and the YWCA. These grew in number to 26 constituent agencies by 1941 .[22]

Founded in 1809 the New York Bible Society began to serve the immigrant's religious needs in 1834. Agents distributed bibles among the families arriving and on board ships for the use of passengers. When Castle Garden was made the exclusive landing place for inmigrants, the work of the agents continued there.

On Ellis Island, the Society had a booth in the railroad room, where it distributed bibles in 53 languages. Mr. Charles A. Carol, a Latvian immigrant worked for over 36 years for the Society at Ellis Island. The Society pursued its goals of temperance and abstinence in the hospitals, in the detention room and on the ships. When the

---

[20]New York Times, Aug. 12, 1909, p. 7:5.

[21]New York Times, Aug. 13, 1909, p. 14:5.

[22]New York Times, Mar. 2, 1941, II, p. 4:8.

inspection was transferred from the Island to the ships, the Society followed immigrants to Brooklyn and Hoboken.[23]

The Daughters of the American Revolution (DAR) commenced its welfare work on Ellis Island in 1923--first with women. It opened a craft shop in 1934, when the society was asked to extend its activities to the hospital area. The three full-time workers taught sewing machine operation and carpentry, and they worked with about 250 persons per day. The sewing class used fabrics that were collected from chapters all over the United States. The operation was managed by Lucille Boss, and she was assisted by Elizabeth Estes, an occupational therapist, and Isabel Rittenhouse.[24]

Over the years the number of services offered immigrants expanded gradually. Representatives of the Social Service Worker Sections on the Island maintained a school and kindergarten and a shop for detainees; they provided clothing and in some cases money, and they contacted relatives and friends. As early as 1923, there was a library in the hospital, which included foreign newspapers, books and magazines in 8 languages. It was inherited from the wartime activities (World War I) of the American Library Association. The librarian, who worked with the Red Cross and received aid from the Rockefeller Foundation, was engaged in much social work also.[25]

The International Institutes

The International Institutes were a major source of assistance to new immigrants after 1910. They began as an adjunct of the YWCA in the industrial cities of America, and they expanded rapidly during World War I, with agencies in Trenton, New Jersey; Lawrence,

---

[23]See New York Bible Society, Among Immigrants (1940).

[24]New York Times, Mar. 2, 1941.

[25]New York Times, Sept. 2, 1923, VII, p. 10:4.

Massachusetts and as far away as Los Angeles, California.

The International Institute of New York City was opened by the YWCA on January 2, 1911 at 341 East 17th Street. In 1919, it became the International Institute for Young Women and then the Foreign Language Information Service in 1921. It had 23 bureaus, each one dealing with a different language, and each one receiving newspapers from abroad in those languages. Representatives of the Foreign Language Service went to Ellis Island daily to interview persons from the respective nationalities. Mrs Johanna Cohrsen, was head of the German bureau for 52 years. It was her job to greet immigrants and to provide them with all necessary information about life in the United States. The YWCA had workers who went to Ellis Island to meet young women. These workers conducted their business and gave their assistance in many languages. When it became known that many single women were being harrassed sexually on ships, the YWCA provided women who acted as chaperones and made the ocean crossing with the young girls and women.

Edith T. Bremer founded the original International Institute in 1911. In an inventory now housed at the national office of the YWCA at 610 Lexington Avenue, New York, Bremer stated that she saw her task as something larger than just helping immigrant women with a few hours' contact on Ellis Island. The YWCA copied ships' manifest lists; which gave names and addresses of all incoming aliens to facilitate what an early commentary termed "A friendly visit in the early days of adjustment." Bremer insisted that only workers who were fluent in the language of the immigrant could operate efficiently. Bremer called them her "nationality secretaries." By 1928, over one-half of all persons employed were drawn from the nationality groups. They were able to provide all the services of the YWCA to foreigners, including adult education, Americanization programs, education for the children, and employment information.

Two workers were assigned to Ellis Island to track immigrants after arrival. Lists of immigrants going to inland destinations were forwarded to Institutes in those cities. In 1928, 6,000 immigrants were assisted in this way.[26]

From the beginning, the YWCA work among immigrants raised quetions of legitimacy. Why, it was reasoned, should groups dedicated to the welfare of women be working with whole families? Why, it was asked by immigrants who were mainly Roman Catholic and Jews should aid be coming from a "Protestant" Institute? Separation from the YWCA was the only proper response. The beginning of independent local affiliates was the creation of the National Institute of Immigrant Welfare (NIIW) in New York City in September 1934. Within two years, 15 additional institutes had withdrawn from the YWCA. These became affiliates of the Federation of the International Institutes of America. Finally, in 1959, the American Federation of International Institutes was merged with the Common Council to establish the American Council for Nationalities Services. Today the Institutes are still rendering services to newly-arrived immigrants (see Appendix for list and addresses).

Since most immigrants arriving between 1892 and 1930 were Catholics or Jews. The immigrant aid societies of the these religious groups command special attention.

The National Catholic Welfare Conference

The great waves of immigration in the early twentieth century brought impoverished Roman Catholics to the United States from Ireland, Italy and the Slavic countries. To protect their interests, the Social Action Department of the National Catholic Welfare Conference (now the U. S. Catholic Conference) organized a Bureau of Immigration, with Bruce M. Mohler, former deputy commissioner of the American Red Cross, as director. The New York office, which had direct contacts with immigrants, was located at 61 Whitehall Street, adjoining the South Ferry. The need for this bureau was very

---

[26]Nicholas V. Montalto, The International Institute Movement: A Guide to Records of Immigrant Service Agencies in the United States (St. Paul: University of Minnesota, 1978), p. viii.

apparent, since from 45 to 65 percent of all arriving immigrants were
Catholic, and since there were already a number of Catholic agencies
working independently on Ellis Island before the NCWC opened its
Bureau.[27]

The experience of one of these agencies (the State Street
Mission) is illustrative. In 1900, it registered 20,000 Irish men and
women and gave aid to 12,000 by caring for the girls in the Mission
until they could be placed with friends or relatives or in jobs. By
1900, Fr. M. J. Henry could report that the girls now landing are
better educated and that they want jobs as saleswomen, stenographers,
operators, and nurses rather than servants.[28]

The Bureau of Immigration of the NCWC was headquartered in
Washington, D. C., and it had branch offices at New York, Ellis
Island, Philadelphia, El Paso and Seattle. Thomas F. Mulholland was
appointed Port Director at New York, and he was assisted by two
trained social workers and a staff of secretaries. The New York
office was located at 61 Whitehall Street, directly across from the Ellis
Island ferry. The NCWC maintained a desk on Ellis Island in an
area allotted to immigration aid societies. (See Figure 22) Elizabeth
Dobbin, Assistant Director of NCWC, Summarized the problems of
the new Bureau as follows:[29]

A day spent at Ellis Island presents such a Kaleidoscope of
motions and emotions that no matter what else we carry
away with us we cannot escape being touched with the
evident loneliness and bewilderment that is so noticeable
among the newly arrived immigrants. . .just now conditions

---

[27]National Catholic Welfare Conference, Bulletin, II (Jan. 1921), p. 5.

[28]NCWC News Service, May 2, 1920.

[29]Elizabeth V. Dobbins, "Assisting the Newly Arrived Immigrant," NCWC Bulletin,
Jan. 1921, 8-10.

on Ellis Island are abnormal. The air is rife with complaints of unnecessary delays and hardships, and in many instances the complaints are true. Accomodations at Ellis Island are inadequate when immigration is at high tide. In one day twenty-four hundred were packed in the detention room. The number of available beds will accomodate about eighteen hundred persons the beds being placed in tiers of three, yet it is a conmon occurrence to have more than two thousand persons detained over a period of a week or longer.

Sarah Weadick, the representative of the Bureau of Immigration, concentrated her efforts on visiting the detained immigrants to assist them whenever possible. Those who were detained were frightened, confused and in some cases terrified. Seldom did they understand the real reasons for their detention, so it was in these rooms that the social worker was most needed. The problems were myriad--some trivial; some grave: wallet left on board ship, relatives not located. phone nunbers lost or even unrecognizable. Weadick related an amusing story of a tall southern Italian woman of 39 years who arrived on Ellis Island with 6 children, intending to join her brother. The Board of Special Inquiry, however, rejected this option because the brother was not obligated to support his sister's children. The woman approached the social worker and asked, "Would not be possible for me and my children to be admitted if I were to marry a man who is an American citizen--a friend of my brother? Weadick

Figure 22   NCWC Bureau on Ellis Island (Photo from the Migration and Refugee Service of NCWC)

was taken back by this "brilliant scheme," and asked if the woman really wanted to marry the man she did not know.   The woman responded, "I grant you, Signorina, I did not come with that intention, but what would you do? They are about to deport me. One must make some sacrifice if one would enter your country."[30]

---

[30]Sarah Weadick, "With the NCWC at Ellis Island," NCWC Bulletin, Mar 1922, p. 10.

Mitchell Mulholland describes his father's work on Ellis Island:[31]

Of coarse my father used to cross to "the Island" virtually every day to help unsnarl the legal tangles that kept immigrants there, and then to get them released. . .Dad was always on the go, between the office, the piers and the Island. Memories do bubble to the surface--the many friends from far-off lands who were helped into the U.S.--the families who were reunited after incredible tangles with bureaucratic red tape and their own unwitting bungles.

Deportation Cases. The New York office of the Bureau of Immigration worked on these cases of immigrants under detention, particularly those about to be deported. It was established in 1922 under the U. S. Department of Labor. It was responsible only to the Attorney General. The Board had jurisdiction over deportation cases, waivers for returning residents, nonquota status, temporary entrants, and bail and parole for violators. The Board accepted *amicus curiae* briefs, which NCWC would file. Its attorney was granted 15 minutes of oral arguments in each case.

The Bureau of Immigration performed many other functions for the immigrant. The Eighth National Conference of Catholic Charities stated, "Our port record has noted 28 conmmon types of assistance rendered." These included recovering wallets left on ships, finding relatives who failed to show up, caring for children in hospitals when they were separated from their mothers, recovering lost Baggage, dealing with incomplete passports and taking care of women when "bridegrooms failed to show up." In addition, the Commissioner of

---

[31]Quoted from letter to author.

the Part of New York suggested that NCWC offer Sunday Masses.[32]

The Bureau, which had a European representative, established working contacts with agencies in Ireland, Germany, Poland, Czechoslovakia, Hungary, Romania, Yugoslavia, Austria and Italy. It served as a general clearing house for coordinating all social activities in the interests of Catholic immigration.

The representatives of the Bureau had authority to board all incoming ships to meet inmigrants referred to it by Federal inmigration officials. This authority was particularly important after the passage of the 1924 law, which provided for examination on shipboard. The doubtful cases (old persons, children and illiterates) and all third class passengers were sent to Ellis Island. They were subject to temporary detention and/or special enquiry.

Between 1921 and 1930, the New York office worked on cases involving quota restrictions, but the 1930's were also years of the "deportation era" at Ellis Island. As the Great Depression placed more new immigrants in dire economic conditions, there was an accelerated effort by U. S. immigration officials for "voluntary removal of aliens who may fall into distress or need public aid" at any time in the first three years of entry.

The NCWC Bureau of Immigration defended aliens who had "fallen foul of immigration laws (the warrant cases)." This work was important, because only one-sixth of all deportation cases were represented by attorneys.

The Johnson Deportation Act of 1929 was concerned with persons who had been arrested and "deported in pursuance of law." The NCWC Bureau of Immigration said that this law "bristled with brutality," because it permanently banished many deportees from reentry even if they left wives and children behind who were

---

[32]Joseph I. Breen, "Our Immigrants, What They Need and How We are Helping Them," NCWC Bulletin, Mar. 1923, 3-5.

American citizens. Fortunately, this feature was removed by the Amendment of May 25, 1932.

In 1932, for the first time in United States history, more persons left the country (103,295) than entered (102,623). Of those who left, 19,420 were deported.[33] In the following year, another record number of deportations was reached (19,865), but the Bureau reported that the New Deal "gave immediate relief to thousands of aliens who were in distress," and it stated that the next year, "some unusual opportunities for service have come to us as a result of the recent unbelievably sympathetic attitude of our government officials." [34] This attitude is manifest in the more than 50 percent reduction in total deportations (from 19,426 in 1932 to 8,879 in 1933.)

Wartime Work of the Bureau. During World War II, the United States continued to be an asylum for oppressed people, but strict government regulations made a large part of the Bureau's clients "aliens of enemy nationality." Italians, Japanese and Germans were forbidden to leave the United States, but refugee children of these nationalities were allowed to enter.

Enemy aliens could file for visas in Switzerland and enter by way of Canada, where the initial screenings were accomplished. Suspicious aliens were detained at Ellis Island, following the declaration of war by the United States. They were placed under the FBI and held in strict confinement, but the District Director allowed Bureau of Immigration representatives to visit detainees to obtain information for pressing their cases.[35] Several enemy aliens were paroled from Ellis Island after the Bureau of Immigration pleaded the merits of their cases.

---

[33]NCWC, Annual Report, 1932, p. 2.

[34]NCWC, Annual Report, 1933, p. 1.

[35]NCWC, Annual Report, 1942, 15.

When the Coast Guard occupied Ellis Island, the U. S. Immigration Service was transferred from Ellis Island to 70 Columbus Avenue, and the NCWC Bureau moved with it. It tried to safeguard the rights of enemy aliens, particularly Germans and Italians.

When Italy surrendered, the status of its aliens changed. All Italians, except those awaiting transfer to Italy, were "released, paroled or transferred."[36] Although the American Consulates in Naples and Palermo were reopened, they could not issue visas because there were no civilian ships to take relatives to the United States, and because Italy was still a combat zone.

The end of World War II did not lessen anxieties for those whom the Bureau of Immigration served. But travel restrictions were eased, visa offices were reopened, and passport limitations were removed. The Bureau worked with the NCWC War Relief Service (now the Catholic Relief Service) in Germany, Austria, Italy, France, Belgium, Poland and Czechoslovakia. In what the Bureau called the "Love 'Em and Leave 'Em" problem, it had to shatter the dreams of many young girls who expected to come to the United States where "everyone has two automobiles, at least one pair of nylons and all one wants to eat." Unfortunately, some guys in Khahi had no intentions of marrying and some already were married.[37]

The D.P's. But the jilted girls were a small problem of the post war. Foremost, was the question of the displaced persons (D.P's). In 1945, when World War II ended, there were countless millions of persons roaming all over Europe searching, for relatives, food and

---

[36]NCWC, Annual Report, 1945, 23.

[37]NCWC, Catholic Action, May 1946, p. 13.

someplace to stay. The allies confronted the resettlement problem.[38] President Truman directed on December 22, 1945 that displaced persons be brought to the United States under quota, if they had a guarantee of support. The entire quotas of nationals in the American Zone of Occupation were allotted to D.P's.[39]

The Bureau of Immigration's three representatives (all volunteers) met the ships arriving with refugees and cleared the D.P's at the pier. The procedure was for the War Relief Service to cable New York City indicating the number of Catholics, Jews and Protestants on Board so that processing could begin. It is interesting to note that there were many more Jews who came under the 1945 directive than Catholics. This probably had something to do with the quotas and also the sympathy for Jews who suffered under the Nazi regime. Between 1946 and 1948, 72 percent of all children admitted as D.P's were Jewish.[40]

The Displaced Persons Act of 1948 authorized 393,500 D.P's to enter the United States.[41] The NCWC pitched in to try to untangle the incredibly complex problem of the nationality of displaced persons. Most of the lands taken by Germans during World War II were inhabited by Catholics, hence they made up the largest share of those who came between 1948 and 1951 (See Table 14).

Under the 1948 act, countries were allowed to borrow quotas from the future, but they could not make use of unused portions of quotas. Thus, while Poland, Romania and Latvia mortgaged their

---

[38]see Mark Wyman, DP: Europe's Displaced Persons, 1945-1951 (Philadelphia: Balch Institute, 1989)

[39]NCWC, Annual Report, p. 6.

[40]NCWC, Annual Report, p. 30.

[41]J. Campbell Bruce, Open Door (New York: Random House, 1954,) p. 53.

Table 14

DISPLACED PERSONS ARRIVING IN THE UNITED STATES

1948-1951

Sponsor	Total	Percentage
Catholic Organizations	114,076	36.3
Protestant Organizations	81,188	25.9
Jewish Organizations	56,736	18.7
Others	61,991	19.1

SOURCE: Mark Wischnitzer, Visas to Freedom: The History of HIAS (Cleveland: World Publishing, 1956, p. 15.

quotas into the twenty first century, over 2.5 million quotas were wasted before 1952.

The Immigration and Nationality Act of 1952

Public Law 414 (The McCarran-Walter Act) was the most thorough overhaul of the immigration laws since 1924. Although the quotas remained substantially the same, the Act set up a preference system. The first 50 percent went to first preference (the highly skilled or educated); the next 30 percent was reserved for parents of U. S. aliens; and last 20 percent (plus any of the unused first and second preference quotas) were reserved for spouses and children of aliens.

Bruce Mohler, in testifying before a Congressional committee supported some features of the Act, including the abolition of sex discrimination in immigration procedures and the attempt to unite families.   But he favored an alternative to the quota system, because there was very much that was wrong with the McCarran-Walter Act. It perpetuated the monstrous theory of racial superiority. The three largest quotas were for Great Britain (65,721), Germany (25,957), and Eire (17,853).   Compare these to the three smallest quotas: China (105), Spain (252) and Greece (307).[42]

How ironic that seven years after we spent billions of dollars and millions of lives to eradicate Hitler, we legislated a theory of Germanic superiority.   Not only did the law discriminate against southern Europeans, but it set up an Asian-Pacific Triangle, lumping together all persons from Afghanistan to Japan.

Section 221 was the second flaw in the Act.   It provided "that no visa shall be issued to an alien if it appears to the consular officer that such alien is ineligible for a visa."   There was no appeal from this section, no right of review.   To see the consequences, let us consider the case of Guido and Dominic Carazzi.   They were born in the United States and taken to Italy by their parents.   In 1938, they applied for visas to return to the United States.   They were denied. In 1951, the State Department admitted Guido, but rejected Dominic. The consular officer stated that he could not be admitted because he had voted in the 1948 Italian elections, and there was no appeal possible.

The case of Pasquale Sciortino is gross inequity.   He was drafted into the Italian army, but deserted to fight with the Americans. He came to the United States, married a Michigan girl and fathered a child.   He then joined the U. S. Air Force at Lackland, San Antonio. Soon he was picked up by U. S. immigration authorities as an Italian fugitive.   He had been tried for desertion earlier in absentia.   He was given a hearing in jail and deported in 1953.   Sadly, in Italy, he was

---

[42]NCWC, Annual Report, 1945, p. 5.

acquitted of all charges. As Cardinal Agaganian said, "I believe it is more difficult to get into your United States than to enter Heaven."[43]

The Hebrew Immigration Aid Society (HIAS)

The story of Jewish aid societies really begins in Russia. Under Czarist rule, Jews were forced to live in the Pale of settlement--in separated areas that were cut off from the main community. In June 1880, a new weekly publication, *The American Hebrew* printed reports of documents that showed that there was a plot to do away with Jews. When Czar Alexander the Second was assassinated, Cossacks rode into Jewish villages destroying them. And so began the pogroms.

When the Russians ignored protests that came in from all over the world, there was only one answer: to sail across the Atlantic to America. They came by the millions; first to Castle Garden, then to Ellis Island. Castle Garden was the official arrival station for immigrants and refugees from 1850 to 1892, when Ellis Island opened. Emma Lazarus, who wrote the famous poem of the "huddled masses yearning to breathe free," worked at Castle Garden aiding mothers and their children. But the numbers were overwhelming. She and a small group of women enlisted the help of businessmen to rent a hall across from Castle Garden.[44] According to Wischnitzer, the first known Jewish aid society in the United States was established in 1870. The Hebrew Emigrant Aid Society was formed "for temporary relief to those here and soon to arrive.[45] This organization did not survive long, and it was replaced by the Emigrant Aid Society, founded on November 27, 1881. These two aid societies were supported by wealthy German Jews and differed markedly from the

---

[43]Bruce, Open Door p. 185.

[44]Eva Merriam, The Voice of Liberty (The Jewish Publication Society of America, 1964.

[45]Wischnitzer, Visas to Freedom, p. 218.

Hebrew Immigration Aid Society, (HIAS) founded and funded by eastern European Jews. The first of the new aid groups was the Hebrew Sheltering House, established in 1889; it was followed by HIAS 13 years later. In 1909, the two were merged into the Hebrew Sheltering and Immigrant Aid Society, later to become famous as HIAS.

HIAS began in a store as one of the *landsmanshaften* established in New York City on the lower East Side. Until 1915, it confined activities to the United States, but during World War I, it helped refugees in Europe and the Far East; since then it has been a worldwide organization. In 1927, it joined with other groups to form HICEM, which assumed the international direction of Jewish immigration.[46] The Presidents of HIAS from its offical founding in 1909 to the time of closing of Ellis Island (1954) are shown in Table 15. Sanders and Bernstein guided the organization through the period of high immigration, while Herman and Telsey concentrated on the refugee problem.

One of the first acts of HIAS was to station a representative on Ellis Island. In 1904, Alexander Harkavy took that post. He worked there until 1909. His main task was to intervene with the Board of Special Inquiry in behalf of immigrants slated to be deported. Another service provided by HIAS was to fight the conditions in steerage, which most Jews travelled. The Hamburg-American Line, especially, was induced to post instructions in Yiddish and to listen to passenger complaints.

The statistics of detainees indicate that HIAS was successful in its main task. In 1913, 103,869 Jewish immigrants landed at Ellis Island. Of these 3,726 were detained. HIAS was able to plead successfully to admit 1944 cases (52 percent). In addition, in 736 cases of appeal, 461 were admitted. Only 1,199 Jews were eventually deported.

---

[46]HICEM stands for HIas-ICa-EMig-direct, the 3 Jewish agencies that agreed to merge.

Table 15

PRESIDENTS OF HIAS

1890-1954

Kasriel H. Sarasohn	1890*
Max Meyerson	1902-09
Leon Sanders	1909-17
John L. Bernstein	1917-26
Abraham Herman	1926-47
Samuel A. Telsey	1947-52
Ben Tousler	1952-54

*President of Hebrew Sheltering House

SOURCE Wischnitzer:Visas to Freedom, p.33.

HIAS also ran an employment bureau for immigrants, which remained open every evening except the Sabbath (Friday). These activities created a need for more space. The society moved to more permanent headquarters at 224 E. Broadway.

In 1908, HIAS began publishing a monthly journal, which was circulated widely in Russia, at the major emigration centers. One purpose of the publication was to inform the Jews not to send unsuitable immigrants to the United States. Editorals preached good citizenship, economy and personal convictions.

The first decade of the twentieth century set a record for the number of persons processed at Ellis Island. In view of the overcrowding and the strained conditions that prevailed, it was natural for those handling the increased load at the Island to (perhaps unconciously) tighten the entrance requirements. A message sent by

cable by HIAS seems to capture the essence of the new conditions.
It went to all leading seaports on December 18, 1910 and it stated:

> The laws are now very strictly enforced at Ellis Island,
> and hundreds of immigrants are being excluded for the
> reason that they come in with prepaid tickets and with little
> or no money on their possession. We believe it is our duty
> to inform the immigrants bound for the United States so that
> they may avoid being detained and subsequently excluded and
> deported. There is hardly any chance for a man or woman
> to land if he or she is not physically and mentally sound in
> very respect. Children under sixteen years of age who left
> their parents abroad are invariably excluded and in most
> cases deported. Only wives going to husbands or children to
> parents may safely come on prepaid tickets. Please spread
> the information broadcast.[47]

Between 1909 and 1914, the Ellis Island Bureau of HIAS was
managed by Irving Lipsitch. He was instrumental in striking down a
ruling of Commissioner William Williams. Although the law of that
time, specified that a $4 head tax was to be paid, Williams imposed
another requirement: that each immigrant must have $25 in cash or
must be sponsored by someone who will pledge that the immigrant
would not become a public charge. Through Lipsitch's efforts the $25
rule was abolished.

One procedure established by HIAS came to be a very important
source of information about Jews. In 1911, the Society set up a
"follow-up" system to keep track of every immigrant who landed in
New York City. It classified imigrants as to whether they remained
in the city or went elsewhere. Those going to the interior were
registered by HIAS at Ellis Island, and their names were forwarded to

---

[47]Wischnitzer, Visas to Freeedom, p. 54.

the representatives in the regions.[48]

During World War I, immigration from Hamburg ceased, but when the war ended, thousands of jews waited to come to the United States, as trains and ships could not handle the numbers. (It took two weeks in 1919 to go by train from Poland to Hamburg). HIAS representatives found a solution: they sent Jews by way of Danzig, which could be reached overnight from Warsaw. From Danzig they took small ships of the Cunard and White Star lines to England and then on to the United States.

The above immigration route was closed by imposition of a quota system. From that time on, HIAS devoted most of its efforts to finding Jews and placing displaced persons and refugees in suitable homes and workplaces.

As the flow of refugees continued, HIAS became concerned with conditions of crowding in the large cities. It responded by setting up experimental farm communities. Many of these Jews had never handled a plow before; they found the pioneering life difficult. But the communities survived in Texas, New Jersey, Louisiana, Kansas and Colorado.

A Brief Backward Look

Someone once said that statistics are bloodless things. True, but they help us to understand the importance of social institutions. The agencies that have been highlighted in the above section made an enormous contribution to the welfare of immigrants and therefore to the United States. Accurate information is difficult to obtain, but we do have one indication. A handful of volunteers in the Bureau of Immigration, of the National Catholic Welfare Conference, received and sent nearly 700,000 pieces of correspondence, located over 150,000 pieces of lost luggage, and they solved nearly 100,000

---

[48]Wischnitzer, Visas to Freedom, p. 64.

problems of interpreting languages between 1920 and 1954.[49]

An Episcopal Priest, who was a Chaplain on Ellis Island from 1948-1954 stated, "Divine rights were as much a part of life on Ellis Island as human rights. Up until its closing in 1954, worship provided by major faiths was an integral part of the atmosphere and a chief factor in morale among detainees." Chaplain John H. Evans, retired, now of the Church of the Holy Cross, Middletown, Rhode Island, 02840 (401) 683-0712, lived at the Seamen's Church Institute at 25 South Street. He worked with Alice G. Palmer on the hospital side of Ellis Island. He was one of an army of volunteers who labored mightily in what many considered to be "God's work." And by their work, the way was made easier for those "huddled masses" who yearned to be free.

---

[49]These totals were calculated by the author from the Annual Reports, 1921-1955.

PART II

CHAPTER V:

THE RESTORATION COMMISSIONS

Conditions of Decay[1]

The years of neglect, vandals and the forces of nature took a large toll on the Island's buildings. Although the Congress authorized $6 million for the Island in 1976 and an additional $24 million in 1978, little money was appropriated, hence the National Park Service had to treat the Island as an appendage of the park system.

Ellis Island is the largest and most complex group of structures on a single site in the National Park Service. Its more than one-half million square feet of space presents a challenge of restoration and interpretation. These conditions are magnified by the neglect and the deterioration of the structures, the environmental requirments and high construction costs.

The main building (the Great Hall), built to serve as the processing center for immigrants, is of primary historical importance. The entire area was landscaped and the site developed between 1933 to 1935. This work included improvements in the ferry house and the recreation hall. The baggage and dormitory building is nearly as large as the main building. It features large tiled dormitory rooms, a modern kitchen and a dining area. After the Island was closed, the lower floors and stairs were severely damaged by the elements, especially rain.

The Power House is located on the north end of Island 1. It was severely damaged on the north side where the brick wall leans outward and was in danger of collapsing. The generating equipment was vandalized, but the large boilers were in good condition, although not operating. The Kitchen and Laundry Building connects to the

---

[1]The following conditions describe Ellis Island as it was before the restoration process began. It would help the reader to refer to Figure 2, Chapter I

Main Building by a corridor. The maintenance staff uses the first floor for offices. There were several areas of severe damage in the structure, particularly the cast iron porch and columns on the south elevation and the entire west wing. According to the National Park Service survey, none of the damage was irreparable. Because of its materials and design, it is a visually-cohesive unit with the Main Building and is important to the historic scene around the ferry basin.

The Bakery and Carpentry Shop also connects the Main Building by way of the Kitchen. Some of the belt-driven power tools remain in the Carpenter Shop. This building also suffered from water damage, but is in sound shape. The interior is sub-divided into shops, storage rooms and offices.

The Ferry Building stands at the northwest end of the ferry basin. It was completed in 1935 to connect Islands 1 and 2. Although the ferry slip and gangway were badly damaged, the building was in good condition, and it was used for toilets and small workshops by the Island staff. The Immigration Building, which is directly behind the Ferry Building was also in good condition and was used by the staff for offices and locker rooms. The Hospital and Administration Buildings are located on Island 1 directly opposite the Main Building. They form the southwest part of the U-shaped buildings which surround the ferry basin. Architecturally, these are elegant structures. Their condition is very similar to the Main Buildings and in some respects are in better shape. With the exception of the attic, nearly all the windows were intact. But severe water damage occurred in drain and skylight areas over stairwells. According to the McCann Report:

> Many finishes are ruined and several interior doorway lintels were rotted away. Whole ceilings have come down in certain rooms. The cellar, however, is relatively dry and no sign of major foundation damage was visible. Some rooms are completely undamaged. Steel structures, when visible, is rusted only in small areas. The sources of most of the water intrusion are the plugged gutter and downspout system,

open attic windows, missing hip and valley flashings on the roof, and broken skylights. Inside, piles of rubbish, in addition to holding moisture, create potentially damaging concentrated loads on the floor system. Although not interpreted at this time, stabilization of the building is not difficult, and it could be valuable for interpretation at a later date.[2]

Island 3 contains the Contagious Disease Wards, a power house, mortuary and the Commissioner's House. The twelve wards are badly damaged and are in poor condition. The mortuary has also deteriorated. But the Commissioner's House is the best preserved on Ellis island. There are living, dining and kitchen spaces on the first floor and bedrooms on the second. Some of the paint peeled, and there is minor plaster damage, but very little water penetrated the interior. Unlike other buildings, there was little vandalism and little structural damage. This building could again be used as a residence, and it is architectually interesting.

Attempted Disposal

After 1924, Ellis Island was no longer used as a primary inspection point for immigrants. During the 1930's the Island served primarily as a detention station, and with the passage of the Internal Security Act of 1950, the population of the Island swelled to 1,500 persons, many of whom were awaiting deportation as subversive aliens. In 1954, the government declared that only those persons "whose release would be inimical to the national security" were to be held at Ellis Island for deportation. By June of 1954, there were only about 24 people still on the Island, and it was clear that it had outlived its usefulness, both as an immigration center and as a deportation center. In November the last official left the Island, and on the following March 4, 1955, the government declared the Island to be "surplus

---

[2]McCann Report, p. A-11.

property." Federal agencies were screened first to determine if there was a need for it under continued federal use. Since no affirmative response was received, GSA put the Island up for sale. During the next 18 months, the Federal government offered to transfer the property to a state or local government agency or a qualified nonprofit institution for any use pursuant to the provisions of the Federal Property and Administrative Services Act of 1949. Since no recommendations were received from an eligible applicant, GSA advertised Ellis Island for private sale by sealed bids.

At one point, Jersey City claimed Ellis Island as its own, and to dramatize its claim the mayor and a landing party seized the Island in the name of the state. State Senator James F. Murray was in favor of converting the Island into an ethnic museum. The boarding party of 25 persons filed "final papers" and announced that a causeway would be built connecting Jersey City and Ellis Island.[3] (Figure 23 shows the proximity of Ellis Island to New Jersey)

During 1958 and 1959, three attempts were made to sell the Island, but no bids received were commensurate with the value of the property. At various times there were forwarded to Washington or to the nation's presses, proposals that included converting the Island into a women's prison, a drug treatment center, a college, a school for international affairs, a gambling casino, an apartment complex, and a commercial center. At this point, GSA suspended its efforts to sell the Island in order to concentrate on the disposal of the property under Section 203(k) of the Act of 1949. The Department of Health, Education and Welfare received several applications for proposed uses of the surplus property, including Ellis Island For Higher Education, Inc.; the Training School of Vineland, New Jersey; the International University Foundation, which suggested that the Island be made into a library

---

[3]New York Times, January 5, 1956, p. 1.

Figure 23

ELLIS ISLAND: regional context

and museum on the subject of American immigration and from Theodore Granik, who suggested that the buildings be used for housing the elderly.[4]

On July 12, 1962, the Committee on Government Operation of the U. S. Senate created the Sub-commitee on Intergovernmental Relations and began to tackle the problem of Ellis Island.   The

---

[4]U.S. Congress, Senate, Committee on Government Operations, <u>Disposal of Ellis Island</u>, Report No. 306, June 9, 1965.

chairman of the committee, Senator Edmund Muskie of Maine, enlisted the support of Adlai Stevenson, the U. S. Representative to the United Nations, and Robert Moses of New York City. Stevenson reported that the possible use of Ellis Island as a UN property had been explored and that there was no UN need at the time. Moses suggested converting the Island into a youth conservation project, like the CCC projects of the 1930's.

The National Park Service, responding to the Congressional initiative, created a study team on December 3, 1963, with Robert E. Lee, Director of the Northeast region as chairman. On June 24, 1964, the Secretary of the Interior forwarded the National Park Service's report on Ellis Island to the Sub-committee. It recommended that Ellis Island be converted to a national area for public visitation and that it be designated as a national historic site with possible secondary compatible uses. The Secretary of the Interior stated that the provisions of the Historic Sites Act of 1935 established a sufficient basis for the Department to begin implementing the general recommendations contained in its study report. Under this legislation, the Secretary of the Interior is authorized to designate the National Park Service as the administering agent, pursuant to Section 2 of the above Act; it also is empowered to enter into contracts and cooperative agreements with "States, Municipal Cooperatives, Associations, or individuals" where this is deemed necessary to "protect, preserve, maintain, or operate" such property; it also may "restore, reconstruct, rehabilitate, preserve, and maintain" the buildings and properties at such national historic sites. The law also authorizes the Park Service to develop educational programs for the purpose of making available to the public facts and information pertaining to these historic sites.

The Secretary's plan for Ellis Island proposed to develop Ellis Island as part of a two-state National Historic Site. The plan would have linked Ellis Island with the American Museum of Immigration (then under construction), and it would use funds from the Federal antipoverty program to have young men from Job Corps Centers assist in the rehabilitation of Ellis Island (an idea that the Restore Ellis

Island Committee returned to in 1976). The plan had one very controversial feature, which probably doomed it: to build a causeway from the New Jersey shore to Ellis Island.[5]

The Presidential Proclamation

President Johnson, noting the positive contributions of immigrants and proceeding under authority of Section 2 of the June 8, 1906 Act, proclaimed the property known as Ellis Island to be made part of the Statue of Liberty National Monument on May 11, 1965, (see Figure 24). Since the State of New Jersey was drafting plans to develop a waterfront park opposite Ellis Island, the Presidential Proclamation made it possible to harmonize the Statue of Liberty national monument and the waterfront park. (Remember that Ellis Island is only 1,300 feet from the New Jersey coast.) President Johnson visited the Statue of Liberty in October 1965 to sign the Proclamation.

Congress next authorized $6 million for the construction of a memorial to the immigrants on Ellis Island, and the plans for the park on the New Jersey shore opposite the Island. Architect Philip Johnson was commissioned to design the memorial, and he proposed a hollow tower 130 feet high which would be covered inside with tiny plaques bearing the names of millions of persons who passed through

---

[5]New York Times, June 16, 1964.

Presidential Documents

Title 3—THE PRESIDENT

ADDING ELLIS ISLAND TO THE STATUE OF LIBERTY NATIONAL MONUMENT

By the President of the United States of America

A Proclamation

WHEREAS Ellis Island in 1890 was placed under the control of the Federal Bureau of Immigration for development as an immigration station; and

WHEREAS between the years 1892 and 1954 Ellis Island was host to more than 16 million aliens entering this country; and

WHEREAS Ellis Island was a temporary shelter for those who sought refuge, freedom, and opportunity in our country; and

WHEREAS the millions of people who passed through the Ellis Island Depot were important to America for their contribution in making the United States of America the world leader it is today; and

WHEREAS the Statue of Liberty is a symbol to the world of the dreams and aspirations which have drawn so many millions of immigrants to America; and

WHEREAS to all Americans the Statue of Liberty stands eternal as the symbol of the freedom which has been made a living reality in the United States for men of all races, creeds, and national origins who have united in allegiance to the Constitution of the United States and to the imperishable ideals of our free society; and

WHEREAS, by Proclamation No. 1713 of October 15, 1924 (43 Stat. 1968), the Statue of Liberty and the land on which it is situated were established as a national monument in accordance with section 2 of the Act of Congress approved June 8, 1906 (34 Stat. 225; 16 U.S.C. 431); and

WHEREAS Ellis Island, consisting of approximately 27.5 acres, with improvements thereon, and of submerged lands in the rectangle surrounding the island, including the above acreage, aggregating 48 acres, is owned and controlled by the United States; and

WHEREAS the public interest would be promoted by reserving this area for proper protection and preservation as the Statue of Liberty National Monument:

NOW, THEREFORE, I, LYNDON B. JOHNSON, President of the United States of America, under and by virtue of the authority vested in me by section 2 of the Act of Congress approved June 8, 1906 (34 Stat. 225; 16 U.S.C. 431), do proclaim that the property known as Ellis Island, as described in the preamble of this Proclamation, which is owned and controlled by the United States is hereby added to and made a part of the Statue of Liberty National Monument, subject to the limitation contained in the last sentence of this paragraph, and shall be administered pursuant to the Act of August 25, 1916 (39 Stat. 535; 16 U.S.C., secs. 1-3), and acts supplementary thereto and amendatory thereof. Henceforth the Statue of Liberty National Monument shall consist of the Statue of Liberty, Liberty Island, and Ellis Island. Unless provided otherwise by Act of Congress, no funds appropriated to the Department of the Interior for the Administration of the National Monument shall be expended upon the development of Ellis Island.

THE PRESIDENT

Warning is hereby expressly given to all unauthorized persons not to appropriate, injure, destroy, or remove any feature of the National Monument.

So much of Proclamation No. 1713 of October 15, 1924, as relates to Fort Wood, New York, and the Statue of Liberty and the land on which it is situated, is hereby superseded.

IN WITNESS WHEREOF, I have hereunto set my hand and caused the Seal of the United States of America to be affixed.

DONE at the City of Washington this eleventh day of May in the year of our Lord nineteen hundred and sixty-five, and of [SEAL] the Independence of the United States of America the one hundred and eighty-ninth.

LYNDON B. JOHNSON

By the President:

DEAN RUSK,
Secretary of State.

[F.R. Doc. 65–5141; Filed, May 12, 1965; 10:08 a.m.]

Figure 24 Source *Federal Register* May 13, 1965.

Ellis Island. As visitors ascended the tower to the top, they could find the names of immigrant relatives or friends.[6] Johnson's plan would have involved leveling all the buildings on the Station except the great reception hall and a hospital building; these structures would have been partially demolished. Partly for this reason, Johnson's plans met with little praise and much hostility and the funds for them were never appropriated.

The National Park Service plan for Ellis Island was to rehabilitate the main immigration building for use as a public museum, to restore one or two smaller buildings for administrative use, and to remove nearly all of the other structures. The plan would have also restored the ferry basin, the sea wall, and it would have landscaped the remaining grounds for a public park, which

[6]This idea of nameplates was revived in 1988 by The Statue of Liberty-Ellis Island Foundation, which is creating "The American Immigrant Wall of Honor." See below.

would have been embellished with sculptures and other depictions of the history of Ellis Island.

To commemorate the designation of Ellis Island as part of the Statue of Liberty National Monument in New York City, the Congress on October 1966 authorized the striking of a medal as the fourth in a series of medals by the New York City National Shrines Advisory Board (Public Law 89-076). The other three medals in the series were (1) Federal Hall National Memorial, (2) The Castle Clinton National Monument, and (3) the Statue of Liberty National Monument, American Museum of Immigration. The National Shrine's Advisory Board was created by Act of Congress in 1955 for the purpose of advising the National Park Service on maintaining shrines.

The design of the medal conformed with those that were previously issued. The face of all medals was identical, presenting the Statue of Liberty National Monument as "Liberty Enlightening the World," which was the theme of the French sculptor August E. Bartholdi. The reverse of the fourth medal depicted the main immigration depot buildings on Ellis Island, through which the millions of immigrants passed. The medals were designed by Medallic Art Company of Danbury, Connecticut. The gross sale of the the the liberty series of medals was limited to not more than 255,000, these to be struck between July 31, 1966 and December 31, 1968, but many fewer were sold. There were 20 gold medals struck, 2,000 silver of .900 fine and an undisclosed amount of bronze -- all 1 5/16 inches in size.

On June 5, 1967, the New York City National Shrines Associates and the Bill of Rights Commemorative Society sponsored a celebration of the 75th anniversary of "Ellis Island as an Immigration Depot." Rear Admiral John J. Bergen, Retired, Chairman of the New York City National Shrines Association, presided over the ceremony, which included the presentation of gold medallions to President Lyndon B. Johnson; Mayor John Lindsay, of New York City; Eva Adams, Director of the Mint; Mrs. Bernard E Gimbel (for her husband, owner if Gimbel's Department Store) and Dr. Vladimir Clain-Stefanelli, of the Smithsonian Institution. Several other persons received silver medallions and the Mayor's "Certificate of Achievment" Scroll Awards. In all, 64 persons received awards.[7]

Ellis Island as a National Monument

The Presidential Proclamation of 1965 made Ellis Island a part of the Statue of Liberty National Monument. Reacting to this move, the Congress placed a $6,000,000 limitation (Public Law 89-129) on expenditures for the Island. In granting this authority, the House Committee on Interior and Insular Affairs specified that, "The plan of the National Park Services is to rehabilitate the main immigration building for use as a public museum, to rehabilitate one or two other structures for administrative use, to remove all or nearly all of the other structures on the Island, to restore the ferry basin, sea wall and utilities, to landscape the grounds for public park use with emphasis through sculpture and otherwise on the importance in history of Ellis Island, and to provide a restaurant and smaller facilities for the visiting public. It may also be that eventually a walkway will be provided to connect the Island with the New Jersey shore."[8]

Although no money was appropriated at that time, the National Park Service drafted a General Management Plan for Ellis Island in 1968. It called for demolition of most existing buildings, leaving only the Great Hall and covered walkways and adding a restaurant, pavilion, maintenance buildings and visitor services. The total development costs for the restoration were set at $8,696,807.

There were two main problems concerning the 1968 plan: it included the raising of the ferry, and it was well over the $6 million limit imposed by Congress. The boat was inspected by representatives of the Regional Office, who agreed that it had deteriorated beyond the

---

[7]I should like to thank Virginia M. Fuentes, Executive Director of the New York City National Shrines Associates, for providing me with this information.

[8]See U. S. House of Representatives, Report No. 585 (1965).

point of salvage.[9]   Also, it included restoration of the exterior of the hospital buildings lining the ferry slip.   There was a question of whether this violated the intent of the Congress.

There was a good deal of support for retaining the hospital buildings.   Architect Philip Johnson, who was asked by Secretary of the Interior Udall to devise a master plan for the Island in 1965, provided for preserving the main building and the hospital buildings. Later, in commenting on the 1968 plan, Dr. Ernest Connally, the Chief of the Office of Archeology and Historic Preservation stated, "Retention of the buildings on both sides of the ferry slip is essential to the architectural composition as a whole.   With removal of any part, the ensemble is destroyed." Connally added, "Some of these spaces can be adapted to use as restaurants, concessions, rest rooms, offices, etc.   It should be a proper function of a master planning to find suitable uses for buildings which are worth preserving as an integral part of an authentic historic environment."

One issue that seemed to be neglected in all of the above discussion was the question of maintenance.   The National Park Service lacked funds to maintain existing parks and the addition of new parks only multiplied the problem.   Once a building is restored, it must be maintained or it wiil require "re-restoration" in a few years.

The rejection of the Johnson plan left Ellis Island to continue to deteriorate in the period after 1965.   In May of 1970, a group of militant Indians attempted to seize Ellis Island to publicize the plight of their people.   They were turned back by the National Park Service guards.   But four months later, members of the National Economic Growth and Reconstruction Organization (NEGRO) did peacfully occupy the Island.   The goal of the group was to provide job opportunities for blacks and to convert Ellis Island into a drug

---

[9]This history is taken from memos in the archives of the National Park Service, 1100 L Street, NW, Washington, D.C.

rehabilitation center for addicts, welfare recipients and former convicts. NEGRO hoped to convert Ellis Island into a number of factories to create jobs for blacks.

The National Park Service permitted this group to use Ellis Island as an experiment. Meanwhile, the Island continued to decay. In 1973, the Secretary of the Interior Rogers C. B. Morton recommended that the National Park Service dispose of Ellis Island by transferring it to the jurisdiction of GSA. He seemed to be giving truth to Santayana's statement that "those who ignore history are doomed to repeat it." The Superintendent of Ellis Island responded properly, "It is simply inconceivable to me that Ellis Island would ever be disposed of for commercial development. Even if an attempt were made to encourage private owners to retain some of the historic structures, the historical integrity of the Island would be irretrievably compromised."

The master plan for 1968 was not acted upon, and the Island continued to deteriorate. As talk of a bicentennial celebration increased, it engendered a new patriotism. All suggestions that the National Park Service dispose of Ellis island ceased.

The Restore Ellis Island Committee

Dr. Peter Sammartino, former President and Chancellor of Fairleigh Dickinson University, is the person most responsible for saving Ellis Island. He created the Restore Ellis Island Committee while serving as Chairman of the International Bicentennial Commission of New Jersey. He visited the Island with Walter Peters, Executive Director of the New Jersey Commission. It is best to quote Sammartino on conditions on the Island:[10]

It was a cold, blustery day with overcast skies. The doors of the main building were banging in the wind. The bats

---

[10]Statement, Fairleigh Dickinson University Archives, May, 1984

and the pigeons were flying around in the cavernous vaults of the central hall. Everywhere, there was crumbling plaster, flaking paint, disintegrating concrete, and odd pieces of furniture scattered throughout; here and there pages from official documents; aging signs in six languages to guide lhe immigrants. And suddenly, I had an emotional reaction. This was the place where my father and mother first landed in America! What Plymouth Rock was to the Pilgrims, Ellis Island was to the millions that came to our shores in the first two decades of our century. My throat choked up and all of a sudden, the stories of my parents' landing became a vivid re-creation.

How appalling that this Island had been forgotten and neglected in spite of the promises of Presidents Johnson and Nixon. What an ugly sight next to the greatest symbol of the world--the Statue of Liberty.

At the next meeting of the International Committee, Sammartino suggested that the New Jersey Bicentennial celebration feature the restoration of Ellis Island and that the Island be opened for tourists in 1976. The plan was received enthusiastically and it was approved unanimously. Thus, the Restore Ellis Island Committee (REIC) was born, with Sammartino as President. Kitty Hoagland, who had gone through Ellis Island herself, was elected Vice President, Dr. Patrick Conway, also of Fairleigh Dickinson University, became Secretary and James Quackenbush, a C.P.A., who was President of the Holland Society, was chosen Treasurer.

Sammartino received the help of various ethnic organizations, including the Polish National Alliance, the Irish American Historical Society, the Steuben Society, the United Hellenic American Congress, the Armenian National Committee, the World Federation of Hungarian Freedom Fighters, the National Italian American Foundation, and the Ukranian National Association. They contacted Congressmen, they publicized the activity in their own bulletins and sent releases to ethnic pubiications, they organized trips to the Island. In all, Sammartino

enlisted the aid of 50 persons, who represented most of the large
ethnic groups, the Congress and the government. (See Table 16)

Sammartino favored using Federal resources to improve conditions on

Table 16

THE RESTORE ELLIS ISLAND COMMITTEE*

William J. Adelman
Vice President, Illinois Labor History Society
Mario Albi
National President, Unico National
Dr. Charles Angoff
Editor, Literary Review
John J. Appell
Secretary, Immigration History Society
East Lansing, Michigan
Henri A. de Bonneval
Engineer, New York City
Dr. Kevin M. Cahill
Pres.-Gen., American Irish Historical Society
Dr. James S. Counelis
Dir. of Research, Univ. of San Francisco
Dr. Nasrollah Fatemi
Dir., Graduate School of Int'l Studies,
Fairleigh Dickinson University
Dr. Carl Fjellman
President, Upsala College
Anthony J. Fornelli
President, Joint Civic Committee of
Italian-Americans
Rev. Andrew Greeley
National Opinion Research Center, Chicago
Professor Victor Greene
Executive Secretary, Immigration History Group,
University of Wisconsin
Dr. Richard Guarino
Vice President, U.S.V. Pharmaceutical Corp.
Ross Harano
Japanese-American Citizens' League
Mrs. F. Richard Hsu
Mgr., R.C.A. for Internat'l Marketing Research
Dr. Vitaut Kipel
Editor, Heritage Review
Dr. Andrew T. Kopan
Chairman, Dept. of Educational Foundations,
De Paul University
Dr. Myron B. Kuropas
Supreme Advisor, Ukranian National Assn.
Dr. Arthur Kron
Chairman, Exec. Comm. Van Brunt & Co., N.Y.C.
George Kruge
Vice President, Grove Shepherd Wilson & Kruge

Joseph Lesawyer
President, Ukranian National Association
Irving M. Levine
Dir., Institute on Pluralism and Group Identity
William J. Mahin
Film Maker, Glen Ellyn, Ill.

Arthur Mann
University of Chicago
George M. Mardikian
G. M. Mardikian Enterprises, San Francisco, CA
Aloysius Mazewski
President, Polish National Alliance
Mary Lynn McCree
Curator, Jane Addams' Hull-House

Robert G. McKelvey
Chairman of the Board, M.M. Enterprises
Mrs. Chester Parker
Sculptor, New York City
Dr. Frank Pellegrini
Joint Civic Committee of Italian Americans
Dr. Andros H. Pogany

Professor, Seton Hall University
Charles C. Porcelli
Attorney at Law, Chicago, Illinois
Bernard Puchalski
President, Iron Workers District Council,
Chicago
Joseph Rosenthal
Chairman of the Board, E.I. Industries
Theodore Saloutos
President, Immigration History Society

Mrs. Peter Sammartino
Dean Emerita, Fairleigh Dickinson University
Dr. J. Harry Smith
President, Essex County College
Michael Sotirhos
Greek Orthodox Church
Edward J. Sussman
National Chairman, Steuben Society of America
Taras G. Szmagala
Office of Senator Robert Taft, Jr

Dr. S. M. Tomasi
Director, Center for Migration Studies
Dennis C. Valenti
Director, Senior Citizen Institute, Newark, N.J.
Dr. Rudolph J. Vecoli
Director, Immigration History Research Center,
University of Minnesota
Vincent Visceglia
Industrialist, Short Hills, New Jersey
Frederick D. Wiss
Executive Vice President, J. Wiss & Sons,
Newark, N.J.

*Philip Lax was added to the Committee and was
elected President in 1978.

the Island. In 1975, REIC made a successful application to the Bergen County Comprehensive Employment and Training Agency for $18,000 to hire seven workers and a supervisor. They met every morning at a Jersey City pier, and the National Park Service boat would take them to the Island where they began the job of clearing away the undergrowth and the debris of twenty years of neglect. They bought 3,500 large plastic bags and filled them with the accumulated dirt inside the building. These bags were then used to strengthen the sea walls around the Island. They were able, through unorthodox bureaucratic means, to start the process of cleaning up Ellis Island.

At the same time, Sammartino worked for Congressional support of his idea to restore Ellis Island. He sponsored dinners in Washington, D.C., and through them he gained the support of Congressman Ed Patten, of New Jersey, who was on the National Park Service Budget Committee, as well as the Chairman, Congressman Sidney Yates of Chicago and Congressman Tip O'Neill of Massachusetts. Patten was very responsive. He submitted Sammartino's request for $1.5 million to clean up the Island for the Bicentennial. The House Committee approved it unanimously, and although the Senate bill did not contain the item, it was added in Conference Committee. President Ford signed the bill during the last days of 1975, just in time for the bicentennial.

Sammartino contacted experienced estimators, who calculated a budget for restoring the island. But one line item turned out to be very controversial; it involved tearing down most buildings on the Island--something that had been a part of the 1968 plan and that did not have universal support.[11]

---

[11] When I joined the Restore Ellis Island Committee in 1976, I was unaware that some members favored the National Park Service plan to demolish all buildings that had "no historic" importance. I made several speeches recommending that the entire island be saved. See, for example, the Christian Science Monitor article for March 25, 1977.

On November 5, 1975, 200 guests gathered on Ellis Island to commemmorate an historic time: the United States flag was raised there for the first time since 1954. On May 28, 1976, ceremonies were held dedicating the Island and opening it to the public. The seats were placed facing the flagpole and the lower end of Manhattan. A government band provided the music. Licia Albanese, of the Metropolitan Opera, sang the national anthem, and the Fairleigh Dickinson Chorus performed. Professor Charles Del Rosso of the University's music department composed a symphonic poem entitled "Ellis Island" and dedicated it to Sally and Peter Sammartino. The New York City fire commissioner collaborated by assigning a fireboat to send up plumes of water as a background just beyond the Island. All present sang the fourth stanza of America the Beautiful," which had much more meaning for the twentieth-century immigrants.

In his dedicatory speech Sammartino reminded us:[12]

It is on this Island that we can pause and think dispassionately of how fortunate we are. Yes, we have problems, we have inequities, and who hasn't? But when all is said and done, we must rejoice in the fact that we are the most favored of any land in the history of civilization. Of all the parks and sites under the jurisdiction of the National Park Service, this will be the most poignant. Let this Island then be a reminder of how the lives of all of us have been affected for the good because of our fathers. Let us remember how they had to save their coins arduously for months and years; how they spent miserable days on the high seas, and then came the morning when their souls were uplifted briefly by the sight of the Statue of Liberty yonder. But when they landed in the baffling frightening stalls of this hall, the fear of rejection hovered as an evil shadow and then--and then that final approval. What courage they had,

---

many not knowing the language, practically all with little or almost no money--to start almost blindly but with an intuitive sense of the greatness of this new land, accepting the snubs along the way as a natural part of working their way up, appreciating every little step ahead; for this was America.

And if we have now become too soft, too demanding, too wasteful, perhaps this Island can be a reminder that we must be thankful for what we have.

In the Bicentennial summer, over 40,000 persons, many of whom had been processed on the island, returned there to "enjoy" the place where they first stepped on American soil. It is fortunate that the National Park Service wisely recorded many of the feelings of these persons by taking their oral histories. The Circle Line provided ferry service to the Island not only from Manhattan but from Jersey City. The Island had been cleared, the main building cleaned up and a regular tour commenced by National Park Service guides.

REIC wanted to sponsor several white-tie dinners on the Island, to which successful executives would be invited (at $100 per plate). Unfortunately, the National Park Service would not allow these events to take place. There was neither water nor sewage, no electrical service, and it was too dangerous to have people ambling about with the possibility of falling beams and chunks of concrete. Instead, REIC sponsored the Ellis Island Awards to successful immigrants (or their children) who had been processed at the Island.

The awards, instead of the usual certificate or plaque, were copies of State Department skippets of the eighteenth century, which were obtained from the Metropolitan Museum.[13] The cover had the official seal of the United States of the early period, and the award and awardee's name were engraved on the underside. The awards ceremonies were full of human tenderness, of nostalgic remembrances,

---

[13]A skippet is a round brass container, about six inches in diameter, which holds the red seal for stamping documents.

and all who attended felt the emotional impact of the brief messages of the day, when several of the awardees broke down and wept openly.

By 1978, Sammartino, who was nearly 74 years of age, felt that it was time for a younger person to take the leadership of the Restore Ellis Island Committee. He proposed Philip Lax as his replacement. Sammartino became President Emeritus, and in 1980, he was honored by the National Italian American Foundation. On April 25, the President of the Foundation John A. Volpe, former Governor of Massachusetts, later Secretary of Transportation and then United States Ambassador to Italy, came from Boston to be the speaker at the ceremony. Licia Albanese of the Metropolitan Opera sang the national anthem. The Superintendent of the Statue of Liberty National Park, David Moffitt, spoke of the part Sammartino played in the Ellis Island restoration movement.

The Ellis Island Restoration Commission

On the resignation of Peter Sammartino as President of the Restore Ellis Island Committee, Philip Lax was elected to that post. Lax, a land developer and interior designer from Short Hills, New Jersey, had been very active in many philanthropic and community activities nationally and internationally, particularly B'Nai B'rith where he was international vice president. Both of his parents went through Ellis Island.

At the next meeting of the executive committee , the name of the committee was changed to the "Ellis Island Restoration Commission, Inc." Three vice presidents were elected, and the number of trustees was increased from 7 to 40. The by-laws were amended to reflect the foregoing resolutions.

The officers of the Commission included the three vice presidents: Jacqueline Beusse, Commissioner of Motion Pictures, New Jersey--Membership; Set Momjian, former U. S. Representative to the United Nations--Development; and August C. Bolino, Professor, Catholic University of America--Research. Dr. Francis P. McQuade, of Seton Hall University was elected Secretary and Alexander B. Lyon,

Jr, President, New York City National Shrines, was chosen as Treasurer. The executive committee included the above officers and Dr. Peter Sammartino; John Bergen, Rear Admiral (deceased); Joseph Brechner President, Mid-Florida Television Corporation (deceased); A. Thorstein Karlsson; Norman Liss; and John Reagan (Tex) McCrary.

Lax insisted that the first order of business for the new Commission was to obtain an agreement with the National Park Service that would designate the Ellis Island Restoration Commission (EIRC) as the primary advisory commission to the Department of the Interior. Senate Report 306, which provided the original recommendations, allowed the establishment of an "Advisory Commission," and such a group was authorized in 1966 as the National Ellis Island Association." Because it accomplished little, EIRC had a more difficult time reaching an agreement with the National Park Service. The first fruit of this effort was for the Interior Department to appoint Martin Schaller as a liaison between the Department and the Ellis Island Restoration Commission. The Commission was given authority to use Federal Hall in New York City.

Meanwhile things were happening on the legislative front. Lax met with Senators McGovern, Case and others, and with Governor Byrne of New Jersey to support reconciliation of the two bills that were written to restore Ellis Island, which authorized $18 million and $12 million. At the same time, Professor Bolino's appearance on the Rosemary Fresino Show in New York City in 1978 came to the attention of Congressman Edward Koch. He submitted a joint resolution to the Congress, which provided that the original authorization of $6 million be increased to $37 million. When Koch was elected Mayor of New York City he turned the resolution over to his friend, Congressman Jonathan Bingham, also of New York. The Koch-Bingham resolution attempted to increase the authorization to $50 million to rehabilitate Ellis Island. During a press conference announcing his resolution, Koch stated that the $37 million figure would be a compromise between the basic stabilization costs for the

Island and the expensive full-scale rehabilitation. He also took special note of the proposal being advanced by the Ellis Island Restoration Commission to restore Ellis Island, to transfer to the Island microfilm of the immigration records and to create a museum there.

On April 28, 1978, Bolino accompanied Congressman Jonathan Bingham to the hearings on the Interior budget before the House Appropriations Committee. In his testimony Bingham supported the Island and he stated, "I would like to see a full rehabilitation of the Island and the establishment there of a national 'roots' center, a center for the appreciation of the immigrant experience. I would envisage a restored Ellis Island with its main building looking approximately as it did in 1907, a peak year of Ellis' operation. The grounds could be opened for festivals sponsored by the various ethnic groups whose forebears came through Ellis. Perhaps we could have a Greek Week, an Italian Week, a Jewish Week, and so on, all centered on Ellis Island."

Although the Congress did not pass the Koch-Bingham resolution, it did authorize an additional $24 million for restoration in October 1978. When President Carter signed this law the National Park Service designated a planning team to draft a master plan. Philip Lax, President of the Ellis Island Restoration Commission, was appointed to this team. The National Park Service drafted a new General Management Plan for the Island.[14] The preliminary plan was ready in December 1980, and it was presented at public hearings in New York and New Jersey.

The Park Service preferred the following options (a) Preserve the three major immigrant service structures on Island 1; (b) Stabilize the main hospital complex, ferry buildings and corridors (Island 2); (c) Retain the contagious disease wards and WPA structures on Island 3 (these buildings would be allowed to deteriorate; (d) Remove the wooden superstructure of the ferry boat and leave the metal hull in

---

[14]"Statue of Liberty, Ellis Island Analysis of Alternatives," National Park Service, December 1980.

the slip; (e) Expand the functions of the American Museum of Immigration (administrative, research, storage, exhibitions) and move these to Ellis Island.

While the hearings on the Ellis Island plan were proceeding, Lax was notified by the National Park Service that it was prepared to sign the agreement that Lax had long sought. The Memorandum was signed on December 12, 1980 As Lax said, "This was a critical agreement, because without the efforts of the Ellis Island Restoration Commission, the Island might have been bulldozed." As the directors of the ElRC were leaving the signing ceremony, Tex McCrary, who serves as a member of the Board of ElRC, then indicated that the transition team for the Reagan Administration was drafting plans for the Department of the Interior. McCrary recommended to Lax that the ElRC postpone action until the new Secretary of the Interior (James Watt) had a chance to analyze the agreement. Upon the appointment of Watts, Garnet Chapin was designated as the new liaison and on June 19, 1981, he met with the Secretary of the Interior to learn the new administration's views concerning restoration plans.

At a meeting of the Ellis Island Restoration Commission, Chapin told the members that we would need a new agreement with the Department and that it was considering new approaches which were consistent with the 1980 Amendments to the Historic Preservation Act, He spoke of RFP's (requests for proposals), and it was clear that the administration intended to lease part of Ellis Island to obtain revenue for rehabilitation. Chapin stated that the plan included saving all the buildings on the Island, and it stressed preserving the view from Island 1 and all the exteriors of existing structures. He indicated that the Department of the Interior wished to rewrite the agreement.

The RFP was released on December 14, 1981, by Secretary James G. Watt (RFP WAS0-82-11). Ross Holland, who was put in charge of the leasing plan, stated, "Secretary Watt and President Reagan's staff prefer to see private investment as an alternative to public neglect." The National Park Service received almost 30 proposals for leasing Islands 2 and 3. The proposals included building 8,200 units of high-rise housing, an office park, theater, restaurants and an aerial tram-way; an international language school; universities, ethnic organization headquarters and printshop for ethnic newspapers.

The leasing of Ellis Island was the first part of the Reagan plan; the second part was to create an umbrella agency to deal with all the organizations that wanted to restore Ellis Island. The National Park Service was concerned with the disrepair of the Statue of Liberty and wished to form a fund raising commission to restore both the Statue of Liberty and Ellis Island. On May 18, 1982, President Reagan and Secretary Watt announced the formation of the Statue of Liberty-Ellis Island Centennial Commission, with Mr. Lee A. Iacocca, President of Chrysler Corporation, as Chairman. Iacocca was one of the very few chief executive officers of a major American corporation who had a link with Ellis Island -- both of his parents had been processed there. Philip Lax was appointed to the Commission, and later he was made Chairman of the Architectural Committee.

The Statue of Liberty-Ellis Island Centennial Commission.

The goals of the Centennial Commission and its operating affiliate, The Statue of Liberty-Ellis Island Foundation, were to raise $230 million to Restore the Statue of Liberty completely by 1986, its centennial year; prevent further decay of the key historic buildings on Ellis Island, and to provide plans for its future use, as a modern living tribute to the ethnic and national origins of all Americans, by 1992, its centennial year; and to plan memorable centennial celebrations.

In addition to Iacocca, commission members included:

Mr. Armen F. Avedisian	Mr. Russell Dickenson
Chairman	Director
Avedisian Corporation	National Park Service
Hinsdale, Illinois	Washington, D.C.
Mr. Kent Barwick	Hon. Angier Biddle Duke

Chairman
New York City Landmarks
New York, New York

Chairman
U.S. Japan Foundation
New York, New York

Mr. Ralph Davidson
Chairman
Time, Inc.
New York, New York

Mr. Douglas Fraser
President
United Auto Workers
Detroit, Michigan

Mr. Marvin Davis
Davis Oil Company
Denver, Colorado

Mr. Roberto C. Goizueta
Chairman
Coca-Cola USA
Atlanta, Georgia

Mr. Lionel Hampton
New York, New York

Mr. and Mrs. Bob Hope
Palm Springs, California

Mr. Peter G. Peterson
Chairman
Lehman Brothers, Kuhn,
Loeb, Inc.
New York, New York

Mr. John Kluge
Chairman and President
Metromedia, Inc.
New York, New York

Mr. Peter V. Ueberroth
President
Los Angeles Olympic
Organizing Committee
Los Angeles, California

Mr. Philip Lax
President
Ellis Island Restoration
CommitteeCommission
Short Hills, New Jersey

Mr. Philippe Vallery-Radot
President
French-American
for the Restoration of
the Statue of Liberty
Paris France

Mr. Nicholas Morley
Chairman
Interterra, Inc.
Miami, Florida

Mr. Robert Zochowski
Attorney-at-Law and Director
Office of Ethnic Affairs,

State of New Jersey

Mr. Morris Pesin   Princeton Junction, New Jersey
Director, City Spirit Program
Office of Mayor Gerald McCann
Jersey City, New Jersey

The restoration of the two landmarks was completed by the New York architectural firm of Beyer Blinder Belle, in association with Anderson Notter Finegold of Boston. John Belle, the architect, supervised the restoration. He is a Welshman, an immigrant, who came to the United States in 1959.[15]

The original schedule called for the completion of the Great Hall in 1986 to coincide with the centennial celebration of the Statue of Liberty.[16] There have been constant delays, and the cost of restoration has escalated. One reason is that this is the largest project of its kind in American history. Lehrer McGovern Bovis, of New York City, which was given the job of restoring the Great Hall, originally set the cost at $100 million, but by 1988, this was raised to $150 million. The firm blamed the increase on the problems of coordinating the 250 subcontracts on the Island, the removal of asbestos, and the need to work without disturbing the "Historic Fabric" of the building. The architectural rendition of the restored Great Hall is shown in Figure 26.

---

[15] There is a fine story on him in the April 9, 1990 New Yorker magazine.

[16] See New York, August 29, 1983, pp. 102-3; Engineering News-Record, May 31, 1984, p.2

Figure 25 Philip Lax and Lee Iacocca View a Model of the restored Ellis Island (National Park Service Photo)

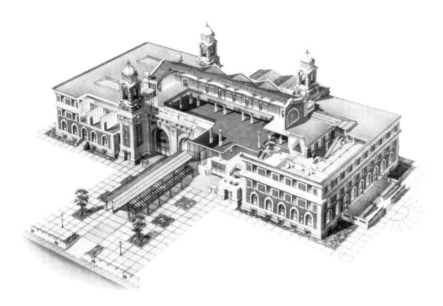

Figure 26   Restoration Design--Main Building Beyer Blinder
Belle, Architects

A temporary bridge was built to connect New Jersey to Ellis Island to
provide materials for rehabilitation. The Plans included restoring the
baggage, railroad and registry rooms; creating an Ellis Island
museum; and installing a computerized genealogy room. When the
plans for the genealogy room were dropped by the Statue of Liberty-
Ellis Island Foundation, the Ellis Island Restoration Commission voted
in October 1986 to plan, finance and to manage a Family History
Center in the Great Hall. (see below)

According to Michael Adlerstein, historical architect of the
Denver Service Center of the National Park Service, the restoration of

Ellis Island proceeded by developing three themes: 1.) The processing of immigrants; 2.) Immigration History; and 3.) American identity (ethnicity). Obviously, the first two were more easily accomplished, and these themes are highlighted in the Great Hall.[17] The Ellis Island Centennial Commission raised over $230 million for the restoration of the two monuments. The completion of the Statue of Liberty was celebrated on July 4, 1986 in a typically American extravaganza that lasted several days (the news networks featured a "Liberty Week").

On July 3, 1986, 300 immigrants from 109 nations went to Ellis Island to join 25,000 others all over the country in becoming United States citizens. Chief Justice Warren Burger administered the oath of citizenship, and shortly after, President Reagan lit the torch of the renewed Statue of Liberty to commemorate its one-hundredth birthday. During the July 4 celebration, Lee Iacocca was replaced as Chairman of the Statue of Liberty-Ellis Island Centennial Commission by Armen Avedisian, a Chicago banker. Iacocca became Chairman Emeritus of the Statue of Liberty-Ellis Island Foundation, which carried out the fund raising efforts of the Commision.

Let us take a backward look to consider the contributions of the Restore Ellis Island Committee and the Ellis Island Restoration Commission. In 1976, Sammartino probably saved Ellis Island when he convinced the Congress to appropriate one million dollars to clean the Island, and in 1978 Lax and Professor Bolino met with Meyer Fishbein, Director of Military Archives of the National Archives, to discuss the possibility of moving documents to Ellis Island and of establishing a computerized research center there. At the meeting with Fishbein, he stated that the Archives would cooperate with EIRC to develop a software program to transfer records to Ellis Island.

---

[17]Some of these issues were discussed at a meeting of the Ellis Island Restoration Commission on October 26, 1984, where Adlerstein summarized restoration plans. These plans conform closely to the suggestions I submitted to the National Park Service. See my "Report on Ellis Island," November, 1979.

The RFP Controversy

The 1981 RFP that was released by Secretary of the Interior James Watt stressed private investment to utilize Islands 2 and 3 (the south end of Ellis Island.) But it also engendered much controversy. After years of indecision, the Interior Department proposed a privately funded luxury hotel and conference center on Ellis Island. The hotel proposal came from William N. Hubbard, President of the Center for Housing Partnerships, of New York. He acknowledged that the 1986 income tax revisions removed some of the attractions for speculative real estate, and would make financing more difficult. But, he maintained that there is a substantial demand for a center in New York City, where people could do "cerebral kinds of things."

The Centennial Commission considered five options: 1) to restore the existing buildings into a conference center and hotel; 2) to restore some buildings to create an ethnic center; 3) to use some buildings for a museum; 4) to stabilize some buildings for a park; and 5) to allow these structures to decay. Of course, none of the options was considered mutually exclusive.

Chairman Lee A. Iacocca, head of the commission, stated that the hotel proposal was an attempt to "commercialize" the historic landmark. Iacocca preferred a "festival/exhibitry/crafts Center," which he likened to Colonial Williamsburg. This idea was supported by New York architect John Burgee, who believed that the $100 million cost could be raised through corporate and private donations.

According to a financial report prepared for the Statue of Liberty-Ellis Island Centennial Commission, the hotel plan is "economically flawed."[18] The finance task force, headed by James R. Galbraith, Vice President of Hilton Hotels, recommended instead that the Interior Department preserve the administration building and two hospitals on the south end of Ellis Island and convert the rest

---

[18]_Washington Post_, April 1, 1987.

158

into an open, grassy park. The cost was estimated at $25 million (compared to $82-100 million for the other two plans). The task force report states that, "This option does present an appropriate, dignified use of the south end of Ellis Island while at the same time it does not produce a horrific financial challenge nor the downside risk of development failure."[19] These proposals were to apply to the south end of the island (the 17 acres of abandoned buildings). The north end, containing the "Great Hall," where millions of new arrivals were processed, is not in dispute. It is restored as a visitors center and museum.

At its meeting of April 24, 1987, the SL-EI Centennial Commission recommended that the three major buildings on the south end be restored as a learning center, without a hotel. The dispute over the south half of Ellis Island led secretary Hodel to replace Chrysler Chairman Lee A.Iacocca as chairman of the centennial commission. The learning center, proposed by Hodel, will include lodging facilities, but Hodel assured Americans that the department would not permit commercial development of the island.

The Restoration Process

While there was disagreement concerning the RFP for Islands 2 and 3, the restoration of the main island commenced in 1984. The SL/EI Foundation engaged the firm of Beyer, Blinder & Belle to do all of the architectural and engineering work. They began by blowing air through the building for one year to dry out the main building, which had "knee-deep rubble and water."[20]

Stephen Briganti, President of the SL-EI Foundation, declared that the restoration would proceed as of 1907--the peak year of

---

[19]But this plan would mean bulldozing most structures on the Island--a proposal that has had considerable opposition since the National Park Service first acquired Ellis Island in 1965.

[20]New York Times, June 15, 1989.

immigration. But he soon learned that it was impossible to stick to a single year or period, because that would mean tearing down structures built at other times (for example, the beautiful guastavino tile ceiling was added in 1918), and it would not allow the Foundation to add the modern adaptations (ie, elevators).[21] When the restorers decided to use 1918 as the focal point of restoration, they had to remove 19 layers of paint to find the original green.

Most of the work was on the Great Hall, where the processing of immigrants took place. A new glass covering replaced the original canopy over the front door, and there are four new copper domes. The 170-foot ceiling was cleaned, and amazingly only 17 of the original 28,258 guastavino tiles had to be replaced. Inside the Great Hall, only the benches were returned to the Registry area. The architects reasoned that any alterations would destroy the feelings of fear and intimidation that immigrants felt during the wait in the Registry area. Perhaps as visitors sit there they will sense that fear and be able to "hear" the babel of their ancestors. John Belle, an immigrant himself, gave testimony to the significance of Ellis Island when he stated, "It's a cathedral of possibilities--all the millions of immigrants who really did find a better life after they passed through here. . . .It's a kind of monument to the possibilities of vast displacements of people, for good or evil."[22] The benches are a story of themselves. They are 12 feet long, made of solid oak. When Ellis Island was closed in 1954, the National Park Service feared that vandals would destroy them, so they were loaned out to museums and educational institutions for safekeeping. The Balch Institute for Ethnic Studies, in Philadelphia, received five benches, which it proudly displayed. Many children and grandchildren of immigrants sat on them reliving the experiences of their ancestors. But when the restoration process began on Ellis Island, these benches were reclaimed.

---

[21] The Guastavinos were also immigrants; they came from Catalan. They also designed the Oyster Bar in Grand Central Station--their other masterpiece.

[22] New Yorker, p. 31

The staff of the Balch Institute found a solution for this loss in the nearby Refugee Vocational Training Center, which trains recent immigrants in woodworking. In December 1986, 45 refugees began to copy the benches, which were completed in August 1987. How appropriate that these new immigrants should honor old immigrants in this fashion.

When the plaster was removed from two rooms, graffiti was found on the walls, which is being saved. It shows immigrant names, dates of arrival, and drawings of faces and boats. Graffiti was also found and preserved on columns in the building. (Figure 27)

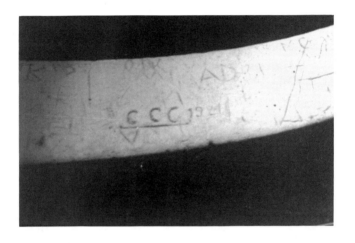

Figure 27   Some Graffiti on Ellis Island   (National Park Service Photo)

The third floor houses exhibit rooms and a library. The west wing contains a re-creation of one of the Special Enquiry rooms, where those who were awaiting deportation could appeal their cases. The east wing was altered more substantially: one can find there two movie theatres, a photo gallery, meeting rooms, a bookstore and a gift shop, bathrooms and a coat check room.   Along the balcony, overlooking the Great Hall, one dormitory room has beeen restored, including the original bunk beds. Other rooms in that area will be used for exhibits. The Kitchen and Laundry Building is "stabilized" and left unrestored, with a new roof and windows. Stabilization means that the building will be made waterproof.

The INS Proposal

The Immigration and Naturalization Service (INS) entered the controversy over islands 2 and 3 on the side of total preservation of Ellis Island. Commissioner Alan Nelson wrote that the Island, "Must be preserved as a national asset."[23] He proposed that Ellis Island "be converted into a multi-purpose center for training, conferences, events, and educational programs related to U. S. history and institutions." He suggested that it be called "The National Historical Center for American Studies," and he quoted Lee Iacocca, that, "Miss Liberty was a symbol of hope. Ellis Island was a symbol of reality." Restoring all the buildings would perpetuate that "symbol of reality;" destroying them would deprive the people of the United States of the "remnants of an emotional part of their history."

The INS proposal emphasized the concept of multiple uses. As a national park, it would reflect the values and institutions related to our traditional hospitality toward immigrants, refugees, foreign visitors, foreign students and in international events.[24]

Because the INS maintains microfilm records of ship manifests of arrivals at Ellis Island from 1896 to 1954, it proposed to donate these records to establish an Immigration Archives and Genealogy Center.

---

[23]Immigration and Naturalization Service,"Ellis Island: A Proposal for a National Center, 1987), p. 2.

[24]Alan C. Nelson, INS Proposal for Ellis Island," INS Reporter, Spring 1986, 15-16.

The Family History Center

The INS proposal for a genealogy center was a fortuitous but welcome development for the Ellis Island Restoration Commission, which had been working since 1977 for such a center. It was natural, therefore, for the two groups to link up to pursue their common goal. On June 9, 1988, The Ellis Island Restoration Commission announced plans for a computerized genealogical center on Ellis Island, which will contain information from the original ship manifests of 17,000,000 immigrants. The Ellis Island Family History Center will offer some 100 million Americans detailed information on their ancestors who were processed through Ellis Island--the gateway to America. $25 million will be needed to finance the Center.

At the press conference, Mrs. Margaret O'Connell Middleton, of Tuscon, Arizona, the granddaughter of Annie Moore, the first person to be processed at Ellis island in 1892, repaid the $10 that was given to the 15-year-old Annie Moore when she arrived on Ellis Island. She was presented with a $10 gold piece by the island's superintendent to commemerate the opening of the center. Also present was one of the original Ellis Island immigrants, 105-year-old Mrs. Mary Kelly Stevenson, of Manchester, Connecticut, who came to Ellis Island in 1920 from Ireland, and her five year old great-great grandchild--a spread of 100 years.

When it is completed in 1992, The Ellis Island Family History Center will be housed in Ellis Island's Main Building, It will open to the public as part of the centennial dedication ceremonies in 1992. It will be designed for easy visitor use--no previous computer knowledge will be necessary and extensive visual aids will be displayed with step-by-step instructions for use. Each entry of immigrants will include: First and' last name of immigrant, name of ship and date of arrival, occupation, literacy, country of origin, ports of embarcation and debarcation, intended destination, race, physical characteristics, data on relatives already in the United States at time of arrival and on relatives remaining in country of origin.

Figure 28 Mary Kelly Stevenson, The Oldest Living Alumnus
(Photo taken by Author)

Visitors will be allowed approximately 12 minutes to search for relatives. For a minimal charge, they will be able to obtain a printed copy of the immigration record that appears on the computer screen.

The Family History Center will be located on the west wing besides the registry room and in front of the railroad ticket office. It will be surrounded by the interpretative rooms, which will relate immigration history from Plymouth rock to Ellis Island. The Center will have 32 computer stations. The design problems are minor compared to the task of creating a database of millions of immigrants, because the exact number of names on the manifests who are immigrants is unknown. There are over 8,000 reels of microfilm, each containing about 5,000 passengers. These total 40,000,000. But about 1,400 reels are useless, and not all passengers were immigrants. The non-immigrant categories include: U. S. citizens returning from overseas (about 7 million), aliens in transit (1 million), passengers arriving from Carribean, African and non-European ports (3.5 million), immigrants returning from a visit to a foreign country (3.4 million), and first and second class immigrants (1.7 million).[25] If we subtract these categories, we obtain a total of 16-18 million immigrants for the database, with 15 questions per name.

In December 1986, AT&T Bell Laboratories submitted a proposal to the Ellis Island Restoration Commission outlining approaches to establishing a database of the 17 million names. It estimated that the total cost would be $10.7 million and the operating costs would total $1.5 million per year. Based on these estimates, The Ellis Island Restoration Commision is seeking $25 million for an annuity to provide for these annual expenses.

On October 16, 1989, a dinner was given in honor of Francesco Cossiga, the President of the Republic of Italy, to commemorate the contribution of Italian immigrants. It was held in the Central Railroad terminal, Liberty State Park, Jersey City, New

Figure 29 The President of the Republic of Italy, Francesco Cossiga, commemorates Italian immigration. At his right are Ira Glazier and Philip Lax of the Ellis Island Restoration Commission

[25]These numbers were computed by Prof. Ira Glazier, of the Temple-Balch Center for Immigration Research.

Jersey, where more than 2,600 persons dined in the restored terminal, where many immigrants boarded trains to reach their final destinations in the United States.

The Ellis Island Immigration Museum

The new Ellis Island museum is the largest of its kind in the world, covering almost 100,000 square feet of exhibits. It is divided into four separate areas. The first, "The Peopling of America," received help from the Ford Foundation, which made a grant of $500,000 for this exhibit. It places Ellis Island within the larger context of immigration in American history.

The second display depicts the immigrants passage through Ellis Island, using a variety of public exhibits featuring historical photographs, motion pictures, diaries and letters, oral history recordings and personal artifacts to illustrate their experiences. Next, the visitor arrives at the "Peak Immigration Years," which deals with larger themes: the decision to leave home, the contribution of immigrants to American life. The final stop is the "Ellis Island Galleries." It features a collection of artifacts, household goods, toys, musical instruments that immigrants brought with them, and a photographic display of the restoration effort.

These exhibits are located in the former railway ticket office. A large, spacious room in the Main Building, it was one of the immigrants' last checkpoints before leaving Ellis Island for outlying parts of the country or for New York City across the bay.

Among the subjects covered are the: ebb and flow of immigration to this country and the major events in U. S. and world history, changes in U. S. immigration policy, distribution of American Indians at the time of the European settlements and subsequent changes in their population, forced migration of black Africans to the New World and the consequences for Africa of losing so many young people to slavery, changes in the proportion of male and female immigrants in the nineteenth and twentieth centuries, patterns of immigrant settlement across the United States, the infuence of immigrants' languages and dialects on the evolution of "American" English, shifts in the geographic regions from which contemporary immigrants come and the reasons why people continue to leave their homelands.

The exhibit also features an electronic counter that shows the average number of immigrants who have entered the United States during the previous twenty four hours. Another feature is a giant American flag composed of a mosaic of photographs of contemporary Americans from a large number of ethnic groups.

The exhibits were developed under the direction of Stephen Briganti, of the SL/EI Foundation. As he said, "We believe that the Peopling of America Exhibit, like the Immigration Museum as a whole, will illustrate that the United States has always had an enormous capacity to benefit from its immigrants, no matter what country they came from, why they came, the languages they spoke, or what their occupations, religious beliefs, or social customs were."[26]

The American Immigrant Wall of Honor

In 1988, The Statue of Liberty- Ellis Island Foundation invited any person to place the name of an immigrant ancestor on the "Wall of Honor." The names are engraved on a copper sheet capping the existing stone wall. The original plans called for the wall to be 755 feet long and and 3 feet high, but when almost 200,000 persons requested space on the wall, it was increased to 1,000 feet, making it the largest wall of names in the world. Each tag on the wall indicates the name of the person and the country of origin. For the minimum $100 donation, the registrant received a certificate and the name of the immigrant was entered into the computer register located on Ellis Island.

The Ferry Boat "Ellis Island"

The steerage passengers were herded from passenger ships at the company's piers onto barges, which were towed to Ellis Island. The steamship companies furnished the barges and tugs that took the steerage passengers to the Island. The Ellis Island ferryboat did not

---

[26]See the Ford Foundation, Letter, August 1988.

bring immigrants to Ellis Island, but instead carried the working staff back and forth and took immigrants who had been processed from Ellis Island to New York City.

Originally, the Immigration Service used a variety of boats for this purpose, but Congress appropriated money for a permanent boat and a contract was awarded to Harland and Hollingsworth, of Wilmington, Delaware.[27] The *Ellis Island* was launched on March 18, 1904. The lower-deck was designed for passengers and baggage and the upper-deck housed the pilot, crew and a room for the Commissioner of Immigration. The boat was 160 feet long, 37 feet at the beam and displaced 660 tons. The hull was steel, but most of the superstructure was of wood. The original power plant was a steam boiler, but this was converted to oil in 1932.

The ferry ran 18 hours per day, and it could make the roundtrip from the Island to the Battery on Manhattan Island in about one hour. The operation was a smooth one until the ferry needed repairs. At various times, in addition to twice-yearly maintenance stops, the boat experienced damage to the rudder, hull and propellers. When the *Ellis Island* needed repairs, the prison ship *Minnehanock* was used to transport aliens. It was a decrepit old boat that listed "now to star-board, now to port," and Commissioner Williams feared that a sudden lurch would capsize the old vessel. But Congress would not appropriate $125,000 for a second ferryboat.[28]

Two incidents stand out in the history of sad Island episodes. In September 1913, a railing of the boat was damaged and repaired improperly. On a subsequent run, the railing gave and 5 persons were plunged into the water, killing an Immigration inspector and an employee.[29] The other incident is more dramatic. On July 30,

---

[27]This history is based on Edwin C. Bearss, The Ferryboat Ellis Island (Washington: National Park Service, 1969)

[28]New York Times, August 6, 1911, p. 8.

[29]New York Times, September 10, 1913, p. 20.

1916, a wharf at Jersey City exploded when German sabateurs made their way to the pier. Some ammunition drifted to Ellis Island and caught fire to the seawall. The terrified aliens were evacuated on the *Ellis Island* with no further damage.

Although Ellis Island closed on November 12, 1954, the ferryboat operated until November 29. Thus, it was in nearly continuous service for 50 years. When the Island closed, the boat was left in the ferry slip and it was offered for sale along with the Island. It became a matter of national concern when it sank in its

berth on the evening of August 11, 1968. While the wooden superstructure of the boat remained under water and the tides continued to bring rapid deterioration, the National Park Service debated the historical importance of the ferryboat. Mr. Henry Judd, chief of the Branch of Preservation of the National Park Service visited New York to study the boat's condition and to make recommendations as to the most feasible plan for salvaging and preserving the boat. At the same time, a National Park Service Historian was assigned to the task of assembling all known data relating to the construction history and the use of the ferryboat.

Unfortunately, although the ferryboat carried many millions of persons to their future homes in the United States, and although the ferryboat is unique in its construction and its usage, the boat was allowed to deteriorate in the water. The Historic Sites Act of 1935 and the Historic Preservation Act of 1966 both would have allowed the National Park Service to allocate funds to raise the boat and to preserve it, because these Acts apply to historic objects as well as to buildings.

Restoring the Ferry

Happily, this is not the end of the ferryboat story. The SL-EI Foundation received help from the U. S. Navy, which offered to raise the sunken boat as a training program. The old boat had to be moved, because it represented a hazard for visitors who will come to the Island when the museum opens.

The diving team included 13 naval reservists from Chicago, 7 regular Navy and 2 women who are students at the Naval Academy. The boat rests in 15 feet of water and lists about 15 degrees. The task of raising the ferryboat was complicated by the estimated 500 tons of mud that covered it. The divers used suction hoses to remove the mud and patched the holes in the hull. The raised ferry was to be put on display next to the slip, but New Jersey has requested that the boat be located there.

Figure 30 The Ferryboat "Ellis Island" Before Sinking in August 1968 (National Park Service Photo)

PART III

CHAPTER VI:

ELLIS ISLAND DOCUMENTS

Ellis Island information is literally scattered across the land. It is in the state historical societies, in the ethnic museums, in church records and in foreign places. As Pitkin said, "The material is in many tongues and scattered in a thousand places.[1] Although much has been lost, the treasure is still rich. This chapter summarizes the records in Washington and elsewhere.

FEDERAL RECORDS

National Archives and Records Administration

There is a considerable body of information about Ellis Island in the National Archives in Washington, D. C. and Suitland, Maryland. The ships passengers lists are a primary source. The National Archives has lists for Baltimore, Boston, New York City, Philadelphia and New Orleans. The New York City passenger lists date from 1820-1931, with indices available for 1820-1846 and 1897-1902. There is an index for the years 1902-1943, but it is restricted under the privacy act; it will not be public until 1993. However, the National Archives staff can search the index for a small fee, the proceeds from which go into the trust fund to pay for some of the employees of the National Archives.[2]

The passenger lists resulted from an act of Congress on March 2, 1819, which specified that the captain of each vessel must supply the collector of customs at the port of arrival with a list of all

---

[1] Pitkin, Keepers of the Gate, p. 211.

[2] The privacy act specifies a 50-year restriction on immigration information and a 75-year restriction on military and Census records. The 1910 Census was made available to the public on July 1, 1982.

passengers. But there was no provision for the storage of the lists, so they are not complete. Some Masters of vessels did not keep lists, some were lost and some were destroyed. But the National Archives has a number of Record Groups that contain thousands of documents about the operation, maintenance, employees and administration of Ellis Island. To understand how these documents are classified, one needs to know the various laws that established the bureaus and whlch transferred records to subsequent bureaus created under later legislation.

The Bureau of Immigration was first established within the Treasury Department on July 23, 1891. On July 1, 1903, the Bureau was transferred to the newly-created Department of Commerce and Labor, and on July 14, 1906, the name of the Bureau was changed to the Bureau of Immigration and Naturalization, when the functions pertaining to naturalization were added. In 1913, the Bureau of Immigration and Naturalization was transferred to the Department of Labor and separated into two bureaus. It remained so until Executive Order 6166, of June 10, 1933, consolidated the two bureaus into the Immigration and Naturalization Service. These legislative changes mean that immigration records in the National Archives are found in three government departments: the Treasury Department, the Department of Labor and the Department of Justice. The National Archives classifies its documents by record groups within the various departments.

Record Group 36. This record group contains passenger lists of vessels arriving in New York, 1820-97. It is designated M237 and is made up of 675 rolls of microfilm. The lists contain passenger's name, age, sex, occupation and nationalities and the name of the country in which each intended to reside.

Record Group 51. In the "General Subject File" there is a report, "Immigration-1921-1928, on the Immigration and Naturalization Service. Chapter IV relates to Ellis Island. This file also contains a 102-page report by J. H. Mackey on the fiscal conditions at Ellis Island.

Record Group 56. These papers consist of the correspondence of the Ellis Island commissioners, which start in approximately 1895 and run to 1933. There appears to be not much known about these papers, and they need to be catalogued and indexed.

Record Group 65. In the records of FBI there are investigative case files of aliens, especially of immigrants in World War I. These files arem dated from 1908-1922.

Record Group 85. This is the largest group of immigration papers in existence; it constitutes 956 cubic feet of records of the Immigration and Naturalization Service. Fortunately, this record group was inventoried in January, 1965, by Marion M. Johnson. The inventory was not published but it was distributed to the National Archives personnel. The papers include correspondence, the education and Americanization case files, card indices, copies of alien registration forms, crew and passengers lists of ships and airplanes, an index to correspondence in case files, deportations, copies of naturalization records in New England courts, medical and other records relating to internment of enemy aliens, and a considerable body of papers of the Services in World Wars I and II. These records are for the period 1789 to 1954. Of particular importance in this record group are the letters received (the early immigration records) dating 1882-1906, 66 feet of records; the letters sent from 1882-1922, 121 feet; the subject correspondence, 1906-1932, 170 feet; the indices to immigration matters, 1893-1932, 20 feet; the education and Americanization files, 1914-1936, 159 feet; and the administrative files relating to naturalization, 1906-1940, 580 feet, We estimate that these pages number over one million and that most of them are not on microfilm. What is on microfilm in Record Group 85 is the index to correspondence in case files (31 rolls), the alien registration forms (6,070 rolls), the passenger and crew lists (9,000 rolls), and the passenger lists indexes (1,300 rolls).

Record Group 90. These records are the medical history of Ellis Island health officials. In addition to these records, we know that Long

Island College Hospital obtained a contract to provide medical services to Ellis Island detainees around the turn of the century.[3]

Record Group 121. This file is composed primarily of records of the public building service of Ellis Island. It contains records pertaining to the upkeep of buildings and has been quite useful in the current rehabilitation efforts.

Record Group 174. This group contains the papers and files of the top officials of the United States Department of Labor for the years 1913-1940, when the records were transferred to the Immigration and Naturalization Service, after its creation. Dr. Jonathan Grossman, the Historian of the United States Department of Labor described this record group as mainly the papers of the Secretaries of labor and the sub-cabinet officials, but he was sure that there is a substantial number of papers dealing with Ellis Island. Grossman believed that no one in the Labor Department has ever researched these papers in terms of their immigration holdings. Dr. William Moye, who worked in Grossman's office, mentioned an inventory of some of the materials in Record Group 174, particularly File No. 19 on "Immigration" and File No. 151 on "Ellis Island." He also cited the Ethelbert Stewart papers involving an investigation in 1918-19 of the inspectors at Ellis Island.

Michael N. Cutsumbis has written a fairly good summary of "The National Archives and Immigration Research."[4] His article covers the Census schedules, the passenger arrival lists, the immigrant passenger lists, the passport applications, the State Department records, records of the INS, and other general immigration records.

Dr. Thomas Pitkin once stated that 60 percent of the documents

---

[3]Correspondence with Long Island University and The New York Historical Society has not yet located these documents.

[4]*International Migration Review,* IV (Summer, 1970) pp. 60-66.

which are supposed to be in the National Archives are not available and are therefore presumed to be lost or destroyed. Much of the general immigration files and some of the Immigration and Naturalization Service records in Record Group 85 were withdrawn and largely destroyed in 1960.[5]

Professor Joseph P. Giovinco, of Sonoma State University, California, who completed a doctoral dissertation on Anthony Caminetti, one of the Commissioners General of Immigration, had considerable difficulty obtaining Immigration and Naturalization Service records from the Department of Justice. He accused J. Edgar Hoover of wholesale destruction of records in 1960 because of what Giovinco thought was a "red scare." According to Giovinco, any immigrant records with a red taint had their papers recalled and shredded. As a result, we have no idea now what papers survive.[6]

There are several regional branches of the National Archives that contain microfilm of the various records mentioned above, as well as extensive Federal manuscript holdings. Their addresses are given in Table 17.

St. Albans Verification Center

The Immigration and Naturalization Service of the Department of Justice maintains records at its Center at St. Albans, Vermont. (Federal Building, PO Box 328, St. Albans, Vermont 05478). The Center houses microfilm of arrivals and departures for all eastern and Canadian seaports. As of June 2, 1986, there were 37,500 reels representing approximately 173 million names. The passenger manifests were discontinued in 1983, but the crew lists are continuing.

---

[5] Keepers of the Gate, p. 212.

[6] When Professor Giovinco made these accusations In August, 1979, I made several telephone calls to a number of offices in the Immigration and Naturalization Service, but I could not locate a single individual who could discuss this matter with me.

The INS records date to 1897. They cover the following time periods:

Seaport arrivals (passenger)	1897-1983
Seaport arrivals (crew)	1897-
Airport arrivals	1942-1969
Land border arrivals	1897-1954
Land border arrivals,Canadian	1906-1954

In addition to the microfilm records of arrivals, the Center has looseleaf notebooks containing names and dates of every ship entering eastern ports after 1897.

Table 17

REGIONAL ARCHIVE BRANCHES

380 Tapelo Road Waltham, MA 02154	PO Box 6216 Fort Worth,TX 76115
Bldg. 22, Military Ocean Terminal Bayonne, NJ 07002	PO Box 25307 Denver, CO 80225
500 Wissahockon Avenue Phila. PA 19144	24000 Avila Road Laguna Niguel, CA 02677
1557 St. Joseph Avenue East Point, GA 30344	1000 Commandore Dr. San Bruno, CA 94066
7358 South Pulaski Road Chicago, 1L 60629	6125 Sand Point Way Seattle, WA 98115
2306 East Bannister Road Kansas City, MO 64131	Washington Nat'l Records Center Suitland, MD 20746

The Papers of the Commissioners

A second major source of information about Ellis Island is the papers of the Commissioners of Immigration. Many of the documents were destroyed personally by officials when they left Federal employment. Recall that Edward Corsi burned his files when he resigned in disgust in 1933. Since most archives collect documents under the names of the persons who donated the papers, a good starting point was a search of the Federal Registry for all the years since 1892, when Ellis Island opened. The search included papers of the commissioners-general of immigration, the commissioners of the Port of New York, the assistant commissioners-general, and the assistant commissioners of immigration. These are shown in Table 12, Chapter IV.

Another aid in finding documents was the *New York Times* Obituary Index (See Table 18). This search yielded few results. The following papers exist in the places named:

The Anthony Caminetti Papers. He was Commissioner General of Immigration from 1913-1920. Some of his papers were discovered in a shed by Professor Joseph Giovinco, of Sonoma State College, Santa Rosa, California. These papers are now in the possession of Professor Giovinco.

The Edward Corsi Papers. He was Commissioner of the Port of New York in 1932 and 1933. His papers are in the special collections division of the Syracuse University Library. According to the National Union Catalog of Manuscripts, they contain 25 feet of materials and were inventoried in 1969. There are also some scattered papers of Edward Corsi in the Immigration History Research Center of the University of Minnesota. These are mentioned in the National Union Catolog entry 75-2019.

Of particular interest is the section dealing with immigration reports and surveys (1883-1922). These papers include materials on the Canadian immigration movement, immigration and deportation statements, Italian immigration, U.S. immigration of Russian exiles, Russian Jewish refugees in America, and the various reports of the United States commissioners of immigration and congressional committees on immigration.

Table 18

New York Times Obituaries of Ellis Island Officials

Percy A. Baker, June 5, 1943, p.15:5.
George E. Baldwin, April 17, 1907, p.9:6.
Anthony Caminetti, Nov. 18, 1923, p.23:2.
Edward Corsi, (funeral Dec. 18, p.29:1), Dec. 14, 1965, p.43:1.
Henry H. Curran, Apr. 9, 1966, p.25:1.
Thomas Fitchie, Sept. 1, 1905, p.9:6.
Fredric C. Howe (portrait), Aug. 4, 1940, p.33:1.
Harry E. Hull, Jan. 17, 1938, p.19:1.
Walter W. Husband, Aug. 1, 1942, p.11:4.
Harry R. Landis, May 1, 1950, p.25:3.
Frank H. Larned, June 23, 1937, p.25:4.
Daniel W. MacCormack, Jan. 1, 1937, p.23:1.
Terence V. Powderly, June 25, 1924, p.23:4
Rudolph Reimer (portrait), July 29, 1948, p.21:1.
Frank P. Sargent, Sept. 5, 1908, p.7:4; Sept. 7, 1908, p.5:7.
John H. Senner (funeral) Oct. 1, 1908, p.9:6; Sept. 29, p.9:7.
Edward H. Shaughnessy, Feb. 3, 1922, p.15:4.
Byron H. Uhl, Nov. 22, 1944, p.19:2.
Frederick A. Wallis, Dec. 23, 1951, p. 22:6.
Robert Watchorn (portrait), Apr. 15, 1944, p.11:3.
John B. Weber, Feb. 6, 1944, p.42:4.
William C. Williams (portrait), Nov. 3, 1945, p.15:6.

The Walter W. Husband Papers. He was the Commissioner-General of Immigration from 1921 to 1924. According to National Union Catalog entry 71-901, his papers are currently housed in the Chicago Historical Society Library.

The Terence V. Powderly Papers. This collection was donated by

Powderly, the second Commissioner-General of Immigration (1897-1901) to The Catholic University of America in Washington, D.C, They are housed in the Archives there and they are well catalogued. They are also on microfilm. Powderly returned to the Bureau of Immigration in 1907 and became the Director of U.S. Office of Statistics. Some of his papers reflect his work in that position. The immigration portion of the Powderly papers includes his correspondence as Commissioner-General of Immigration and Chief of the Information Division, which was originally divided into eight parts by the Catholic University library staff. Much of the correspondence was put on 35 mm microfilm by the Microfilming Corporation of America. Parts 1A, 1B and 1C are arranged alphabetically by the last name of the sender, while Parts 1D, 1E, 1F and 2A are arranged chronologically. Part 1G includes six letter-press copybooks, 1897-1903, covering Powderly's period as Commissioner-General of Immigration.

Part 2 contains the correspondence, arranged alphabetically, of the Information Division, Bureau of Immigration (1906-1922). Included in this correspondence is Powderly's 1906 report (mentioned above) in which he investigated the illegal entry of English machinists and other abuses of our immigration laws.

Part 3 includes reports on deportation cases, memoranda, statistics and reports of the Immigration Bureau, speeches, newspaper clippings, and a lengthy transcript of the Luigi Graziano case (1900), that pointed out corruption in the Bureau of Immigration.

Part 4 contains twenty-two immigration pamphlets (1883-1903) and the Annual Reports of the Commissioners-General of Immigration (1898-1902).

The Robert Watchorn Papers. He was Commissioner of the Port of New York from 1905 to 1909. No substantial amount of his papers have been found to date, but some materials of his are in the Theodore Roosevelt Papers.

The William Williams Papers. He was also Commissioner of the Port of New York from 1902 to 1904 and from 1909 to 1913. His papers are in the New York Public Library. They are in five boxes and are inventoried. There is also a small collection of his papers in the Yale University Library, and there is mention of him in Folder 1579 of the William H. Taft Papers in the Library of Congress.

The papers in the Manuscript and Archives Division of the New York Public Library include Williams correspondence from 1902-1918, foreign language newspaper clippings, speeches on immigration matters, a guest book, and Ellis Island scrapbooks.

Although Fredric C. Howe, the former Commissioner of the Port of New York, was alleged To have burned his papers when he resigned in 1919, there are scattered mentions of him in other collections. The Lynn Haines Collection in the Minnesota Historical Society covers some of Howe's work (see National Union Catalog item 60-1374). Also, the Walter P. Eaton Papers contain some correspondence with Howe (see National Union Catalog 61-1628).

Other sources of Ellis Island papers would include the annual reports of cabinet members, the annual reports of the commissioners-general of immigration (1895-1931), and the debates on immigration in the Congressional Record (for example, "To Regulate Immigration," (House Report No. 3792, 50th Congress 2nd Session, January 19, 1889). *The Abstracts of Reports of the Immigration Commission* (two volumes, Washington, D.C,, 1911) is a good summary of the 42-volume report of the Commission. It contains voluminous records of immigration. The annual reports of the Secretary of the Treasury, the Secretary of Labor and of the Immigration and Naturalization Service are excellent sources of Ellis Island material.

Several persons related their Ellis Island experiences in books. These include Edward Corsi, *In the Shadow of Liberty* (New York, 1935); Philip Cowen *Memories of an American Jew* (New York, 1932); Henry H. Curran, *Pilar to Post* (New York, 1941); Frederic C. Howe, *The Confessions of a Reformer* (New York, 1925); Fiorello H. LaGuardia, *The Making of an Insurgent: An Autobiography, 1992-1919* (Philadelphia, 1948); Elting E. Morison (Ed.), *The Letters of Theodore Roosevelt* (8 volumes; Cambridge, 1952-1954); Lewis E Post, *The Deportation Delirium of 1920: A Personal Narrative of an Historic Personal Experience* (Chicago: 1923); Victor Safford, *Immigration Problems: Personal Experiences of an Official* (New York, 1925).

The Work Projects Administration

The Works Progress Administration (WPA) was established in May, 1935, to take over the responsibilities for the work relief programs of the Federal Emergency Relief Administration, which were expiring that year. WPA was first an independent agency and continued as such until July 1, 1939, when it was made a part of the new Federal Works Agency and its title was changed to Work Projects Administration.

The WPA in the 1930's did surveys of naturalization and immigration records. Most states participated in this effort and the results of the survey may be found in *Index of Published Guides From the WPA Historical Records Survey*. The Historical Records Survey of the WPA was "the most ambitious archival survey ever undertaken in the United States."[7] It was a work relief program which began in 1935 and ended abruptly in 1942. During that time, thousands of persons surveyed every kind of public document and a large number of private documents also. This effort produced more than 2,000 published inventories.

Over the next three decades the HRS materials were stored and largely forgotten. In 1970, Leonard Rapport, of the National Archives, began to locate the unpublished materials in the United States.[8] In 1977, the Society of American Archivists received a grant from the

---

[7]Loretta L. Hefner, The WPA Historical Records Survey: A Guide to the Unpublished Inventories, Indexes and Manscripts (Chicago Society of American Archivists, 1980).p 1.

[8]See his article, "Dumped from a Wharf Into Casco Bay: The Historical Records Survey Revisited," American Archivist, XXXVII (April, 1974), pp, 201-210.

National Endowment for the Humanities to conduct a survey of the unpublished inventories. There were approximately 2,000 published checklists, but nine-tenths were not published. The Library of Congress has about 400 cubic feet of these unprocessed materials.

The Connecticut WPA records are indicative of the rich treasure that this agency has left us. The WPA office in Connecticut was first established in New Haven, with district offices opening in several other cities. These records of the WPA are now part of Record Group 33 of the Connecticut State Library in Hartford. The records include interviews with immigrants, although it is not known at this time exactly how many of them were processed on Ellis Island. Of primary importance is the Ethnic Groups Survey, which was part of the Writers Project initiated in 1935 as part of Federal Project Number 1. The survey was sponsored by the Yale University Department of Sociology, and it resulted in a large collection of material on the various ethnic groups in Connecticut at the time. Boxes 67-73 include papers on ethnic groups for 1936 to 1938, and Boxes 92-95 are detailed interviews with members of ethnic groups concerning their history, status, and opinions on life and the community.

The Library of Congress

There are three parts of the Library of Congress that contain some immigration documents. These include the American Folklife Center, the Manuscript Division and the Rare Books Room. The Library has a large number of prints and photographs. In addition, the Archive of Folksong has an extensive collection of music of the immigrant population. The Archive houses over 225,000 sheets of manuscript material, including the 180,000 pages compiled by the Federal Writers' Project of the WPA. The recordings include Jewish, Polish, French and other European music. The Library of Congress has been able through an exchange program, to obtain recordings published elsewhere.

ELLIS ISLAND RECORDS OUTSIDE OF WASHINGTON

There are approximately 11,000 archives and museums in the United States. Most of the documents they collect are not on microfilm, because it is very expensive and because curators need to utilize their scarce resources to arrange and display artifacts in their archives and museums.

In the sections that follow, we review the nature of these documents that can be found in museums, archives, multi-cultural centers, reprint collections, churches and foreign sources.

Immigrant Historical Societies[9]

The first immigrant societies in the United States sprang from a national consciousness and the desire to revive or keep alive an ethnic identity. These societies are still an important source of immigration materials, although many records have been destroyed and others have been transferred to places that have space to store them and persons to preserve them.

The flood tide of Irish immigration was between 1849 and 1870. When Ellis Island opened in 1892, Irish immigration had already peaked. At that time, there were about 12 million of "Irish stock" and only about four and one-half million were Catholic. From the middle of the 19th century, the Catholic and Protestant Irish made war against each other; thus, the orange and the green went their separate ways, settled in different places and established their own historical societies. At the end of the 19th century, three-fifths of all Catholic Irish lived in Massachusetts, New York, Pennsylvania and Illinois. By contrast, the Scotch Irish (Protestant) were scattered throughout the southern states and the rest of the United States.

The Scotch-Irish Historical Society. The Scotch-Irish Historical Society was organized in May, 1889, at Columbia, Tennessee, to collect materials of the Scotch-Irish in the United States. One of its

---

[9]This section is based on John J. Appel, Immigrant Historical Societies in the United States, 1880-1950 (New York: Arno Press, 1980).

first accomplishments was to publish a ten-volume study of *The Scotch-Irish in America, Proceedings and Addresses* (Cincinnati: R. Clark and Co., 1889-1901). Unfortunately, much of the efforts of this society was spent trying to convince Americans (and themselves) that there was an essential difference between the Scotch-Irish and the Catholic Irish, even though the charter of the group claimed that the Society was a racial organization," not a religious one. "But the Scotch-Irish Historical Society never tired of calling for the collection of family documents and the pursuit of genealogical researches."[10]

The American-Irish Historical Society. The American Irish (Catholic) Historical Society (AIHS) was formed in 1896, at a time when pressure was mounting for the formation of a Catholic group to counter the anti-Catholic literature that was pouring from the nation's presses, particularly from the "Orangemen" and the American Protective Association.

The problem of the AIHS was that there already were a number of Catholic historical societies in the United States (i.e., Boston and Philadelphia). The membership declined between 1904 and 1908, but thereafter, the Society and its chief publication, *The Journal of the American-Irish Historical Society*, grew rapidiy. The papers of the Society were housed at first in the New York Public Library, but later they were moved to 132 East 16th Street and now are preserved at 991 Fifth Ave., New York City, 10028. The collection includes 12,000 books, 250 periodicals and personal papers, dissertations, and correspondence.

The American Jewish Historical Society. The idea for some kind of historical society for Jews seems to have surfaced in the debate over the "Jewish question"--whether Jews were indeed patriots and whether they had fought for their country in the American Civil War. By implication, the question put a label of "foreign race" on American

---

[10]Appel, Immigrant Historical Societies, p.89.

Jewry. Just as the Catholic publications, in the same time, had to defend the patriotism of Roman Catholics, so too do we find the *Jewish Messenger* circulating roll calls of Jewish soldiers who fought for the Union and the Confederate sides.

Professor Cyrus Adler, of Johns Hopkins University, began, as early as 1889, to solicit support for an historical society to counter anti-Jewish publications, particularly the *North American Review*. Finally, on June 7, 1892, forty one persons attended an organizational meeting at the Jewish Theological Seminary in New York City. At the first annual meeting, the President of the Society reminded the members that "the objectives were not sectarian but American."[11] Given this charge, the Society grew to 450 members by 1925, but the Great Depression, Hitler's rise to power, and some disagreement as to publication policies put the continuation of the Society in jeopardy. That old question facing all immigrant groups arose again: should the Society emphasize its American character or its racial and nationalistic distinctions?

The American Jewish Historical Society survived the post-World War II period, as it survived the earlier ones, by avoiding controversy and steering clear, especially of political topics. Its publications did not treat adequately the subject of the immigration of Russian and eastern Jews to the United States. In an attempt to upgrade the publication, the name was changed to the *American Jewish Historical Society Quarterly* in 1950. Finally in 1968, the Society moved to Waltham, Massachusetts, on the fringe of Brandeis University."[12] Ten years later, the chief publication of the Society was changed to the *American Jewish Historical Society*.

The archives of the Society consist of approximately 4,000,000 items which relate to all aspects of American Jewish history. The

---

[11]Appel, Immigrant Historical Societies, p. 214.

[12]"See the June, 1968, Quarterly for details of the move and plans for the buildings.

language of the archives is primarily English, although some papers are found in German, Hebrew, Yiddish, French and Russian. The archives also contain a large collection of American newspapers, microfilm, photographs and portraits. The most important immigration documents are:

1. The papers of the Woodbine Colony of New Jersey from 1890 to 1932.

2. The records of the Woodbine Agricultural School for the years 1893 to 1922.

3. The records of the Baron de Hirsch Trade School of New York for the years 1890 to 1935.

4. The records of the Baron de Hirsch Fund for 1870 to 1935.

5. The papers of the Jewish Immigration Committee of New York for 1908 to 1917.

6. The records of the National Jewish Immigration Council for 1910 to 1919.

7. The papers dealing with the Galveston Immigration Plan for 1907 to 1918.

8. The papers of the Industrial Removal Office for the years 1899 to 1922.

9. The papers of the National Refugee Service for 1935 to 1946.

10. The records of the United Service for New Americans for 1947 to 1954.

11. The papers of the Hebrew Immigration Aid Society of Boston for 1930 to 1965.

12. The personal papers of Max J. Kohler; which deal primarily with the problems of immigration for the period 1888 to 1934.

13. The papers of Louis Marshall, which represent the problems of restrictive immigration legislation for 1906 to 1929.

The manuscript collections of the Society were catalogued as of January, 1968 - June, 1969.

The Scandinavian Historical Societies. Although immigration from Scandinavia reached a peak in the 1880's, before Ellis Island opened as an Immigration Station, the statistics of Scandinavian immigration place it in fourth place for the years 1892-1914. Scandinavians were attracted to the promise of free land in the central states of Illinois, Wisconsin, Minnesota, Iowa and the Dakotas. These Scandinavians were considered to be solid, progressive, hard-working and usually ranked at the head of the non-English speaking immigrants. They were welcomed because of their Nordic ethnicity.

Although Scandinavians Americanized quickly, they did not desire to ignore their roots; the historical societies were the means of retaining their Scandinavian identities. The Swedish-American Historical Society was the first, organized in 1888 in Illinois, by persons associated with the Swedish Lutheran Church or the Swedish American Newspapers. The Scandinavians were deeply attached to their churches and newspapers.

In 1905, the original Swedish-American Historical Society was reorganized at a meeting in Illinois as the Swedish Historical Society of America. The 1905 meeting coincided with the dissolution of the Norwegian-Swedish dual monarchy that had existed since the Congress of Vienna (1815). The Swedish-American Historical Society sought a constructive emigration policy in Sweden, encouraged affiliation with the Augustana Lutheran Church, and the retention of the Swedish language for immigrants.

The documents of the Society were housed at the Swedish Methodist Theological Seminary at Evanston, Illinois, until 1918, when they were moved to the Denkmann Library of Augustana College, Rock Island, Illinois. The first six yearbooks contained membership lists, sketches of pioneers, reminiscences of immigrants and bibliographies of Swedish books and articles.[13]

In 1921, the Society agreed to move to St. Paul, Minnesota, so that the Society's library could be merged with that of the Minnesota Historical Society. This move brought the Swedish-American Historical Society into contact with many professors from nearby universities, and the Yearbook became more professional. In 1926, it was changed to a quarterly. Unfortunately, all the scholarly research was put on the shelf in the Great Depression, and the Society expired in 1932. Since then, the Swedish historical foundations have become more scattered, with organizations being established at the University of Washington, Seattle in 1942, in Philadelphia in 1948, and in Chicago in 1948.

The Chicago organization, the Swedish Pioneer Historical Society was established to honor Swedish pioneers, and to observe the 100th anniversary of the arrival of Swedes to the Midwest. The archive is at North Park College in Chicago, and it contains books, pamphlets, magazines, newspapers clippings, diaries, letters, photographs and records of Swedish-American organizations. The Society sponsors and publishes a journal and books dealing with the history of the Swedish presence in the United States, as well as books on personal reminiscences.

The Society's purpose is to stimulate and promote interest in Swedish-American contributions to the development of life in the United States. Some of the publications of the Society include H. Arnold Barton, *Letters From the Promised Land: Swedes in America,*

---

[13]Appel, Immigrant Historical Societies, p. 344.

1840-1914 (Minneapolis, 1975); Allan Kastrup, *The Swedish Heritage in America* (Minneapolis, 1975); Sture Lindmark, *Swedish America, 1914-1932* (Uppsula and Chicago, 1975).

The idea for a Norwegian-American Historical Society was first discussed in Decorah, Iowa, the "Norwegian Capital," in 1907 by Prof. O. E. Rolvaag, of St. Olaf College, Northfield, Minnesota. This led to the establishment of the *For Faedrearven* Society to preserve the Norwegian culture and language. This society proved ineffective and it was replaced by the Society For the Preservation of Historical Relics and Records of Norse-American Pioneer and Cultural Life to prepare for the observance of the bi-centennial of Norwegian-American immigration. The chief organizers were Prof. Rolvaag, Kristian Prestgard, editor of the *Decorah-Posten* and Prof. Knut Gjerset, of Luther College. They signed the incorporation agreement in 1926, and they assembled an impressive list of historians to tell the story of the Norwegian people in the United States. In the 1930's, the Norwegian-American Historical Association was supporting the work of Marcus L. Hansen, Lawrence M. Larson, Einar Haugen, Paul Knapland, Brynjolf J. Hovde, Carlton C. Qualey and Theodore Blegen.

Between 1926 and 1950, the Association published 16 volumes of *Studies and Records* and 5 volumes of *Travel and Description*. Most of these dealt with Norwegian settlement in the Middle West.

The documents of Norwegian immigration were divided into two parts in 1925. The archival materials were given to the Norwegian-American Historical Association at St. Olaf College; the historical collections were expanded and given to *Vesterheim*, the Norwegian-American museum at Decorah, Iowa. The *Vesterheim* Museum is one of the oldest immigrant societies in the United States. There are also Norwegian-American documents scattered throughout the upper Midwest, particularly in places like Moorhead State University, Moorhead, Minnesota and the University of Minnesota at Duluth.

The American Italian Historical Association. The American Italian Historical Association (AIHA) was founded in December, 1966, by a

190

group of historians, educators and sociologists who met at the LaGuardia Memorial House in New York City. The Association encourages the study of the American-Italian experience, and it collects, preserves and popularizes this experience. It accomplishes these objectives through regional and national meetings. At present, there are ten regional chapters. AIHA also sponsors joint conferences with such groups as the Center for Migration Studies (New York); the Balch Institute (Philadelphia); the American-Jewish Historical Society (Waltham); and the Canadian Italian Historical Association. In addition, AIHA sponsors resource depositories that collect and preserve the historical records of Italian Americans, including printed materials, private papers, photographs, and oral history tapes.

The 1989 conference of the AIHA was the twenty second-- nineteen of the proceedings have been published. The following are of particular interest to those who investigate immigration history:

Volume 9 -- Hubert Nelli (ed.) *The United States and Italy: The First Two Hundred Years* (1976);

Volume 10 -- Betty Boyd Caroli, Robert E. Harney and Lydio F. Tomasi (eds.) *The Italian Immigrant Woman in America* (1977);

Volume 11 -- George E. Pozzetta (ed.), *Pane E. Lavoro: The Italian American Working Class* (1978);

Volume 14-- Rudolph J. Vecoli (ed.) *Italian Immigrants in Rural and Small Town America* (1984);

Volume 15 -- Rocco Caporale (ed,) *The Italian Americans Through the Generations: The First One Hundred Years* (1984).

Volume 18 -- Jerome Krase and William Egelman (eds.), *The Melting Pot and Beyond: Italian Americans in the Year 2000* (1985).[14]

---

[14]For a history of AIHA and a list of meeting places and publications, see Frank J. Cavaioli, "The American Italian Historical Association: Twenty Years Later, 1966-1986," in Italian Americans: The Search for a Usable Past, Proceedings of the 19th Annual Conference, (1989), 282-293.

All of the above volumes were published by the Center for Migration Studies, 209 Flagg Place, Staten Island, New York, 10304.

We should note, also, that the American Italian Historical Association published a directory of membership in 1988.

The State Historical Societies

In general, the state historical societies were not very helpful in locating Ellis Island documents. Directors of several societies stated that their records tended to emphasize the early to middle nineteenth century, rather than the period of the new immigration. Most of them indicated, however, that they were making attempts now to correct this deficiency in their holdings. This is true for Ohio, where the Cleveland Ethnographic Museum was merged with the Ohio Historical Society.

The New York Historical Society has only three items about Ellis Island--an incredible void, considering the number of persons involved--and these are dated 1796, 1809-1812, and 1875-1898.[15]

This society has failed to document the greatest migration in world history. However, the New York Archives do contain the papers of former Mayor Fiorello La Guardia, which includes his work as an inspector on Ellis Island in the 1930's.

There are some Ellis Island materials in the state libraries or archives. For example, the Wisconsin State Historical Archives contains records of "Germans in the United States," for the years 1816-1937. These are mainly the papers of Joseph Scheben of the University of Bonn. There are six boxes, some of which have been translated.

The Rhode Island Historical Society has been working with the Rhode Island Heritage Commission, and with Providence College,

[15]See Arthur J. Breton, A Guide to the Manuscript Collections of the New York Historical Society (2 volumes; Westport:Greenwood Press, 1972).

where there is an ethnic archive. According to Harold Kemble, the Archivist, there may be several letters and diaries of Ellis Island in the manuscript collection of Providence College.

MULTI-CULTURAL IMMIGRATION RECORDS

Immigration History Research Center

This center was founded in 1965 to foster an understanding of how immigration shapes American society. Although Professor Rudolph J. Vecoli, the Director of the Immigration History Research Center at the University of Minnesota, did not found the Center, he was responsible for bringing it to its current rank. Today, the Center contains nearly 23,000 volumes, 2,500 rolls of microfilm and approximately 2,000 feet of manuscripts. There are 3,000 serials and 900 newspaper titles. The manuscripts include foreign language and English documents for 25 ethnic groups. Included in the holdings are the records of ethnic organizations, churches, and the personal papers of important leaders in many fields. The collection includes over 10,000 letters sent by Finnish immigrants in the United States to places in Finland; papers of James V. Donnaruma, the publisher of *La Gazzetta Del Massachusetts*; the official correspondence, reports and minutes of the First Catholic Slovak Union, the largest Slovak benefit society in the United States and the letters of an immigrant priest who served in Illinois and Minnesota.

Suzanna Moody and Joel Wurl (Comps.), completed a guide to the Center's collections: *The Immigration History Research Center: A Guide to Collections* (Greenwood Press, 1989). This is a cumputerized index and guide.

The Balch Institute for Ethnic Studies

The Balch Institute of Philadelphia, founded in 1971, emphasizes ethnic, racial and minority immigrant history. While the Balch is a national institution, it does concentrate on the middle-Atlantic region and particularly Philadelphia history. The archives includes 50,000 books, almanacs, newspapers, brochures, parish records, and organization papers. Of particular importance is the Permanent Gallery, which shows an ocean crossing in steerage and inspection at Ellis Island.[16]

The Balch Institute is involved with a variety of projects. It has done considerable work on women as an ethnic group; it has a number of phonograph records of radio shows of the 1930's, some of which contain immigrant experiences and it also has a large group of photos of ethnics in World War II.

A very large project is the Center for Immigration Research, a joint endeavor of the Balch Institute and Temple University. Professor Ira A. Glazier is the Director. It is computerizing the original passenger lists--a task which involves dealing with 11 tons of manifests for the years 1820 to 1924. These original manifests were transferred in 1978 from the National Archives. Since 1981, the Center has put about 2 million names into its computers, so the completion date will be in the 21st century.

The Bentley Historical Library

The Bentley Library is part of the Michigan Historical Collections, which was established in 1935, to collect, preserve and to make available primary source materials concerning the people and institutions of the State of Michigan. The Library is located at the University of Michigan. Its collection includes 13,500 cubic feet of manuscript material, 30,000 books and pamphlets, 225 photographic images, 1,700 maps, and various newspaper clippings. One interesting immigration source is Keijo Virtanen's bulletin on the "Finns in Michigan," which was published in June 1976. It contains Virtanen's translation of immigrant letters sent by Michigan Finns to their homeland.

The Immigration Sources Project of the Bentley Library is

---

[16]See Mark Stolarik, "The Balch Institute for Ethnic Studies," The Immigrant History Newsletter, XIII (November, 1980), p, 15.

working to locate information regarding historical documents of immigrants and their descendants who settled in the State of Michigan. This project, with the financial assistance of the National Endowment for the Humanities, produced a guide describing the kinds of historical documents available in the Library. The foreign phase of this project involved sending researchers to Europe to find information about life in the "new land."

Jane Addams Hull House

The Hull House is a treasure of immigrant material both because of its location in South Chicago and because of its history as a settlement house. The museum opened in 1968, and is concerned with the history of the neighborhood. Because Hull House is on the edge of the University of Illinois, Circle Campus, there are cooperative efforts between the two to develop immigrant and neighborhood sources.

In 1908, the founders of Hull House created the Immigrants' Protective League to tackle the problems of immigration. It was situated in a predominately foreign speaking neighborhood, with Grace Abbott as its superintendent. From its beginning, the Italians, Greeks and Mexicans of Halsted and Polk Streets were offered free services designed to hasten their adjustment to their adopted country.

So successful was the Protective League, that in 1919 the State of Illinois took over its functions and renamed it the Immigrants' Commission of Illinois and attached it to the State Department of Registration and Education. And so the work of the League was extended to the entire state, and it was charged with conducting studies and publishing documents relating to immigration problems of Illinois. Among its publications were: *The Educational Needs of Immigrants in Illinois* and *The Immigrant and the Coal Mining Communities of Illinois.*

In 1921, the Governor of Illinois vetoed an appropriation bill for the Commission and there began a period of uncertainty for the League. In 1925-26, the agency was reorganized and it reverted back to its original mandate: "with the responsibility of helping the immigrant after his admission into the U.S." At that time, the League's staff included workers fluent in the following languages: Czechoslovakian, Danish, French, German, Italian, Lithuanian, Norwegian, Polish, Russian, Spanish, Swedish, Ukranian, and Yiddish. The records of the League are in the Preston Bradley Library at Hull House. They include the papers of the Immigrants' Protective League, the minutes of the various refugee relief committees, monthly statistical reports, case histories of immigrants (1920-1954), dissertations on Chicago's ethnic groups, and other papers pertaining to immigration policies.

Center for Migration Studies

The Center, located at 209 Flagg Place, Staten Island, N. Y. 10304, was founded in 1964. Besides documenting the immigration movement, its program includes the publication of the *International Migration Review*, conferences and seminars. It claims to have "the most comprehensive library on migration in the world."

The Center has microfilmed the records of the Italian Commissioner of Emigration in 1980-81. In 1984, it received a grant from the National Endowment for the Humanities to continue filming for the years 1902-1933. The extensive records of the Center for Migration Studies may be located through the CMS Archival Guide Series. These records, while primariiy Italian, do cover other ethnic groups.

Another project of the Center was the publication of a Guide to the records of the Italian Welfare League, which was completed in 1988. This was one of the oldest immigrant aid societies in the United States--its papers dating from 1916 to 1987. It was the only Italian group that gave aid to immigrants on Ellis Island.

PAPERS OF SPECIFIC ETHNIC GROUPS

Jewish Archives[17]

The YIVO Institute for Social Research in New York City has extensive records of Ellis Island immigration. In particular, Record Group 245.2 is the records of the Hebrew Sheltering and Immigration Aid Society (HIAS) on Ellis Island for the years 1905-1923. These files are the records of Irving I. Lipsitch and Samuel Littman, Lipsitch was the first general manager of the Ellis Island bureau. These records deal mainly with cases of detention and impending deportation of Jewish immigrants and of the HIAS intercession on their behalf. The records also consist of correspondence of HIAS to certain individuals to locate relatives in the United States, the Baron de Hirsch fund (1890-1903), correspondence and reports relating to Ellis Island (1913-1934), Statistical Reports of HIAS activities on Ellis Island, and minutes of meetings, reports and memoranda of various Jewish organizations dealing with immigration problems for the years 1909-1963.

The YIVO Institute received a grant from the National Historical Publications and Records Commission for a two-year research on the *Landsmanshafn*. This grant preserved these documents as a 100-year history of the many Jewish groups that came to this country -- records which were in danger of destruction as the older organizations declined. The project located and collected these records, developed and published a guide to the collection, and prepared and disseminated an institutional records survey. These *Landsmanshafn* records supplement an earlier study done in 1938 by the Yiddish writers' group of the Federal Writers' Project of the WPA. At that time, about 3,000 *Landsmanshafn* existed in New York City alone.

---

[17]I do not wish to enter the controversy between orthodox and reformed Jews as to What is a Jew?" By placing the Jews in the "ethnic" category, I am assuming that the activites of Rabbis were tangential to the activities of such groups as HIAS. I do not believe that any major American Jewish Archives separate records as to their religious or social character. The bulk of the records (by my examination) appears to be civil and social, hence I am describing these records under "Major Ethnic Groups." No slight of the religeosity of the Jews is intended.

The Philadelphia Jewish Archives Center was established in September, 1972, as a joint project of the Federation of Jewish Agencies and the Philadelphia Chapter of the American Jewish Committee. It has been collecting official records, personal papers, manuscripts, photographs and artifacts of Jewish history. It has the HIAS records for Philadelphia for the years 1884-1921, which are on microfilm, and which have been copied by the Latter-day Saints (Mormons). It also has the passenger order books for the years 1894-1934, and the Jewish newspaper, *The Exponent*, copies from 1887 to the present. These are in the Pennsylvania Free Library.

Other Jewish sources include the Council of Jewish Women Records, 1905-1927, (Cincinnati), minutes and correspondence; the Jewish Family and Children's Service Records, 1924-1951, American Jewish Archives--correspondence, case files of immigration; and the Jewish Archive Project of the University of Washington, Seattle, 1849-1975-- organizational records, photos and ephemera on immigration.

Documents of Italian Immigration

The chief archive devoted mainly to Italian-American immigration is the Center for Migration Studies of Staten Island, established in 1964 by Father Lydio Tomasi. Because it is sponsored by the Scalabrini Fathers, it has had a heavy emphasis on religion and immigration, but its archives contain a substantial amount of secular documentation of Italian immigration.

The Center has an extensive publication program, including the *International Migration Digest*, the *International Migration Review*, and the *Migration and Ethnicity Series*, which includes several volumes on Italian-American immigration. It is not confined exclusively to the Italian experience, however, because it has published volumes on the Germans and Arabic speaking communities, as well as a bibliographic guide to materials on Greeks and Portuguese. The Center's collection of press material is rich in the Italian-American experience. For example, there are the *Bollettino dell 'Emigrazione* for the years 1902-1927, published in Rome; *El Carroccio*, for the years

1915-1932, in New York City; *Christoforo Colombo*, 1891-1894, New York City; *Eco dell'Ofanto*, 1893-1900 from Avellino, Italy; *Il Lavoro* 1916-1930, New York City; *Leonardo*, 1905-1907, Florence, Italy; and *Rivista d'Italia e d'America*, 1923-1926, Rome and New York.

In 1989, the Immigration History Research Center, at St. Paul, Minnesota completed a three-year project to locate and identify the records of the Orders of the Sons of Italy in America, under a grant by the National Historical Publications and Records Commission. These papers span the years from 1905 to 1988, and involve lodges in 17 states and 2 Canadian provinces. The archives houses more than 2,000 linear feet, but only 700 of these are deposited in Minnesota. They include hundreds of photographs, tapes and film; artifacts (vests, hats) and ceremonial regalia); minutes of meetings, correspondence and speeches.

In Boston, Massachusetts, there are items on Italians who went through Ellis Island in East Boston and in the North End. Salvatore Tarbi and Victor Casaburi are the co-publishers of the *East Boston Times*, and they are very active in the East Boston Historical Society, of which Michael Laurano is President. He has collected postcards, photographs, and other personal-type documents.

Scandinavian Immigrant Documents

The Emigrant Institute. The Emigrant Institute is a joint project of Vaxjo, Sweden, and East Moline, Illinois. The project received funding in Sweden for an inventory and microfilm project, which recorded the history of the Swedish immigrant in the United States and Canada. The objectives of the Institute are to develop contacts between Swedish descendants in America and their ancestors in Sweden, and to establish libraries and archives for this purpose. Since the institute was formed in 1968, it has acquired a half million index cards of immigrants to the United States, and the library contains the largest book collection on Swedish immigrants next to the Swedish National Library. Professor Lennart Setterdahl was appointed to the Emigrant Institute Chair at East Moline, Illinois. His work was supported by the Wallenberg Foundation in Stockholm.

The giant microfilm project of preserving Swedish-American church records and other organizational material, which was begun in 1968 with a few county documents in Minnesota and Wisconsin, has now been completed. The Emigrant Institute carried its work into the American Midwest, the Northeast, the Plains States and into the Far West and Canada. In all, 34 states and five provinces were researched and documents microfilmed. The records of about 1,600 Swedish-American church archives have been inventoried and microfilmed, and these records include information about 1.25 million Swedes who emigrated to the United States between 1840 and 1930. Most of these records are of members of the Augustana Synod of the Lutheran Church in America, which kept good records of dates of birth, transfers, deaths and other important personal information.

The Baptist General Conference Archives is a non-Lutheran source. Its papers date from 1850 to 1920 and are located at the Bethel Seminary Library, St. Paul, Minnesota. The papers reflect the church's work with Swedish immigrants.

The Dan-America Archives Society. This Society is an American branch of the Emigrant Archives, established in Denmark in 1974. The Archives collects unpublished and published material, including letters, diaries, autobiographies, newspapers, pamphlets and books, and other historical works. The American Branch was established with a donation of $10,000 by William S. Knudsen, a former vice president of General Motors Corporation. There are several other Danish-American societies that are collecting historical documents. These include the Danish-American Heritage Society, which publishes *The Bridge* and the Danish Immigrant Archival Listing, which is part of The Grandview College Archives.

Letters to Finland. Probably the largest body of Finnish-American materials is located at Suomi College, Houghton, Michigan. Since most of the Documents are in Finnish, the College invited Keijo Virtanen, of the Institute for General History at the University of Turku, to translate and catalogue the materials--many of which were letters from immigrants to their previous homes in Finland. Virtanen also arranged to copy the twelve thousand American letters from his

Institute for the Bentley Library at the University of Michigan, where he was a visiting scholar. The joint microfilm project produced excellent results.[18]

Slavic Sources

The Czech-American Archives. The largest Czechoslovakian archive in the United States is at the University of Chicago, under the direction of Professor Zbemek Hruban, a professor of pathology. This collection consists of printed books in several languages, 1,000 issues of newspapers, photographs, the Martinek papers (1912), the *Calendar* dating from the 1800's into the twentieth century, and the bi-monthly *Hospodar*--the collected histories of individuals. The *Calendar* has been indexed.[19]

According to Hruban, three-fourths of the material in the archives is in the Czech language and about one-quarter is in Slovak, although there are publications in German, French and in English. He believes that we should collect journals and books published in places outside of the United States and Canada because of the ideological and economic factors affecting Czech history.

Another important collection is the Czech heritage holdings of the University of Nebraska, Dr. Joseph Svoboda, archivist. This collection includes 50 oral histories (some second generation), the *Calendar* for 1870-1950, and reminiscences of early immigrants, which Svoboda says is a very *"large collection."* Most of the material is in the Czech language.

Jednota. The Slovak Museum and Archive Institute, of Middletown,

---

[18]Keijo Virtanen, "Letters to Finland," Bulletin No. 26 (Ann Arbor: Michigan Historical Collections, 1976).

[19]See Esther Jerabek, Czechs and Slovaks in America (New York: Czechoslovak Society of Arts and Science in America, 1976).

Pennsylvania, is under the leadership of Vincent Drobniak. He has been collecting memoirs, books, histories, and other archival material. According to him, the materials are not classified, but he is certain that many of the Slovaks came through Ellis Island. He donated some of these materials earlier to the American Museum of Immigration on Liberty Island. His estimate is that he has 100 feet of material and oral histories. In addition, the organization publishes *Jednota* a weekly that was begun in 1890.

German Documents

German-American Studies. The Society for German-American Studies was established in Ohio in 1968 to support scholarship and to disseminate information relating to German-Americans. It publishes a quarterly newsletter, yearbook and holds annual meetings and symposia. The contact is Robert E. Coley, 330 E. Charlotte St., Millerviile, PA 17551.

Hungarian Heritage Center

The Hungarian-American institutions in the United States collected a sizable library and archival collection of over 30,000 volumes. These holdings were in three places: The American Hungarian Foundation, New Brunswick, N.J. 08903; the Hungarian Cultural Foundation, Stone Mountain, GA 30087; and the Hungarian Scout Association in Exile, Garfield, N.J. 07026. On May 21, 1989, Hungarian-Americans dedicated a new Hungarian Heritage Center at New Brunswick, New Jersey to consolidate records, photographs and artifacts.

The Center includes a museum, library and craft shop. The library expects to add 1,750 volumes per year. A special feature of the library is the Vasvary Collection of 24,000 entries on Hungarian history dating from 1600. It is currently an affiliate of the Rutgers University Library and may be accessed by using the Research Library Information Network (RLIN). The Center is directed by August J. Molnar. He may be contacted at 300 Somerset St., PO Box 1084,

New Brunswick, New Jersey 08903.

Another important Hungarian source is the two volumes edited by Albert Tezla, a retired Professor of literature at the University of Minnesota: *Valahol Tul, Meseorszagban: Az amerikas magyorok, 1895-1920* (Budapest: Europa Publishing, 1987. The topics include "descriptions of ocean crossing and reception at Ellis Island. He combed the archives of Hungary and the Austro-Hungarian consular reports in selecting his inclusions.

Miscellaneous Document Sources

American Sokol Educational and Physical Culture. This American School of, Berwyn, Illinois, contains books, theses, pictorial materials and manuscripts. It also published *The American Society* from 1879 to the present.

Museum of Lithuanian Culture. Stanley Balzekas, President, has the largest Lithuanian archives in the United States in Chicago, at 6500 S. Pulaski Rd. There are over 15,000 books, 10,000 periodicals and other printed and unpublished photographs and materials A large genealogy collection is on microfilm.

Center for the Study of Ethnic Publications in the United States. Attached to the School of Library Science at Kent State University, under the direction of Professor Lubomyr Wynar, the center has a wide range of research projects on the history, content of ethnic presses, ethnic organizations and ethnicity in general.

Grand View College. This library, sponsored by the Lutheran Church is under the direction of Thorwald Hansen. Founded in 1896, its consists mainly of unpublished and published materials and pictures of American immigrants. It is located at Des Moines, Iowa, 50316.

Baltic Collections. Dr. John Cadzow, the Director of the Ethnic Heritage Program at Kent State University, has received funds from both the Rockefeller and the Ford Foundations for the preservation of

Finnish, Latvian, Estonian, Lithuanian, Romanian, Hungarian and Ukranian collections. Kent State University is the center of the largest Baltic collections in the United States. It is particularly strong in the Lithuanian and Latvian materials. In addition to the Kent State University holdings, Gunars Rutkovskis, who works at the Boston Public Library, has pre World War II Latvian materials, and Monsignor Francis Juras, of the Lithuanian Archives in Putnam, Connecticut has documents from the Baltic countries which discuss immigration, the reasons for leaving, and their destinations.

The Netherlands Museum. The Netherlands Museum was founded in 1937 to celebrate the 90th anniversary of the city of Holland, Michigan. This archive is a rich collection of materials relating to Dutch immigration to western Michigan. Its value is enhanced because many of the documents have been translated from the Dutch into English. In 1967, Herbert Brinks served as general editor in the preparation and publication of a guide to these archives, *Guide to the Dutch American History Collections of Western Michigan.* The Dutch American archive contains personal papers, business records, church and school records, newspapers, pamphlets and books. The 200 pamphlets in the museum's collection are now indexed and available for use by scholars. We note also, that the Moeryk papers have been added to the collection.

Irish Documents. In 1977, the American Committee on Irish Studies surveyed more than 600 colleges and universities in the United States to determine the extent to which Irish studies were being taught. One result was a "Guide to Studies in the United States," published by Professor Maureen Murphy, of Hofstra University. Although this Guide is concerned with Irish studies, it may be an important source of materials on immigration and, especially, Ellis Island documents. The American Committee for Irish Studies can supply a number of places and names where documents of Irish immigration may be found. These include the the Irish Social Club of Dorcester, the American Irish Immigration Committee of New York City, the Irish Historical Society of Boston, and the Irish Embassy in Washington.

Lancaster Mennonite Conference Historical Society. Although founded in 1958, this archive in Lancaster County, Pennsylvania, contains thousands of books and personal papers. Emphasis is on the Amish-related German groups of the region. This library participates in the Kutztown folk festivals.

Nationality Rooms and Intercultural Exchange Rooms. These rooms were built in 1926 at the University of Pittsburgh, and they are gifts to the University from ethnic groups in Pennsylvania. The rooms are authentic in architecture and interior furnishings of the heritage of the 18 groups which are represented. The ethnic groups include Chinese, Czeckoslavak, English, French, German, Greek, Hungarian, Irish, Italian, Lithuanian, Norwegian, Polish, Romanian, Russian, Scottish, Swedish, Syrian-Lebanese, and Yugoslavian. The entire collection includes 5,000 books, personal papers, correspondence, unpublished records, pictures, and current records.

Goodwill Industries. Since all units of the Goodwill Industries are autonomous, it is difficult to determine the involvement of this organization on Ellis Island. The New York City branch, now at 421 27th Avenue, Astoria, New York, had workers on the Island, according to Phyllis Miller, who worked for Goodwill Industries for 20 years. The history of the experience is covered in a book, *For the Love of People,* published by the organization.

American Express. The American Express Company provided currency exchange services on Ellis Island during the early part of the 20th century. The earliest record in its archives is an entry for the minutes of the meeting of June 19, 1905, relating to a contract for the exchanging of immigrants' foreign money into U.S. currency. In the same year, on July 6, the company entered into a contract with Cesare Conti for cashing checks of the Bank of Naples. On May 16, 1910, a contract was entered into by American Express with the United States government for the privilege of purchasing gold from immigrants. In 1913, American Express entered into an agreement with the U. S. Department of Labor for the installation of a telephone in one if the company's booths on the Island. In that same year, the company agreed to pay by check to the Commissary Contractors on the Island for the gold, silver and foreign currency accumuiated by the company each day. Copies of the above agreement are in the American Express archives, as well as other materials relating to its operations on Ellis Island.

The Boston Public Library. According to Gunars Rutkovskis, the library has sound recordings and other material of 40 ethnic groups in Boston. These cover the years 1892 to 1930, In addition, the Charlestown Public Library has several pamphlets of the proceedings of the Boston 200 (Bicentennial) Celebration, which includes the histories of several ethnic groups.

The following sources, all containing general immigration materials in the locations noted, may contain references to Ellis Island.[20]

University of Colorado Libraries, Boulder. Western Historical Collections. Josephine Aspinwall Roche Papers, 1910-70. Josephine Aspinwall Roche's writings of her work as director of the Foreign Language Information Service in New York.

University of Illinois Library, Chicago Circle. Martin H. Brickham Papers, 1905-76. Brickham's papers contain photos and scrapbooks of immigrant families.

Records of the German Aid society of Chicago, 1878-1949. This collection includes case histories of German immigrants and records of the Women's Trade Union League's Immigration Department.

Records of The Immigrants' Protective League. These records include case histories, photos and press releases.

---

[20]These sources are taken from Andrea Hinding, Women's Library Sources (New York: R. R. Bowker, 1979).

Western Reserve Historical Society, Cleveland. Records of American Polish Women's Club, 1933-72. Records of the movement to bring Polish immigrants to the U. S., along with membership records and scrapbooks.

Records of the Young Women's Christian Association. This collection contains histories, scrapbooks and bulletins of immigration.

Ohio Historical Society, Columbus. Mary Louise Mark Papers, 1903-68. These papers contain her reseach for the U. S. Immigration Commission.

Bartlett Memorial Historical Museum, Eau Claire, WI. Skavlem and Odegaarden Family Papers, 1839-1976. These papers contain the histories of Norwegian settlers plus photos and genealogies,

University of Nebraska-Lincoln Archives, Lincoln. Grace and Edith Abbott Papers, 1897-1954. These papers contain correspondence, lecture notes, scrapbooks, and photos of immigration.

University of Minnesota Special Welfare History Archives. Records of the American Immigration and Citizenship Conference, 1932-68. This organization attempted to influence immigration and naturalization policy and to assist immigrants.

Minnesota Historical Society, St. Paul. Consolidated Biographies File. This file contains biographies of 19th and 20th century immigrants.

Records of the St. Paul Planning Board, 1934-1948. These records contain information on the foreign-born population of St. Paul.

Nebraska State Historical Society. Hattie (Plum) Williams Papers, 1884-1959. Research notes on Immigration of German-Russians.

New York Public Library. Records of Inter-Municipal Research Committee, 1906. Report on immigrants' conditions.

University of North Dakota. Icelandic Immigration Collection, 1853-1922. This collection contains correspondence, diaries, interviews of immigrants most of whom were Icelandic.

Balch Institute, Philadelphia. Ann Kobryn Boyko Papers, 1910-73. These papers contain Ukranian correspondence, diaries and clippings of immigrants.

University of Pittsburgh. Archives of Industrial Society. Rauh Family Papers, 1903-51. Archives primarily on immigrant Jewish women.

The Huntington Library, San Marino, California. Ciyde H, Porter Papers, 1928-56. Contains information on immigration into Texas.

American Jewish Historical Society, Waltham, Massachusetts. Records of University Settlement Society of New York, 1899-1919. These records concern the intellectual development of immigrants and include minutes and yearbooks.

Women's Bureau, Record Group 86, 1918-67. This collection includes several bulletins on immigrant women.

North Bennet Street Industrial School, 1879-1965. This school served as an immigrant community and its records include annual reports, ledgers and correspondence.

CHURCH RECORDS

The LDS Records

The Mormons are the Mecca of family history, because for them, genealogy is a matter of religious teaching.[21]

The Church of Jesus Christ of Latter-day Saints (Mormons) has embarked on one of the most ambitious microfilm projects ever. It

---

[21]One of the sections of Doctrine and Covenents and Pearl of Great Price (compiled by Joseph Smith after a series of revelations) commands the Mormons to do work for the dead. The Mormons have interpreted this to mean that they should find ancestors and baptize them to give them eternal life.

began collecting ancestral records in 1894, and when microfilming was invented in 1938, it began to copy records in earnest. It has filmed Census data, local county records, ship lists, passenger lists, church records, conscription records, and they have been seeking these records both in the United States and in many foreign countries. In this country, it is working with a one-tenth sample of families by surnames. This sample includes lists of government employees and passport records. Jaussi and Chaston describe the card indices of immigration and emigration in their *Register of L.D.S.Records* (Salt Lake City: Deseret Book Company, 1968). This European Emigration Card index sometimes referred to as "Crossing the Ocean" and "Shipping File Index," includes names of persons who emigrated from European countries. The majority were associated with the Mormon Church and registered for passage through the L.D.S. Church in Liverpool, England. Most ofthe indices have been compiled from the Immigration Registers of the British Mission, the Scandinavian Mission, the Swedish Mission, and the Netherlands Mission, The card index is arranged alphabetically by surname and usually shows the name of the head of the household first with accompanying individuals following. All of these records are on microfilm and are classified by the Library of Genealogical Society. The Immigration Registers of the British Mission, which date from 1849-1885 and 1899-1925, were compiled by the L.D.S. Church agents at Liverpool, England. Nearly all persons emigrating from Europe to Utah were processed through this office. These records include emigration from Scandinavia, Italy, France, Poland, Germany, Holland, Belgium, and Switzerland. These records are also on microfilm.

The size of the Mormon library is staggering. Approximately two *billion* names have been recorded on 1.5 million rolls of microfilm--almost one-third of all persons who has ever lived! The Mormons used over 100 microfilm cameras in all parts of the world, and they added 40,000 to 50,000 new rolls each year. One drawback to this project is that it is concerned only with persons who are deceased, and this tends to limit the number of names of persons who went through Ellis Island, which opened in 1892.

Most of the data are stored in Little Cottonwood Canyon, about 20 miles from Salt Lake City. These are buried hundreds of feet below the surface, as protection from an atomic bomb blast. But the main library is in Salt Lake City, and there are 800 family history centers in North America and 12 other countries. The card catalog is automated and includes 70 million names by place of birth.

The National Catholic Welfare Conference

The documents of the original Bureau are of two kinds: the Annual Reports of the National Catholic Welfare Conference and the reports of the New York and Washington offices. These records were donated to the Center for Migration Studies of Staten Island. In addition, there are copies of the *Catholic Action Bulletin* at the Archives of the Catholic University of America.

The University of Notre Dame has on microfilm the records of the Vatican Society for the Propogation of the Faith. Since the United States Catholic Church was a mission church until 1908, all of the papers of the church before that time are in this collection. There is undoubtedly a large amount of information about immigrants, especially those who entered Ellis Island between 1892 and 1908. Unfortunately, there is a 100-year restriction on the use of these data.

The Archdiocese of New York

What is now the Saint Elizabeth Ann Seton Shrine at 7 State Street, New York (10004) was at one time an important part of the Ellis Island story. From 1883 to 1930, it was the "Mission of the Immaculate Virgin for the Safekeeping of Irish Girls." As the young, single girls were processed at Ellis Island, they were provided shelter, food, and jobs by the pastor of the church, Fr. M. J. Henry. He told the *New Nork Times* that in 1900 his mission had served 12,000 young Irish women, who were cared for until they could be sent to relatives or friends. Between 1883 and 1900, 262,000 young women were accomodated.[22] The records of this mission survive in the form

---

[22]New York Times, September 29, 1900, p. 9.

of letters, newletters, news clippings, etc.

The Leo House, which has not survived, was another important structure in this complex. It housed German immigrants. All of these papers are part of the records of the Archdiocese of New York. They are under the jurisdiction of Sister Margharita Smith of Saint Joseph's Seminary, Dunwoodie, Yonkers, New York 10704. She started microfilming the collection in 1979, but did not complete the task.

Seaman's Church Institute of New York and New Jersey

The Institute has records which date from 1834. They include merchant seamen scrapbooks, passenger lists, glass slides and a card file of these items. Part of The documents are at the Cathedral of St. John the Divine (of the Episcopal Church) and part are at the Seamen's Institute, None of these records are on microfilm. Robert Wolk is in charge of the archives. The address is 15 State Street, New York, New York 10004.

The Lutheran Church in America

Dr. Joel W. Lundeen, the Associate Archivist of the Lutheran Church in America, has important letter collections of the later Swedish immigration to America. These are letters dealing with official business of presidents and other leaders of the former Augustana (Swedish) Lutheran Church. These include papers of T. N. Hasselquist, Eric Norelius, L. P. Esbjorn, Jonas Swensson, Jonas Ausland, Olaf Olsson and others.

The first three sets of letters are extensive and they have been microfiimed, The Lutheran collection also includes a number of immigrant diaries and autobiographical reminiscences. The collection includes many printed histories, anniversary books and materials of that kind (mostly secondary in nature). Dr Lundeen suggests other sources of important Swedish archives: the Denkmann Library of Augustana College, Rock Island, Illinois, which, he says, is the largest and most complete collection of Swedish-American materials in the United States; the Swedish Pioneer Archives of Chicago Illinois; the Bernadotte Library of Gustavus Adolphus College, St. Petersburg, Minnesota; and the Library of Upsala College of East Orange, New Jersey. The Archives contains 1,000 books, 500 periodicals and 2,000 feet of manuscripts. The object of the Archives is to preserve the documents ofthe Lutheran Church, which includes Swedish, Danish, Norwegian, Finnish, and Icelandic records. Certain portions of the holdings are on microfilm.

Bethlen Otthon

This Home for the Aged in Ligonier, Pennsylvania has a significant archive of the Presbyterian church in the area, which is Hungarian-American. The Reverend Paul Kovacs is administrator of the records. They contain historical materials from churches, minutes of meetings and other papers. There is no inventory. These records were shipped to Youngstown, Ohio for safe keeping.

OTHER RECORDS

Ethnic Presses

Foreign language newspapers have served immigrants for over 200 years. They played an important role in socializing immigrants by providing information about the United States and the old home country. This dual objective fostered the Americanization of aliens, but it also created conditions for the ultimate decline of these newspapers.

The peak years of these presses coincided with the peak years of Ellis Island activity (In 1917 there were 1,325 immigrant newspapers in the United States).[23] These papers were in 40 languages and served an estimated 13 million readers. One can see the process of decline

---

[23]"The Ethnic Press: Many Voices," Spectrum, III (March, 1980), p.1.

in the case of the German-language newspapers. They "suffered most, dropping from 800 in 1894 to 554 in 1910 and to 234 in 1920.[24] Although their number declined steadily, they survive, because they helped to establish an ethnic identity. But more importantly, they printed letters, editorials and experiences of new arrivals (and returning immigrants).

The standard materials in the foreign language press included news of fraternal organizations, churches, social events, poetry, humorous stories and educational matter. Stories were usually provided in the foreign language and English. The estimated readership in 1940 was 5-8 million. The largest dailies of that time were the *Jewish Daily Forward* (103,337); the Italian *Il Progresso Italo-Americano* (78,811) and the German *Staat-Zeitung und Herold* (51,800). These were unusual because most of the foreign dailies had a circulation of under 5,000.[25] The distribution of these dailies by language and by frequency of publication is given in Table 19. It can be seen that most publications (55 percent) were weeklies and that the next category was the monthly papers.

The Immigrant Genealogical Society informs us that there are "at least" 58 ethnic newspapers published in Los Angeles County today. Some of these are quite old, and probably involve some Ellis Island history. For example, the *California Staats-Zeitung* dates to 1890 and still has a circulation of 30,000; the *California Magyarsag* began in 1922 and its circulation is 7,500; the *California Jewish Press* began in 1935 and has 151,000 readers; and the *L'Italo Americano*

---

[24]Marion T. Marzolf, "A Vital Link: The Ethnic Press in the United States, Michigan Alumnus (July/August 1986), p. 43.

[25]Frances Kalnay and Richard Collins, The New Americans (New York:Greenberg Publications, 1941), p. 245.

dates to 1908, with a readership of 4,000 today.[26]

Michigan, too, has foreign-language newspapers that have a long history. *The Detroiter Abend-Post* was founded in 1854 and still publishes today. It reached its peak enrollment of 28,864 in 1940. *The Polish Daily News*, founded in 1909, publishes two edition, in Polish and English.[27]

The Immigration History Research Center is microfilming Italian American newspapers that were published in the United States by immigrants. From 1836 to the present, more than 2,000 titles were printed, but many have been lost or destroyed. For this reason, the Center is appealing to libraries, historical societies and universities to make copies available. The Center has also published a guide to Polish newspapers: Frank Renkiewicz and Anne Bjorkquist, *Guide to Polish American Newspapers and Periodicals in Microform*, 1989. The Guide offers a list of 69 Polish American publications.

The Balch Institute for Ethnic Studies has available the company records of the *Gwiazda* (the Star), which was published in Philadelphia from 1902 to 1985. It was founded by a Polish immigrant, Stephan Nowaczyk, and at its peak the circulation reached 7,500 Balch has also published Arlow W. Anderson, *Rough Road to Glory: The Norwegian-American Press Speaks Out on Public Affairs, 1875-1925*, (1989).

The corporate records of *Atlantis*, the first Greek-American newspaper in the United States, for the years 1894-1973, are located at the Balch Institute for Ethnic Studies, Philadelphia, Pennsylvania, 19106. These papers contain correspondence files, scrapbooks and business records.

---

[26]The Society is located at 5043 Lankershim, North Hollywood, CA 91601. See its Newsletter, February 1988

[27]Marzolf, *Michigan Alumnus*, p. 45.

Table 19

FOREIGN LANGUAGE PUBLICATIONS in the UNITED STATES

(1940)

	Total	Daily	Semi-Weekly	Weekly	Semi-Monthly	Monthly	Other
Albanian	1	—	—	—	1	—	—
Arabic	9	4	3	2	—	—	—
Armenian	17	3	2	6	—	4	2
Bulgarian	5	—	1	3	1	—	—
Chinese	11	11	—	—	—	—	—
Croatian	16	—	2	8	4	2	—
Czech	50	6	13	17	1	13	—
Danish	16	—	—	10	2	3	1
Dutch	16	—	1	9	—	5	1
Esperanto	1	—	—	—	1	—	—
Estonian	2	—	—	1	—	1	—
Finnish	23	5	6	4	1	7	—
Flemish	2	—	—	2	—	—	—
French	36	6	1	20	3	4	2
German	172	13	8	109	6	29	7
Greek	28	3	2	12	5	6	—
Hebrew	11	—	2	—	—	4	5
Hungarian	57	2	2	45	2	6	—
Italian	126	8	4	90	6	18	—
Japanese	19	8	3	6	—	2	—
Korean	1	—	—	1	—	—	—
Ladino	1	—	—	1	—	—	—
Latvian	1	—	—	1	—	—	—
Lithuanian	31	5	2	10	4	8	2
Norwegian	26	—	2	14	4	5	1
Polish	69	12	1	49	1	6	—
Portuguese	18	1	—	12	1	3	1
Roumanian	6	—	2	3	—	1	—
Russian	21	5	2	6	3	5	—
Serbian	5	2	—	2	—	1	—
Slovak	37	2	3	17	5	10	—
Slovene	15	5	—	7	—	3	—
Spanish	74	8	1	42	4	17	2
Swedish	30	—	—	20	1	7	2
Ukraian	15	2	3	6	2	2	—
Welsh	1	—	—	1	—	—	—
Wendish	1	—	—	1	—	—	—
Yiddish	49	8	3	11	2	22	3
TOTAL	1019	119	69	548	60	194	29

Source: Kalney and Collins, p.245.

The Fraternal Organizations

From the time most immigrants came to the United States, they sought out the assistance of persons who had come earlier from the same villages, provinces, or countries. They sought individuals with common languages, memories and cultures. By joining one of the several fraternal societies or associations, they were able to purchase a small amount of security, since most of these associations offered insurance against sickness, disability and a dignified burial. The fraternal organizations also published their own newspapers, books, and almanacs, they encouraged members to become better citizens by sponsoring evening classes in Americanization, and they supported orphanages, homes for the aged and social clubs. There were hundreds of benefits associations, but Table 20 encompasses the most important. The membership number is approximate.

The records of these associations, where they still exist, have been described as "the largest single source of ethnic documentation which has not been systematically gathered and utilized for historical research."[28]

The International Institutes

When Dr. Nicholas Montalto was the Executive Director of the New Jersey International Institute, he completed a major study of the International Institutes.[29] Working for the Immigration History Research Center at Saint Paul, Minnesota, he supervised the acquisition of papers of the American Council for Nationalities Services in New York City, and he helped to determine which records would

---

[28]The Immigration History Research Center Grant Application to the National Endowment for the Humanities, August 29, 1977. The Minnesota Center received two grants from the National Endowment for the Humanities since 1976, to conduct a survey of these ethnic records. The project prepared a list of 106 national internal organizations through the use of mail surveys, telephone inquiries and some personal visits.

[29]He informed me by telephone that most early records were destroyed, but that there are still records that have survived from five or six institutes. He mentioned, in particular, Boston, St. Paul and St. Louis. In addition, the Providence papers went to Rhode Island College and the Bridgeport records are in private hands.

be moved to Minnesota.

Where records have not been destroyed, there is some question as to access. Lucretia L. Stoica, of the Cleveland Nationalities Service Center believes that the century-old records in that depository are confidential and are not available because they contain cases of some living persons. Madeleine J. Douet, Director of the Archives Center of the YMCA National Board, also objected to the microfilming of records.

Table 20

FRATERNAL BENEFIT SOCIETIES

(1940)

Name	Approximate Membership
Polish National Alliance of the U.S. of N.A., Chicago, Ill.	275,000
First Catholic Slovak Union, Cleveland, OH	92,000
Croatian Fraternal Union of America, Pittsburgh, PA	90,400
Workmen's Circle, NYC (Jewish)	72,000
Lutheran Brotherhood, Minneapolis (Norwegian)	63,200
Greek Cathlolic Union of Russian Brotherhoods, Munhall, PA	60,000
The Order of Vasa, Chicago, IL (Swedish)	60,000
Workmen's Benefit Fund, Brooklyn, NY (German)	58,300
L'Union St. Jean Baptiste d'Amerique, Woonsocket, RI	57,500
Slovene National Benefit Society, Chicago, IL	52,000
Western Bohemian Fraternal Association, Cedar Rapids, IA	45,200
Verhovay Fraternal Ins. Assocation, Pittsburgh, PA (Hungarian)	41,300
Ukranian National Association, New Jersey	36,300
Czecho-Slovak Society of America, Pittsburgh, PA	32,000
Sons of Italy, Philadelphia, PA	30,000
Armenian Democratic Liberal Association, Boston, MA	—
Macedonian People's League of USA, Detroit, MI (Bulgarian)	—

SOURCE: Kalnay and Collins, *The New American*, pp. 232-41.

FOREIGN SOURCES

We complete this chapter by surveying the chief foreign sources and the persons who are pursuing these sources in foreign places. The European sources of Ellis Island materials are considerable. According to Pitkin, the Italian goverment had the finest system of keeping track of immigrants of any nation. To quote him, "Every citizen that goes out or comes into the country is registered." [30] Other countries have rich holdings of immigration information and it was inevitable as the "roots" phenomenon spread that it should reach Europe. In fact, Europeans have always been more ethnically and genealogically minded than the United States citizens.

A run down of some of the research on European places is indicative. Professor Robert Swearinger, of Kent State University, is doing immigration research from the Dutch side. Prof. Ira M. Glazier, of the Immigration Archives at Temple University, is doing research on the ships' manifests to identify towns, regions, and families from Italy, and he is creating computer links with Italian sources. He is working with Dr. Gianfausto Rosoli, of the *Centro Studi Emigrazione*, of Rome, Italy. Glazier also has established links with the University of Bari on this project. Dr. Mark Stolarik, of the Balch Institute, has good Slovak sources and Dr. John Kromkowski, of The Catholic University of America and the National Center for Urban Ethnic Affairs, has been working with the Jagiellonian University in Krakow, Poland, where he has been doing research on American roots of Polish citizens. He is collaborating with Prof. Theodore Gromada of Jersey City State College. Countless other persons have been developing overseas contacts to expand our sources of immigration information. Some sources are particularly noteworthy, and we need to discuss them in more detail.

---

[30] Pitkin, Keepers of the Gate.

Canadian Archives

The public archives of Canada is a source of Ellis Island information, because several persons who were processed at Ellis Island went directly to Canada. There was no registration of immigrants in Canada before 1906, but records are very good after that date. Most persons migrating to Canada were met at the labor exchanges, especially those who came to work on construction projects. In particular, Record Group 76, which contains Papers of the Departments of Interior, Labor/Agriculture, and Immigration is of special importance. One large file entitled "Inspection of Immigrants at New York," dating from 1897-1921 (microfilm reel C-7351), deals with the activities of Canadian officers working at Ellis Island, especially medical officers.

In the fall of 1976, a group of academics, archivists and librarians formed the Multicultural History Society of Ontario. They began efforts to record the province's immigrant and ethnic past. The objectives of the Society were to promote and advance studies in the history of all ethnocultural groups within the Province of Ontario, and to collect and to prepare guides to material relevant to the history of these groups. They made contacts with 40 different ethno-cultural groups. The work of the Society is publicized through its journal, *Polyphony*. The Society has a variety of historical collections, including letters, photographs, ethnic newspapers, and oral testimony.

Italian Sources

The *Archivio Centrale dello Stato*, Rome (The Central State Archives) was established in 1862. The original holdings were documents of the administration of the Pontifical State, the Civil State of House of Savoy and Heraldic Registers. Between 1875 and 1953, there were two archival systems, the Central in Rome and the regional in the provinces. After 1953, the distinction between the two was resolved when the government created the *Minestero per i Beni Culturali* (the Minister of Cultural Welfare) to administer documents all over Italy. This office publishes a General Inventory of State Archives, which includes information about the Regional Archives in

Abruzzo Molise, Calabria, Basilicata, Sicilia, Campania, Liguria, Puglia, Lombardia, Sardegna, Umbria, Friuli-Venezia, Giulia, Trentino Aito Adige, Marche, and Piemonte. Of particular importance in the Archives of the Province of Naples is the Center for Emigration from Naples, 1894-1961.

The Italian government began to collect immigration data in 1876.[31] These data are flawed, however, because not all Italians left by Italian ports (some went by way of Le Havre and Hamburg) and some entered the United States through Canada. In addition, there were the illegals and the undocumented emigrants. For these reasons, the Italian data understate immigration when compared with U. S. data. After 1902, the *Commissariato Generale dell'Emigrazione* compiled statistics on the number leaving Italy each year in the 1920's, and the International Institute of Statistics of the International Labour Office did extensive research on immigration, including Italian.

The *Bollettino dell'Emigrazione* is a major Italian source. Published from 1902-1927, by the *Commissariato Generale dell'Emigrazione*, it relates the experiences of Italians in the many nations to which they emigrated. In all, 345 issues were published, totaling over 36 thousand pages. Each of the issues contains articles, notes, reviews and monographs on all aspects of emigration. Publication was suspended in 1918 because of World War 1.[32] Many Italians did not intend to emigrate permanently; they returned to their Italian homes each year. These were counted after 1905 by the

---

[31]This information was provided by Fr. Gianfausto Rosoli, of the Centro Studi d'Emigrazione, Rome. See his <u>Un Secolo di Emigrazione Italiana, 1876-1976</u> (Rome: CSER, 1978).

[32]Professor Francesco Cordasco compiled a massive bibliographical guide to the <u>Bolletino</u> (see the Bibliography). It contains 4,711 entries.

Commissariato.[33]

Italians who are doing research on emigration, including American immigration, include Dr. Pietro Russo, of the *Universite degli Studi di Firenze,* who compiled a 9000 item bibliography of Italian-American publications, which is computerized; Professor Giorgio Fondati, of Cigini, Venice, and Professor Anna Maria Martelone of the University of Florence.

The Catholic church in Italy entered the emigration question on a scholarly level when the Scalabrini Fathers, a missionary order dedicated to the care of emigrants, established the *Centro Studi d'Emigrazione* in Rome in 1963. In the following year, the Order began publishing a journal, *Studi Emigrazione* and other publications on Italian immigration. Many of these publications deal with Italian emigration to the United States.[34]

The Swedish and Scandinavian Emigrant Registers

The Emigrant Register in Karlstad, Sweden, was founded in 1960 by the Varnland Historical Society and the Vasa Orders Karlstad Lodge to strengthen ties between Swedes and Swedish-Americans in the United States. The Register includes writings of emigrants in the form of diaries, letters, and memoirs; newspapers in English and Swedish; magazines and books. The Register also publishes a quarterly magazine, *The Bridge,* which is circulated in the United States and Canada. The House of Emigrants (Emigrantinstitulet), located at Vaxjo, is also devoted to documenting Swedish emigration. It has microfilmed over one thousand Swedish Lutheran congregation records in the United States and Canada, and it contains over seven thousand letters sent to the United States, each classified by American

---

[33]Another important source of Italian immigration data is the <u>Sommario di Statistiche Storiche Italiane</u> 1861-1955 (The Instituto Centrale di Statistica, Roma).

[34]For example, Gianfausto Rosoli, "La Colonizzazione Italiana delle Americhe tra Mito e Realta," <u>Studi Emigrazione</u>, IX (October, 1972), pp. 296-376.

geography.[35] The *Folkminnessamling* (folklore archive) in Stockholm is another important archive, because it documents Swedish immigrant women who were in domestic service in the United States.[36]

The Uppsala Migration Research Project, centering on Swedish emigration statistics, utilizes local population registers, passports and passenger lists from emigration ports. The project was directed by Hakan Berggren from 1962 1966; Sune Akerman from 1966-1973; and by Harold Runblom from 1973 to the present. The researchers have tried to follow emigrants from place to place, and thus do research on migration streams, return migrations, and ultimate destinations in the United States.

The largest immigration of Swedes to the United States came in 1868-73, 1879-93, 1900-13, and 1920-29.[37] Many came through Ellis Island, but many returned home--the estimate is 19 percent of all Swedes who came between 1880 and 1930. The Swedes (like the Italians) considered immigration as a means of accumulating an income to purchase land back home. They, too, did not naturalize quickly for they considered immigration a reversible project.

On Christmas Day, 1978, Swedish television ran a series of nine one-hour programs about Swedes in America, which was filmed on location by Swedish television crews. According to Swedish authorities this nine-hour program resulted in a new wave of America Fever." Swedes from all over the land began to phone Emigrant Institutes in attempts to locate relatives who lived in the United States

---

[35]Cf. Ulf Beijbom, "A Decade with the Emigrant Institute in Vaxjo," Swedish Pioneer Historical Quarterly (1976), pp. 178-88.

[36]See Joy K. Lintelman, America is the woman's promised land":Swedish Immigrant Women and American Domestic Service," Journal of American Ethnic History, VIII (Spring 1989), 9-23.

[37]H. Runblom and H. Norman (eds.), Fom Sweden to America (Minneapolis: University of Minnesota Press, 1976).

and who had not been heard from for some time. The producer of the programs, Lars Holmquist, emphasized that there was much more "Swedishness" in the United States than he thought. The nine hours of television included scenes of Brooklyn, New York; Galesburg, Illinois; St. Pete, Minnesota; Kansas, and California.

The Swedish research projects summarized above are part of a larger project, "Nordic Emigration,"[38] that has been supported by foundations, universities and businesses throughout Scandinavia. Dr. Kristan Hvidt is in charge of the Danish section, Professor Thorhallur Vilmundarson of the Icelandic research, Professor Ingrid Summingsen of the Norwegian, Dr. Reino Kero of the Finnish, and Dr. Sune Akerman of the Swedish project. With the support of the *Letterstedtska* Foundation, the researchers were able to map emigration from Scandinavia during the years, 1865-1915 and to survey immigration by areas and country for 5-year periods.

The Danish emigrant archives at Aalborg include letters from Danish pastors to the United States. Professor Marion Marzolf, of the Journalism Department of the University of Michigan, made some important discoveries in Danish archives.

In the summer of 1984, the Henie-Onstad museum, near Oslo, Norway, presented an exhibition on Norwegian immigration called "The Promise of America." It told the story of how 800,000 Norwegians emigrated to America and the hardships they faced. The exhibition included a replica of The statue of Liberty, experiences crossing the ocean, how the ship arrived at Brooklyn and the processing at Ellis Island. It concluded with a journey by horse-drawn coach to the midwest prairie. The exhibit featured famous Norwegian-Americans, including Knute Rockne, Chief Justice Earl Warren, and Ole Rolvaag.

German Immigration Records

---

[38]Sune Akerman, "The Research Project 'Nordic Emigration', Immigration History Society Newsletter, VII (May, 1975), pp. 1-4.

Since German immigration peaked before Ellis Island was opened as an immigration station, most early research on German emigration was concerned with the analysis of the 19th century, particularly of colonization and the political aspects of migration.[39] The more recent migrations have been studied since World War II. Since then German historians have shown an upsurge in interest in the causes of emigration, especially to the United States.

Rolf Engelsing, Gunther Moltmann and Peter Marschalck have investigated the growth of port traffic and the changing patterns of emigration by German states. Much of this research is part of a large-scale project, centered at the University of Hamburg, that is directed by Moltmann.

The Museum for Hamburg history has an Historic Emigration Office, in which 5 million names are stored on microfilm. These are the only complete German emigration records from 1850-1914, and they assume more importance because more Americans (28 percent) consider themselves of German ancestry than any other ethnic group. These names exist because of German law, which required that every ship agent provide a complete list of all passengers by age, occupation, family and home city. The Historic Emigration Office can provide (usually in one hour) an official certificate with an excerpt of the original ship's list. The German archives also contain a sizable body of information about Jews, including many who emigrated to the United States in the 1930's. The government required Germans to produce a family tree to prove that there was no Jewish blood, and this tree had go back at least three or four generations.

Other Foreign Sources

Between 1976 and 1983, the Bentley Historical Library of the University of Michigan investigated the extent of the documentation of

---

[39]Peter Aarschalck, "Public Opinion and Scientific Interpretation of German Emigration In the 19th and 20th Centuries," Migration History Society Newsletter, VII (May, 1965), pp. 5-8.

the great migration in four foreign countries: The Netherlands, Poland, Ireland and Finland. This project's emphasis was on the migrants to Michigan. Researchers went first to Scandinavia to visit archives in Norway, Denmark and Finland. The Finnish archives are more relevant to Michigan history, because There are more Finns there than in any other state. Visits to the University of Turku and discussions with Professor Reino Kero confirmed that Finnish migration to the United States is well documented.

In the second Phase of the Immigration Source Project, four persons did research in foreign countries to explore immigrant documents there. Professor Herbed Brink, of Calvin College, went to the Netherlands; Professor Jo Ellen Vinyard, of Maygrove College, travelled to Ireland; Keijo Virtanen of the University of Turku, conducted the survey of Finnish sources, and Stephen Corrin travelled to Poland. Their search led the project directors to conclude, "Clearly sources important to the study of migration exist scattered all over the globe."[40]

American research on Polish immigration sources has stressed the work of the Polonia Research Institute, at the Jagielonian University in Krakow. This Institute, under the direction of Hieroniun Kubiak, emphasizes studies of Poles who emigrated to the United States, China, Denmark, Lithuania, Great Britain, The Netherlands, France and South America. ♦

Austrian-Hungarian materials are widely scattered. Statistics on emigration from Austria-Hungary before 1918 and from Austria after 1918 may be found in the publications of the *Osterreichisches Statistisches Zentralamt*. Some information on emigration from Austria to the United States may be found in the appendix to Richard Riedl, *Die Oganisation de Auswander in Osterreich* (Wein: Handlesministerium gefurhten Untersuchung, 1913). Additional information about Austrian archival materials may be obtained from

---

[40]Francis X. Blouin and Robert M. Warners, Sources for the Study of Migration and Ethnicity (Ann Arbor: Bentley Historical Library, 1979), p. 23.

the Haus-, Hof and Staats Archiv, Vienna.

English language information about Hungarian emigration to the United States is rare. In fact, Julianna Puskas gave us the first such volume in 1982[41] Puskas works for the Historical Institute of the Hungarian Academy of Sciences. She searched old imperial records, Hungarian papers and various county archives, she interviewed return migrants and she used many Magyar publications that originated in the United States.

Although Dutch emigration was much smaller than that of the Irish or the Italians, until World War I, 75 percent of the migration was directed to North America, mostly to the United States.[42] Until very recently, this migration was largely ignored by Dutch scholars, and the leading research was conducted by Dutch-Americans. The ethnic revival of the 1960's resulted in the first Dutch-American historical workshop at Calvin College in 1977 and the formation of the Dutch-American Historical Society to promote the study of Dutch immigration. Although the major collections of Dutch immigration are in the United States, the Dutch archives contain important materials. The *Koninklijk Bibliotheek* in the Hague has serials, pamphlets and books; and the Netherlands Historical and Economic Archives houses the records of the 20th century immigration societies.

---

[41]See her From Hungary to the United States, 1880-1914 (Budapest: Akademiai Kiado).]

[42]This information concerning Dutch immigration is taken from Robert Swierenga, "Dutch Immigration Historiography," Immigration History Society, Newsletter, XI (November, 1979), pp. 1-6.

CHAPTER VII:

ORAL HISTORIES

Some say oral history is a controversial manner of telling a story (it may be exaggeration, historical puff, mental rambling of the aged and just not history). Several important historians have denounced oral histories in their way. Barbara Tuchman claims that oral history leads to a mountain of trivia; Forrest Pogue, a former president of the Oral History Association, suggested that many oral history interviews resulted in historical fiction, and Corneluis Ryan once stated that he rejected 90 percent of his oral testimony in writing his famous book, *The Longest Day*.

Despite the difficulties presented by the oral history approach, there is no question that this technique has a definite role to play in historical research. William Moss, the past president of the Oral History Association, provided the best response to the critics. In his "Oral history, An Appreciation," he states, "Oral history has a proper place in the system of evidence, experience, and analysis that produces good history and properly used it can make an important contribution. Improperly used it can be mischievous and destructive. Oral history to be most effective, must itself be well grounded in sound analysis and in thorough knowledge and understanding of all the other available and pertinent sources, if it is to produce the best and most reliable oral documentation."[1]

FEDERAL HISTORIES

Smithsonian Institution

The oral history and folklore materials of the Smithsonian Institution concerning Ellis Island are found in three collections: (1) The Family Folklore collection, which are interviews done at the

---

[1] *The American Archivist*, XL (October, 1977), p. 429.

Festival of American Folklife in 1976 and later years. This collection is indexed by subject and was under the direction of Steve Zeitlin; (2) The Ethnic American Collection Project, which were interviews made during the 1976 festival; and (3) The field work and performance records of the Ellis Island programs of the 1977 and 1978 festivals. These include audio and video tapes of persons interviewed and some who were selected to perform at the festivals. Susan Kalcik coordinated the last two programs. In addition, there were some oral histories taken in connection with the regional meetings of the Smithsonian Associates. The latest information is that there are about 300 oral histories completed. These are on tape and are available at the Smithsonian Archives.

The Ethnic American Collection Project consists of 118 90-minute cassett tapes made during the twelve weeks of the 1976 Festival of American Folklife. The tapes are of two kinds: program tapes made of workshops and interview tapes made mainly by interns in folklore and American studies, working under Susan Kalcik and Dr. Patricia Averill of the University of Maryland and Dr. Caroline Golab of the University of Pennsylvania. This project is indexed. The index number tells the person who was interviewed, the interviewer, the ethnic identity or ethnic group and the genre.

National Park Service

The National Park Service completed oral histories at both the Statue of Liberty and at Ellis Island. Some of these were summer projects when many Ellis Island "alumni" returned to the Island. The first 157 persons were interviewed between August 1973 and November 1983. Of these, 126 were immigrants--23 Russian, 12 German, 10 Italian, 9 Polish and 8 Austrian. These were stored at The American Museum of Immigration, located at the base of the Statue of Liberty. Most of the interviews were taken in New York City. The 157 cassettes include transcripts for most of the tapes (these can be duplicated at cost) and they include former employees who worked on the Island. Among the interviewees are a medical inspector a former attorney for deportation cases, and several public health physicians.

Because of the urgency of the situation (the advanced ages of Ellis Island immigrants), the National Park Service issued a Request for Proposal (RFP) on July 3, 1983 for an "Oral History Recording Project." The contract was awarded to AKRF, Inc. for 200 oral histories. These were to include immigrants, former employees, voluntees and military personnel.

The interviews were completed in 1989. The leading ethnic groups covered were Italian 31, Russian (mostly Jews) 26, English 11, Hungarians 11, Polish 10 and Ukranians 10. Of these, 11 were former employees. In the same year, an additional 60 interviews were completed by Nancy L. Dallett Productions of Brooklyn, New York. In this group, there were 6 Russians, 6 Germans, 5 Swedes, 3 Poles and 2 Italians.[2]

OTHER ORAL HISTORIES

Following are brief annotated summaries of some of the more important oral histories that have been completed. Each of them has an Ellis Island component.

The Armenian Assembly.

The Armenian Assembly of Washington D.C. has completed 400 oral histories, with survivers of the Turkish-Armenian massacres during 1915-1923. Transcription, indexing and translation are completed. The tapes are located at 1420 N Street N. W., Washinglon D. C. 20005.

The Ashland-Cleveland Projects.

---

[2]The total number of National Park Service tapes on June 15, 1990 was 434, but the number continues to grow, because as Marcy Cohen, Curator of Exhibits, Statue of Liberty-Ellis Island National Monument, told me, "The project is ongoing."

Professor Charles Ferroni, of the Department of Social Services at Ashland College in Ashland, Ohio, conducted an oral history project, with his students as intewiewers. Of the 100 interviews, about thirty percent are immigrants and the remainder are children of immigrants. Ferroni previously obtained a PhD for a study of Italians in Cleveland.

Baltimore People, Baltimore Places.

Professor Jean (Vincenza) Scarpaci, formerly of Towson State University, and W. Theodore Durr of the University of Baltimore collaborated on an oral history project in Baltimore under a grant from the National Endowment for the Humanities. This project, under Durr's direction, involved six ethnic areas of Baltimore: black, Jewish, Italian, American, Polish, and Irish. There are over 600 hours of interviews.

Battle Creek

The Culture Fusion and Urban Development Oral History Project, 1977-78, of Battle Creek, Michigan, includes 40 interviews of businessmen and women who are first and second generation immigrants to Battle Creek. These are housed in the Willard Library.

Center for Migration Studies.

Several persons, working under the direction of Father Lydio Tomasi, completed oral histories for publication by the Center. Most of these involve the Italian-American experience. Included in this group are the histories done by Professors Salvatore LaGumina, Betty Boyd Caroli, Virginia Yans McGloughlin, and Remigio Pane.

Center for Oral History--University of Connecticut.

Established as the Oral History Project in 1968, it became a Center in 1981. Completed projects include "The Peoples of Connecticut" and "Connecticut Workers and a Half Century of Technological Change, 1930-1980." The Center transcribes tapes for oral historians and stores them at the University.

The Chicago Polonia Project

This project, directed by Mary Cygan, was funded under Title IX of the Ethnic Heritage Studies Act in 1976. It is a series of taped interviews with Poles who immigrated to the United States between 1880 and 1930. The project, which collected over 140 life histories on tapes, is the largest Polish project of its type in the United States. It involved 32 interviewers, many of whom, were fluent in Polish. The materials on the Polonia project may be obtained from the Chicago Historical Society.

Greater Cleveland Ethnographic Museum

The Greater Cleveland oral history project was under the direction of Annette Fromm, folklorist, immigrant experience project. The museum is located in the Old Arcade in Cleveland.[3] The project includes 94 histories of several ethnic groups, which were taken from December 1977 to February 1979.

Czechoslovakian Heritage Museum and Library

Founded in 1854, this is the oldest Czech archive in the United States. Located at Berwyn Illinois, its holdings include unpublished records, personal papers, correspondence, dissertations and oral histories of immigrants. Since 1897, it has published the Journal *Czechoslovenskych Spolku V Americe,*

Croatian Ethnic Institute, Inc.

This Croatian Franciscan Archive, located in Chicago, has developed a centralized collection to preserve its ethnic heritage and culture. An oral history research project was conducted on

---

[3]After this project was completed, the museum was merged into the Ohio Historical Society.

immigrants entering the United States before 1910.

Delaware Oral History

The oral history project at the University of Delaware is part of the Historic Media Center for the History department, and is under the general direction of Professor George Basalla.

Emigrantinstitutet

This project, which is based at East Moline, Illinois, began in the early 1960's as a result of efforts of Lennart Setterdahl, It was supported by the Swedish Government. The project interviewed more than 1,000 Swedes who immigrated to the United States.

The Ethnic Heritage Studies Program

Ethnic studies grants were first authorized under Title IX, Part E of the Elementary and Secondary Education Act, as amended in 1967. The grants were meant to encourage the creation of curriculum materials for the teaching of ethnicity in the American schools. The first grants were made in 1974 by the Office (now Department) of Education. To facilitate the dissemination of information about the ethnic programs, The Ethnic Heritage Studies Clearing House was created in Boulder Colorado, as a project of the Social Science Consortium, Inc., with the support of the U.S. Office of Education.[4]

The projects listed below relate particularly to immigration and Ellis Island history.

---

[4]The writer conducted a mail survey of all programs that were funded between 1974 and 1979 to learn which of these programs were relevant to the Ellis Island story. For a list of all projects, see "Bibliography of Ethnic Heritage Studies Program Materials," The National Center for Urban Ethnic Affairs and the National Education Association, 1976.

1. Connecticut. The Peoples of Connecticut Multicultural Ethnic Heritage Series", The University of Connecticut, Storrs. In particular, see the Irish, the Italians and the Jewish Americans "In Their Homeland, In America and In Connecticut".

2. Florida. "A Project in Multicultural Learning: Greek-American Contributions to American Society," Florida State University, Tallahassee.

3. Illinois. Chicago Consortium for Inter-Ethnic Curriculum Development, "Self Reliance," Chicago Features video tapes of four ethnic groups: Lithuanians, Greeks, Jews and Ukranians.

4. Massachusetts. "Jewish Immigration to America," Ethnic Studies Project, Brandeis University, Waltham.

5. Minnesota. "Minneapolis Multi-Ethnic Curriculum project," Ethnic Cultural Center, Minneapolis.

Friends of Ellis Island

Incorporated as a non-profit organization in the State of New York, the Friends of Ellis Island is a citizens group interested in establishing the Island as a "memorial to the American immigrant." The group completed 30-40 oral interviews in five boroughs of New York. It also presented a sound and light show on Ellis Island to raise cash for minor repairs on the Island.

Finnish-American Cultural Society of Baltimore.

This small archive (contained in one file cabinet) consists of personal papers, correspondence, unpublished materials and photos. There is also a collection of oral histories to document the Finn's awareness of their history and contribution.

Oral Histories in Florida

Professor George Pozzeta, of the University of Florida at Gainesville, interviewed about 30 Italian Americans. These interviews were donated to the oral history collection at the University of Florida. Professor Gary Mormino, another Floridian doing oral histories, is associated with the University of South Florida in Tampa. He completed 25 interviews in that area. He has a cooperative arrangement with the project at the University of Florida at Gainesville. He previously did interviews of Italians in St. Louis and some of these materials are at the University of North Carolina in Chapel Hill.

The Immigration Ethnic Archives--San Francisco

Professor Joseph Giovinco, of Sonoma State University, received a grant from the Rockefeller Foundation to conduct oral history studies for the Immigrant Ethnic Archives in San Francisco. There are 57 histories, including many Danish and Italian. Some of these persons came to San Francisco by way of Ellis Island. These interviews are "transcribed in rough."

Immigrant Voyages--Massachusetts

The emphasis of this oral history is the journey from Europe to the United States. Professor R. Wayne Anderson, of Northeastern University, interviewed shore workers, fishermen, and merchant seamen, many of whom are immigrants. These ethnic groups tend to be concentrated: Italians in Gloucester, Portuguese in New Bedford.

Italians In Boston

Judith K. Dunning, who worked for the National Park Service in the Lowell Historical project, did a major oral history project on Italians in Boston. Under a grant from the National Endowment for the Humanities, she conducted oral interviews in the North End of Boston. She interviewed 50 Italian women who spanned three generations. Their ages ranged from 20 to 95. Theinterviews are all transcribed and they are in her personal possession. Some of these discussions included Ellis Island experiences.

Dunning was involved also in a three-year bilingual project for the National Park Service involving several hundred interviews of Greeks, French Canadians, English, Irish, Polish and Portuguese who worked in the textile mills of Lowell. There are some questions in the survey concerning Ellis Island.

The Italians in Chicago

This project, under the direction of Professor Domenic Candeloro, formerly of the University of Illinois, Circle Campus, now of Governors State University, was financed by a grant from the National Endowment for the Humanities; it resulted in the completion of 105 oral histories of Italian Americans in the Chicago area.[5]

Institute on Pluralism and Group Identity

In this oral history study, Corinne A, Krause interviewed three generations of Jewish, Italian and Slavic-American women to obtain their views on ethnicity. The project involved 225 grandmothers, mothers and daughters. Some of the grandmothers related their Ellis Island experience. These histories are available from the Institute in New York City.

The Latvian Heritage Foundation

This Foundation, located in Jamacia Plain, Massachusetts, has preserved Latvian culture in the United States in a collection of about 1,000 radio broadcast tapes of the show, "Spotlight on Latvia." It includes features of the annual Latvian Song Festival in June and July.

---

[5]Professor Candeloro has very generously donated these oral histories to the Ellis Island Restoration Commission.

LDS Church Archive

This collection, completed between 1972 and 1974, includes interviews with emigrants who came to Utah to become part of the Mormon church and its organization. There is a published guide: *Guide of the Oral History Programs of the Historical Department, The Church of Jesus Christ of Latter-day Saints* (Salt Lake City: Historical Department, 1975).

Media Studies--Bridgeport

Professor Steve Ross, of Sacred Heart University in Bridgeport, Connecticut, produced a 2-reel film for television involving interviews of four ethnic families. In addition, between 1977 and 1979 he completed 25 oral histories of Hungarian immigrants in the Fairfield-Bridgeport area. They are part of the "Media Studies" program at Sacred Heart University

The Minnesota Historical Society

The oral history collection of the State of Minnesota is housed in St. Paul and in the various regional society locations. This project commenced in 1949, and there are now over 600 tape recordings of Minnesotans, many including immigrant experiences. The Minnesota Regional Research Centers tend to have oral histories of specific ethnic groups, for example, of the Finns, the Norwegians, the Danes. All of these tapes are available from the Audio-Visual Library at St. Paul, Minnesota.

Moorhead State University.

Professor Kenneth Smemo conducted several projects involving oral histories of Finns, Norwegians, Swedes and Danes as part of the Sandinavian-American ethnic retention project. He completed 100 tapes, some of which mention Ellis Island experiences. Smemo also did a film for the Federal government involving the narratives of some of his interviewees, most from the Minnesota Red River Valley area.

National Council of Jewish Women--Pittsburgh

The archival materials in this collection date back to 1893. They are housed the Hillman Library Archives of the University of Pittsburgh. The oral history program documents the Jewish immigrant experience.

Oral History in New Jersey

The oral history project in New Jersey was directed by Dr. Ronald J. Grele, formerly of the New Jersey Historical Commission. He published a directory of these projects,[6] which gives a county-by-county inventory of oral histories in New Jersey, and it is clear that many of these histories involve Ellis Island immigrants.

Dr. Giles Wright, replaced Grele as the coordinator of the oral history project. This project now totals 1,500 interviews and covers several counties and several colleges in the State of New Jersey, including Brookdale, Cumberland, Essex, Rutgers and William Crawford.

The New York State Education Department

This ethnic heritage project was intended to develop curricular and instructional materials designed to integrate Italian-American studies into the K-12 social studies curriculum. The project involved the selection of a community or region in New York State which had a large number of residents of Italian descent and cultural background. It also involved the selection of a community in Italy from which at one time or another many residents emigrated to the United States and to which some may have returned in retirement years.

The project produced dozens of hours of oral history on audio

---

[6]Oral History in New Jersey: A Directory (Trenton, 1979).

cassettes, but unfortunately these are not transcribed and edited. The tapes were made in the subject communities of Pozzallo, Giugliano and the Pozzallese section of Brooklyn. A number of them deal with immigration and with Ellis Island.

The Pennsylvania State Archives

The Pennsylvania oral history project centers on Slavic immigrants who settled in that region. Dr. John Bodnar directed the approximately 1,200 interviews, some of which include Ellis Island material. The results of this project may be obtained from the Pennsylvania Museum and Historical Commission, Harrisburg, Pennsylvania.

Professor Bruce Weston, Director of the Ethnic Heritage Center at California State College in California, Pennsylvania, conducted 80 interviews of coal miners in Pennsylvania, using Bodnar's questionnaire. He found some Ellis Island history in these interviews. They are now stored in two places: at the William Penn Museum in Harrisburg and at California State College. Only nine of these have been transcribed. Some of these are described in the "Daiseytown Oral History Booklet."

Plymouth's Little Portugal

The Plymouth, Massachusetts County, under a grant from the National Endowment for the Humanities, collected oral histories of the Portuguese in southeastern Massachusetts. Several national groups are represented, including Italians, Germans and Portuguese.

Purdue University Department of Education

This project, of approximately 130 immigrants of Romanian descent living in the Calumet region, involved interviews of early immigrant experiences in America. Although none of the interviews were intended to have a specific Ellis Island dimension, many of the persons interviewed did refer to their apprehensions and experiences upon landing at Ellis Island prior to their admission to the United

States. This project was conducted by Dr. Mary Leuca, who served as chief investigator and who directed the interviews.

Rhode Island Jewish Historical Association

This association preserves publications from other Rhode Island associations. The archive consists of correspondence, unpublished papers, personal papers and other manuscripts. Also included is an oral history collection.

Ribbons of Memories

Edward E. Sundberg and Gerda Sundberg, of Watsonville, California travelled 15,000 miles into 16 states, 70 towns and cities to interview 450 immigrants or their children. They produced 70,000 items and names and a 400 page index of these stories. The 200 oral tape interviews include at least 48 references to Ellis Island. Professor Sundberg, who taught at Cabrillo College, concentrated on obtaining interviews with Scandinavians who settled in the Santa Clara Valley, for which they received a small grant from San Jose State University. Many of the oral tapes are in Danish, Swedish, Norwegian and Icelandic, because Mrs. Sundberg could communicate in these languages. The Sundbergs made arrangements to leave their collection to California Lutheran College at Thousand Oaks, California, which has a heritage center as part of its library.

The St. Cloud State University Gerentology Project

Dr. Dena Shenk, an anthropologist at the Department of Interdisciplinary Studies, compiled field notes on older Americans in Minnesota. She completed 16 interviews and she found that some of these people came through Ellis Island. All of her work is with Lebanese Americans.

Steel Shavings

First published in 1975, this magazine is the work of the Calumet Regional Archives and the Indiana University Northwest, of

Gary, Indiana. This archives contains the records of the Gary International Institute, many of which contain letters and references to Ellis Island. "Steel Shavings" results from family histories written by students, of which the best are published.

Ukranian Workingmen's Association

Founded in Scranton, Pennsylvania in 1910, the archive contains the weekly, *Narodna Volya*, on microfilm from 1911, and other original publications, personal papers, correspondence, and printed material. This fraternal organization provided life insurance for members, thus the archives includes membership lists since 1910. An oral history program documents further the activities of the Association.

University of Maryland-SUNY Oral History Tapes

The University of Maryland, under an Ethnic Studies Project, did video histories of southern and eastern Europeans in the Baltimore and Washington, D.C. areas. These were under the direction of Diane Gayeski, now of Ithaca College and Edward Jurewcz, now of Kent State University.

Professor Frank Femminella, of the State University of New York at Albany, worked on the videotapes of the University of Maryland project. He went to Ellis Island to produce the narratives and the films under the Maryland grant, He is in possession of the tapes that were conducted in Baltimore and Washington, D.C. He also received an Ethnic Heritage Studies grant (1979-80) to study the peoples of eastern and southern Europe. Under this grant, there were a dozen interviews done by Peter Stoll, a student at SUNY. These interviews were conducted in the Albany area. There are a total of 70 hours of videotapes in the SUNY collection, including those of the University of Maryland. Stoll has transcribed a number of these.

Dr. Jane Deren, also of the University of Maryland, received a grant from the National Endowment for the Humanities to produce a series of radio shows on immigrant women. She sought first person narratives in all of the leading archives containing information about women. She collected documents and put information on index cards. According to her, she found "lots of Ellis Island histories." The radio shows which she produced are entitled "These Are Our Mothers"--a series of eight productions for National Public Radio. Assisting in this project were Dr. Maxine Seller, Dr. Barbara Klaczynska and Dr. Corinne Krause.

The University of Pittsburgh Libraries

The University of Pittsburgh has two oral history collections that are housed in the Archives of Industrial Society. There are detailed inventories for each, These are The National Council of Jewish Women project and the Pittsburgh Oral History project. The National Council of Jewish Women began in 1969 to gather information of the immigrant experiences of European-born Jews, who arrived in the United Stales between 1890 and 1920 and who later settled in Pittsburgh. The initial results of this effort was the book, *By Myself I'm A Book* published in 1982 by the American Jewish Historical Society. In June 1975, the oral history program for western Pennsylvania was established at the University of Pittsburgh. Using interviewers from the University, oral histories were taken in the Jewish, black, Croatian, Italian, and Polish communities in the Pittsburgh area.

Utah State Historical Society

This oral history project consists of tapes and transcripts of 41 interviews with women, some of whom emigrated to Utah from England, Denmark, Sweden and Finland. The interviews were conducted between 1953 and 1976.

Vermont Department of Education

The Barre Ethnic Heritage Studies Project was directed by Karen Lane and Tina Bielenberg in 1977 and 1978. This grant was made to assist the State Department to gather together books and manuscripts, personal papers and photographs, ethnic society records, oral histories, and other materials relating to the multi-cultural heritage of the "Granite City" and the Greater Barre area. They identified over 30 ethnic groups. Copies of the results were deposited in the Aldrich Public Library. There are a few items in the taped library that refer to Ellis Island.

In connection with Vermont ethnic history, it is important to note that many of the immigrants who went there arrived by way of Boston and Canada and some entered illegally.

The Western Historical Manuscript Collection

The oral history program at the University of Missouri at St. Louis contains 120 recorded interviews with immigrants from 32 separate countries. The faculty and students conducted the interviews. The holdings showed the following ethnic categories: Italian, 22; Irish, 13; German, 13; Russian, 12; and Polish, 5. The remaining interviews were scattered among the other ethnic groups. These interviews cover the 19th and 20th centuries. There is more material on Germans or descendants of Germans who settled in St. Louis, but there are many references to Ellis Island, according to Irene Cortinovis, the former Associate Director of the Western Historical Manuscript Collection.

Wisconsin Jewish Archives

This collection, housed in Madison, is a special part of the State Historical Society. It documents the growth of Jewish communities in Wisconsin, especially the recollections (oral histories) of first generation settlers and immigrants. The tape collection is indexed.

Table 21 summarizes many of the oral history projects that were described above.

Table 21

SUMMARY OF ORAL HISTORY PROJECTS

Person or Project	Place of Interview	No. of Interviews	Present Location	Major Ethnic Group(s)
American Museum of Immigration, NPS	New York, NY	157 (126 Immigrants)	Statue of Liberty Liberty Island	Russian, Italian German, Austrian
Armenian Assembly	Washington, D.C.	400	Washington, D.C.	Armenian
Ashland Cleveland	Cleveland, OH	100	Cleveland, OH	Italian
Baltimore Heritage Project	Baltimore, M.D.	(600 hours)	Baltimore, M.D.	Jewish, italian, Polish, Irish, Italian, Romanian
Joseph Barton	Cleveland, OH	25	Evanston, IL	Slovak
George Basalla	Delaware		DE	Multi-cultural
Battle Creek	Battle Creek, MI	40	Battle Creek, MI	Multi-cultural
Joseph Bentivegna	Loretta, PA		Loretta, PA	Italian
Richard Bernard	Milwaukee, WI		Marquette Univ.	
John Bodnar	Pennsylvania	1,200	Harrisburg, PA	Slovak
Betty Boyd Caroli	NY		New York City	Italian
Croatian Heritage Institute	Chicago, IL		Chicago, IL	Croatian
Czechoslovak Heritage Museum	IL		Berwyn, IL	Slovak
Jane Deren	MD		University of Maryland	Women Immigrants
Judith Dunning	Lowell, MA	100	Lowell, MA	Irish, Greek
Judith Dunning	Boston, MA	50	Personal Collection	Italian Women
Emigrant Institute	USA	1,000	E. Moline, IL	Scandinavian
Ethnic Fraternal Orgn.	Pittsburgh, PA	144	University of Pittsburgh	Jewish, Italian Croatian
Frank Femminella	Albany, NY	10-12 Videos	SUNY-Albany, NY	Italian
Charles Ferroni	Ashland, OH	30	Ashland College	Italian

Table 21 (Continued)

Person or Project	Place of Interview	No. of Interviews	Present Location	Major Ethnic Group(s)
John J. Fox	Lynn, MA	50	Salem, MA	Multi-cultural
Friends of Ellis Island	Bronx, NY	30-40	Bronx, NY	Jewish
Lawrence D. Geller	Plymouth, MA		Plymouth, MA	Portuguese
Greater Cleveland Ethn. Museum	Cleveland, OH	94	Cleveland, OH	Jewish, Italian, Greek, Hungarian, Slovak, Scand.
Immigration Ethnic Archives, Jednota	Middletown, PA	57	Middledown, PA	Slavic
Immigration Ethnic Archive	San Francisco CA	57	Sonoma State University	Danish, Italian
Immigration Voyages	MA		Northeastern University	Italian, Portuguese
Indiana Univ.	Gary, IN		Indiana Univ., Gary, IN.	Multi-cultural
Institute on Pluralism and Group Identity	New York City NY	225	New York City NY	Jewish, Italian Slavic
Italians in Chicago South	Chicago, IL	100	Chicago, IL	Italian
Corinna A. Krause	Pittsburgh, PA	225	New York	Jewish, Italian, Slavic
Salvatore La Gumina	New York, NY	12	Staten Island NY	Italian
LDS Church Archives	UT		Salt Lake City UT	Multi-cultural
Latvian Heritage Foundation	MA	1,000 (radio)	Jamaica Plain MA	Latvian
Gary Mormino	St. Louis, MO Tampa, FL	20-28 25	Univ of. So. Florida	Italian
Minn. Hist. Society	Minneapolis, MN	600	St. Paul, MN	Norwegians, Danish Swedish, Finnish, Jewish
Multicultural Hist. Soc. of Ontario	Toronto	Thousands	Toronto, ONT	Over 50

Table 21 (Continued)

Person or Project	Place of Interview	No. of Interviews	Present Location	Major Ethnic Group(s)
Festival Bostonian	Boston, MA	50-100	Boston, MA	Multi-cultural
Alixa Naff	U.S.		Washington, D.C.	Syrians
Nat. Council of Jewish Women	Pittsburgh, PA	168	University of Pittsburgh	Jewish
National Park Service	U.S.	260	Statue of Liberty	Italian, Russian English,Hungarian Polish
Nebraska State Hist. Soc.	Lincoln, NE		Lincoln, NE	Scandinavian
New York State Dept. of Education	NY		Albany, NY	Italian
New Jersey Hist. Comm.	NJ	1,500	Trenton, NJ	Jewish, Italian
Norwegian-Amer. Hist. Assoc.			St. Olaf College	Norwegian
NYC Board Of Education	NY		New York	Italian, Jewish
Remigio Pane	NJ		Library Rutgers Univ.	Italian
Polish Nat. Alliance	Chicago, IL	140	Chicago Hist. Society	Polish
George Pozzetta	Gainsville, FL	25-30	Univ. of Florida	Italian
Purdue Univ.	Calumet, IN	130	Dept. of Education	Italian
Rl Jewish Historical Association	Rl		Providence, Rl	Jewish
Stephen Ross	Bridgeport, CT	25	Univ., CT	Hungarian
Carmella Santoro	Rl			Italian
Vincenza (Jean) Scarpaci	Baltimore, MD		Personal Collection	Jewish, Italian, Polish
Maxine Sellers	Buffalo, NY		SUNY-Buffalo NY	Women

Table 21 (Continued)

Person or Project	Place of Interview	No. of Interviews	Present Location	Major Ethnic Group(s)
Dena Shenk	St. Cloud, MN	16	St. Cloud, MN	Lebanese
Roger D. Simon	Bethlehem Steel, PA	16	Lehigh Univ.	Slovak
Kenneth Smemo	Minnesota	100	Moorhead State Univ.	Scandinavian
Smithsonian Institute	Washington, D.C.	300	Washington, D.C.	Multi-cultural
State Dept. of Educ.	Albany, NY		Albany, NY	Multi-cultural
M. Mark Stolarik	Bethlehem, PA	25	Lehigh Univ.	Slovak
Edward F. Sundberg	U.S.	450	Luther College, Iowa	Scandinavian
Joseph Svoboda	NE	50	Univ. of Nebraska Lincoln, NE	Czechoslovakian
Ukranian Workingmen's Assocation	PA		Scranton, PA	Ukranian
University of Maryland	MD		SUNY, Albany NY	Eastern and Southern Europeans
Utah State Historical Society	UT	41	Logan, UT	Scandinavian
Bela Vassady	Elizabethtown, PA		Harrisburg, PA	Hungarian
Vermont Dept. of Education	VT		Barre, VT	Multi-cultural
Western Hist. Manus. Coll.	St. Louis, MO	120	St. Louis, MO	German, Irish, Polish, Jewish, Italian
Bruce Weston	California, PA	80	California State College	Slavic
Wisconsin Jewish Archives	WI		Madison, WI	Jewish
YIVO Institute	Farmingdale, NJ	116	New York City NY	Jewish
Finnish-American Hist. Archives	Hancock, MN		Suomi College	Finnish

CHAPTER VIII:

ELLIS ISLAND AND THE SEARCH FOR ROOTS

The American Bicentennial was a spectacular binge of patriotism, of celebration with rockets, firework, tall ships and a regaining of national pride. But it was also the death of the "melting pot" idea and the revival (if it ever died) of ethnicity in the United States.[1] With good reason, Michal Novak called the 1970's the "Decade of the Ethnics."[2]

The Bicentennial was the crest of a flood of books, articles and research papers on the role of ethnicity. As we approached 1976, many states created commissions to develop themes for this celebration. In nearly all cases, the themes involved ethnic aspects of American life. The Bicentennial coincided also with the search for identity and personal origins. Americans reclaimed the heritage that was submerged in the drive toward assimilation and Americanization.

Ellis Island is an important stopping place in the search for the past, because it was the place where immigrants first stepped on American soil, and because its records are the records that many seek to recover. The search for identity is an antidote to the ills of the past, and at the same time it is an expression of the security of a mature population.

Ellis Island is also the place where immigrants were thrown into a strange country, with strange customs, a difficult language and where many found their names misspelled as they began their conquest of barriers to a better life. At Ellis Island they were forced to leave their culture behind them, to destroy their past and to make it on America's terms. Now they are retracing those steps to recover

---

[1] Professor Jamer Potter of the London School of Economics suggests that "salad bowl" is a better term to explain American society than "melting pot", because each component retains its identity but mixes in its way.

[2] The Rise of the Unmeltable Ethnics (New York: Macmillan, 1975).

some of that identity. As it turned out, the melting pot was just warmed over and the homogenization process was incomplete. Glazer and Moynihan stated flatly that the "melting pot did not happen."[3]

In place of the melting pot, we find a new sense of ethnic awareness, and Ellis Island is an integral part of the new trend. For Novak, it is a rebellion against "The Bleaching of America," against WASP ideals and Anglo-Saxon Americanism. As he said, "Jews were the model, and Blacks were the catalyst." It was in response to the "Black is Beautiful" theme that other ethnics began to revive dormant cultural traits, that were manifest in the formation of associations, the holding of festivals, the search for roots. And so it was that for many genealogy leapt to the front of the movement.

One can get an idea of the true scope of American ethnicity by analyzing the *Harvard Encyclopedia of American Ethnic Groups*, which was produced from 16,000 card items covering 110 categories of ethnic groups.[4] Two-thirds of the project was federally financed (the National Endowment for the Humanities); one-third came from the Rockefeller Foundation. In addition to group entries, the Encyclopedia is cross-referenced and indexed, and it includes maps and glossary of key terms and concepts. The entire project was under the supervision of Dr. Stephan Thernstrom, with Ann Orlov as managing editor. For Ellis Island purposes, this Encyclopedia tells us more than we need to know about ethnic groups, but it points to the difficulty one encounters in trying to define an ethnic group.

GENEALOGICAL RESOURCES

---

[3]Nathan Glazer and Daniel P. Moynihan, Beyond the Melting Pot. (Cambridge: Harvard University Press, 1965).

[4]Harvard Encyclopedia of American Ethnic Groups(Cambridge: Harvard University Press, 1980).

Searching in Washington

There are many genealogical resources in Washington, D. C. to aid those who want to know from whence they came. The search should properly start at the National Archives or one of its branches. The Archives has a recorded message about services which it provides. Information is available about population censuses, military records and passenger arrival lists by port. It has guides for beginners: *Getting Started: Beginning Your Genealogical Research in the National Archives* (800 Pennsylvania Ave. N. W., Washington, D. C. 20408). There is also the *Guide to Genealogical Research in the National Archives.*

The National Archives and the Board for Certification of Genealolgist will search a family history for a fee. (PO Box 19165, Washington, D. C. 20036) The Board's fee is considerably higher, running about $7 to $25 per hour.

Because Ellis Island opened in 1892, Census records are a limited Resource. Nearly 99 percent of the records of the 1890 Census was destroyed by fire in 1921. The 1900 and 1910 years are available to the public, but the 1920 Census will not be opened until 1992. For 1900 and after, the Census if available on Soundex--this is the method of grouping all names that sound alike, regardless of their spelling.

The Library of Congress has a major collection of genealogy and local history. It has many family histories, but most are of families that have a long history in the United States, and it is not very useful for families seeking Ellis Island roots.

The Daughters of the American Revolution (DAR) specializes in local history. It has many family and town histories and it did considerable work in recording information from tombstones.

The Heartstone Bookshop is the only bookstore in the Washington D. C. area that is devoted entirely to genealogy and local history (Potomac Square, 8405-H Richmond Highway, Alexandria, VA 22309). It supplies genealogical software and search services.

"Genealogical Computing" is a newsletter on computer

applications for genealogy. It is published by Data Transfer Associates, Fairfield, VA 22032.

Searching Elsewhere

It is important to know the name of the ship that brought your ancestor. For this purpose, the Morton Allen directory is essential: *Directory of European Passenger Steamship Arrivals for the Years 1890 to 1930 at the Port of New York and for the Years 1904 to 1926 at Ports of New York, Philadelphia, Boston and Baltimore,* (New York: Immigration Information Bureau, 1931). *Ships of our Ancestors,* by Michael J. Anuta is also useful, as well as *Lloyd's Index.* The former shows hundreds of photographs and drawings of ships for the 19th and 20th centuries, and the latter gives information on ownership and construction of vessels.

The Church of Jesus Christ of Latter Day Saints (Mormon) has the largest genealogical library in the world. Much of this information can be researched in one of its 800 family history centers in the United States. The Mormons offer many genealogical aids. Its *Genealogical Helper* (Everton Publishers, PO Box 368, Logan, Utah, assists in locating members of the same family.

If one wishes to search for roots in earnest, then membership in a genealogical society is required. The Genealogy Club of America was formed in 1974 for "People who are serious about discovering their heritage." It offers discounts on searches, books and histories and genealogy tours. Its address is 420 S. 425th West, Bountiful, Utah 84010. Another society is the Federation of Genealogical Societies (PO Box 2307, Olathe, Kansas 66061). This Federation is centered in Missouri and Kansas and offers many of the same services as the Genealogy Club of America.

AN ANNOTATED BIBLIOGRAPHY

The single best source of genealogical information comes from the Genealogical Publishing Co., Inc., located at 1001 North Calvert St., Baltimore, Md. 21202. A good "how-to" book is Harriet Stryker-

Rodda, *How to Climb Your Family Tree* (1983). It introduces the beginner to Census records, church records and birth, marriage and death records. Another beginning book is William Dollarhide, *Managing a Genealogical Project* (1988). It emphasizes organizing research: how good notetaking minimizes research time. He compares the various methods of numbering descendants, and he covers the growing importance of computers in genealogy. Dollarhide also collaborated with William Thorndale to produce a *Map Guide to the U. S. Censuses, 1790-1920.*

Val D. Greenwood provided an all-purpose reference: *The Researcher's Guide to American Genealogy* (1983). He interprets records as to their genealogical importance. Although less useful for Ellis Island immigrants than for older immigrants, Finding Your Roots, produced by the Staff of Action for Independent Maturity (Washington, D.C., 1982) is a good "Beginners Guide to Genealogy." It includes lists of official records, places to search, research tips and forms for searching family histories. The "Genealogical Research, Methods and Sources," published by the American Society of Genealogist, is available in most libraries. One can learn of current and inactive family organizations and family periodicals devoted to surnames by contacting the National Index of Family Associations and Periodicals, Chino, California, (91710).

GENEALOGY BY ETHNIC GROUPS

The data shown in Table 22 are for the years up to 1948, long after Ellis Island immigration had peaked. It presents immigration by nationality for the leading ethnic groups. In this section, we offer some genealogical sources for some of these groups.

German Genealogical Society of America

Anmyone seeking German ancestors should begin with Angus Baxter, *In search of Your German Roots* (Baltimore: Genealogical Publishing Co, 1987). Next communicate with the German Genealogical Society of America. This German Society, located in

Los Angeles, was organized in 1986 to help members to trace their roots. The GGSA's library of German books and manuscripts is located at 1420 N. Claremont Boulevard, Claremont, California. The Society will search its indices, the Index of the Genealogical Society of Utah and German telephone directories. To obtain a Research Request Form, write to GGSA, PO Box 291818, Los Angeles, CA 90029.

The Immigrant Genealogical Society is also a German Society. It was formed in 1981 to promote research in the United States and Germany. Elisabeth, an American, and Gerda Haffner, a German, were the original founders. A committee--The Genealogical Exchange Group--handles questions pertaining to roots. The Society publishes a newsletter--"Immigrant Library" which disseminates results of genealogical searches. It has a library at 5043 Lankershim Boulevard, North Hollywood, CA 91601.

Preserving Italian Heritage

The Italian Genealogical Society was established in 1988 by Dr. Thomas E. Militello, of Rancho Palos Verdes, California. His magazine *POINTers*, an acronym for Pursuing Our Italian Names Together, 6 is a computerized data base of 6,000 Italian surnames from 800 persons in 46 states and several foreign countries. The names represent 850 Italian cities and towns, as well as those from France, Corsica, Gibraltar, Greece, Spain, Switzerland, and Russia.

According to Jayare Roberts, of the Family History Library of Salt Lake City, 7,300,000 new pages of documents from Italy were added to the Library in 1988. There are 475,000 births and marriages listed in the "International Genealogical Index," which may be researched in Salt Lake City. The new acquisitions were obtained from Italian state archives. Most of these records are for the years 1809 to 1865, but some go to 1900. The largest number were for the following locations: Palermo--1150 rolls, Campobasso--1,000 rolls, Cosenza--885 rolls, Bari--625 rolls, Catania--545 rolls, Siracusa--490 rolls and Benevento--375 rolls.

Table 22

NUMBER of IMMIGRANTS by NATIONALITY

1850-1948

Nationality	Number Admitted
Germans	6,064,653
Jews	5,000,000
Italians	4,752,735
Irish	4,597,429
Russians	3,300,000
Polish	2,905,859
Swedes	1,200,000
Czechoslovakian	1,000,000
Hungarians	662,068
French	624,561
Norwegians	800,000
Greeks	434,418
Yugoslavians	383,393
Dutch	372,384
Danish	338,085
Finnish	284,240
Romanians	158,208
TOTAL	32,888,033

Source: "The Immigration and Naturalization Systems of the U.S.," 81st Cong. Senate Report 1515, Apr. 20, 1950.

Joseph G. Fucilla revised his 1949 study of *Our Italian Surnames* in 1987, also by Genealogical Publishing Co. It is the most comprehensive analysis of Italian names ever done.

Polish Genealogical Sources

There are Polish research facilities in Poland and in the United States. The Polish Surname Network advertises surnames in major genealogical magazines and periodicals and with Polish societies.

At the same time, a Name Bank was set up in 1989 by the Genealogicval Research Center in Pultusk, north of Warsaw. It promises to help Polish-Americans to find their Polish roots. Information is available by writing: Osrodek Badan Genealogicznych "PIAST," UL. Zaulek 22, Pultusk, Poland.

Croatian Genealogical Society.

Some information about Croatians who passed through Ellis Island may be contained in the many records of the Croatian Genealogical Society, which collects church, cemetery, birth, death, marriage, naturalization, passenger, and other records of Croatians in the United States. It is affiliated with the Slavic-American Society. The Croatian archives contain over 120,000 names on 3 x 5 cards. The Society, which is San Carlos, California, also has a publication program with the Ragusan Press.

Slovak Genealogy

The Czechoslovak Genealogy Society, of St. Paul, Minnesota, publishes a newsletter, "Nase Rodina," and it collects maps and family histories for research. Write to Box 16225, St. Paul, Minnesota 55116.

The 1928 Census of Hungary, which included Slovakia, lists heads of households and other information concerning Slovak families.

Irish Genealogy

A good starting point for this search is Angus Baxter, *In Search of Your British and Irish Roots* (Baltimore: Genealogical Publishing Co., 1989). Irish-Americans can search their roots in the United States or in Ireland through the Ancient Order of Hibernians, the oldest Irish-American organization. Its Irish address is Hibernian Research Company, Ltd., 22 Windsor Rd, Dublin 6 Ireland. The Irish Genealogical Society will help Irish-Americans find their Irish ancestors for a $15 fee.

Tracing Your Welsh Ancestors

If your family emigrated from Wales, there is available to you Registers of births, marriages and deaths for each county since 1875. There are also copies in the National Library of Wales, Aberystwth, Dyfed SY23 3BU. The Association of Family History Societies of Wales, Pen Lon, Menai Bridge, Gwyneded 5LW., is willing to search records for those unable to get to Wales. In addition, The Association of Genealogists and Record Agents, 64 Oakleigh Park North, London N209 9AU, has a list of experienced researchers.

Additional Search Helps

For those tracing their Slovak roots, they may order the "Slovak Genealogy Research Kit" from Ray Plutko, 16455 E. Prentece Place, Aurora, Colorada 80015. Norwegians may contact the Rowberg File at St. Olaf College Library, Northfield, MN 55057 which is a collection of obituaries from 1914 to 1970. A standard reference on Scottish genealogy is Gerald Hamilton-Edwards, *In Search of your Scottish Ancestry* (Baltimore: Genealogical Publishing Co., 1986).

For those who want to purchase a family registry and crest, Halbert's will research your name and provide a personalized registry. It claims to have researched "100 million names or records in Europe, Canada, the United States and Australia." Their address is: 3699 Ira Rd, Bath, Ohio 44210.

Some Ethnic Centers

The Ohio Ethnic Center

The Ohio Historical Society, like most of its counterparts in other states, was concerned chiefly with historic sites, museums in rural areas and gathering the histories of important citizens of the States until very recently. All this changed in the 1970's. In 1971, the Western Reserve Historical Society established the Cleveland Regional Ethnic Archives. This included a large number of pamphlets, books and photographs which are now inventoried in a *Guide to the Ethnic Pictorial Resources of the Western Reserve Historical Society.*

In June, 1974, the Ohio General Assembly approved the establishment of a branch of the Ohio Historical Society in Cleveland. There followed the creation of the Urban Museum in downtown Cleveland. The Greater Cleveland Ethnographic Museum acquired artifacts and documents to represent all facets of the Ohio heritage. At the same time, several ethnic authorities began meeting at John Carroll University to discuss the formation of an academic organization. The Ethnic Heritage Studies Act of 19T2, provided funds for the establishment of a program for Cleveland. Dr. Lubomyr Wynar was its first president and Dr. Karl Bonutti was one of the two vice-presidents, Wynar is director of the Center for Study of Ethnic Publications at Kent State University. He has published numerous guides to ethnic museums, archives and libraries. Particularly important are his *Encycopedic Directory of Ethic Organizations* (Littleton, 1975), and his guide *Guide to Ethic Museums, Archives and Libraries* (1978). Bonutti served as director of the Ethnic Heritage Studies Series -- a list of 16 studies of ethnic groups.

The Wayne State Folklore Archive.

The Wayne State University Folklore Archive is a part of the Department of English, Professor Janet Langlois, director.

The Archive has been collecting ethnic information since 1939, and it now provides annotated lists of these materials. The first list in 1977 was an Afro-American inventory. The second one, which is important for Ellis Island, is the "Polish and Polish American Folklore Collection," 1978. Also of importance is the Wayne State Ethnic Heritage Committee, formed in 1973.

The Wayne State Archive contains approximately 3,250 collections, with analysis made by professional collectors. Other holdings include student studies and commercial recordings. Some of the materials are restricted under limitations imposed by the donors. A brochure describes the many ethnic newsletters, newspapers and other ethnic material. Included in the Wayne State holdings are the "Asian Folklore Studies Group Newsletter," "Jewish Folklore and Ethnology Newsletter," "Finnish Center Association Newsletter," and "Curiosita."

Chicago's Ethnic Museums

Chicago is the home of several ethnic museums, and these often are located in the communities where the ethnic group first settled. The most famous of these is the Polish Museum of America, the oldest ethnic museum in Chicago, which began in 1937, and the Archives and Museums of the Polish Roman Catholic Union of America. The main exhibit hall contains items such as costumes, utensils, dolls and woodcarvings. It also has an art gallery and library.

The Maurice Spertus Museum of Judaica, at 618 South Michigan Avenue, contains an important collections of gold, silver, bronze, textiles, scrolls and other ethnic materials spanning many years of Jewish History. It also houses the only holocaust museum of its kind in the United States.

The Italian Cultural Center, which was opened in May, 1970, offers programs of Italian immigration. It is a unique collection of artistic and historical objects relating to Italian-Americans.

The oldest ethnic artifacts and documents in Chicago may be found at Jane Addams' Hull House on the Chicago River. Between 1908 and 1963, there was a 13-building complex on that location, but only two of the original houses survive. These are now the focal point of a varied ethnic collection.

Ethnic doings in Maryland

Professor Jean (Vincenza) Scarpaci, formerly of Towson State University, compiled a bibliography of ethnic experiences in Maryland, which was sponsored by the Maryland Bicentennial Commission. This effort began in a series of courses at Towson State, where persons doing oral or family history were encouraged to do research and to deposit their materials with area historical agencies. Participants were asked also to contribute to the bibliography which Professor Scarpaci compiled. Although this is called a Maryland ethnic experience, a considerable part of the bibliography deals with Baltimore and vicinity. After compiling "the ethnic experience of Maryland," Professor Scarpaci worked on *Ambiente Italiano: Origins and Growth of Baltimore's Little Italy.*

The Oklahoma Image Project

Oklahoma Image was sponsored by the Oklahoma Department of Libraries deals toexamine the impact of Europeans and other groups on the state's heritage. An important part of the Image project was the booklet series, edited by Dr. H. Wayne Morgan, of the Department of History of the University of Oklahoma. Ten titles were included in the project, reflecting the ethnic history of ten different groups. Included in this "Newcomers to a New Land" series are the immigrant experiences of Germans, Russians, Poles, Jews, Czechs, Italians and British.

CHAPTER IX:

FILMS, PHOTOS AND VISUALS

There is a surprisingly large body of visual information about Ellis Island. It too is scattered geographically. In this chapter, the films, photos, slides, drawings and sculptures are described and located.

EARLY SILENT FILMS AND DOCUMENTARIES

When motion pictures were developed in the 1890s, photographers turned to immigrant life as subject matter. Although these early films were very brief, they have historic value. One of the earliest is the 3-minute film of scenes of the New York City ghetto fish market by Thomas Edison completed in 1903. Also, in 1903, the American Mutoscope and Biograph Company produced a 2-minute film entitled, "Emigrants Landing at Ellis Island." In 1906, Thomas Edison produced another 3-minute film of "Arrival of Emigrants, Ellis Island." The United States Bureau of the Mines in 1913 produced an 18-minute documentary entitled "An American in the Making," which shows the lives of immigrants from south-central Europe who went to work in the Gary, Indiana steel mills.

A very early fiction film is "Fights of Nations," produced in 1907 and lasting ten minutes. In 1916, Samuel Goldwyn produced a 15-minute film, "Hungry Hearts," depicting the story of a Russian Jewish family that emigrated to New York City. But by far the most popular immigration film of its time was the 25-minute movie featuring Charlie Chaplin as a young immigrant who meets Edna, also an immigrant, aboard ship in steerage. Another famous immigration film is the 70-minute "My Boy," produced in 1921 and featuring Jackie Coogan, who plays a young immigrant boy who is detained on Ellis Island because his mother died during the Atlantic crossing. The plight of immigrant girls is shown in the film, "Mariana," a 1915 film by Carl Laemmle. In this 15-minute film, an immigrant Italian girl in the tenements of New York City falls victim to prostitution. A 1920 silent film, "Astray From the Steerage," was produced by Mack Sennett. In this film, we are given the immigrant's view of the United States. The film is somewhat incredible and approaches surrealism. A copy is currently at the Museum of Modern Art in New York City.

THE NEWS COMPANIES

The most important films of Ellis Island activities were those from the five news companies: these include Movietone News, Pathe News, Paramount News, Hearst Metrotone News, and Universal News. There are also film libraries and museums which have material of Ellis Island. The John Allen Company of Park Ridge, New Jersey, has a film of immigration, of the ferryboat and of the east side of New York. The Sherman Grinberg Library of New York City has early footage also.

Hearst Metrotone News produced a motion picture about Ellis Island entitled, "The Golden Door." The film was part of an award-winning educational series, *The Screen News Digest*, and makes much use of motion picture archives which depict the arrival of early American immigrants.

The Hearst Metronome Newsreels are part of the UCLA archives. This archives includes 12,000 film titles, 20,000 radio scripts and 40,000 television programs. In 1982, materials from RKO General were added to the UCLA collection. The RKO collection was catalogued after 1958, when the studios closed, by Vernon Harbin, who worked there for 50 years.

MORE RECENT FILMS

As far as we have been able to determine, only one Hollywood movie was ever made on Ellis Island. It was entitled, "Gateway," and it starred Don Ameche, Arlean Whelan, Gregory Ratoff, Vinnie Barnes, Gilbert Roland, John Carradine, and Harry Carey. The *New York Times* Film Review for August 10, 1938, called the film, "mildly ridiculous." This, it said, was due to the armed riot which the film depicts of persons about to be deported in the final scene.

In 1967, McGraw-Hill produced a film called, "The Island Called Ellis," which was a recreation of how immigrants were processed on the Island and what happened to them as they moved on. The film was narrated by Jose Ferrer. It included a number of still photographs and much footage of the Island. Another film showing the Ellis Island experience is "The Uprooted." This British documentary shows the tremendous cost of immigration to America--the social and cultural dislocations, the rootlessness, and the stresses on the family and the individual. It includes many excellent photographs by Jacob Riis. Another film, by the Anti-Defamation League of B'nai B'rith, was produced for the New York World's Fair of 1964-65. It attempts to convey to non-Americans the uniqueness of The United States as a nation of immigrants. The film tends to gloss over many of the problems immigrants faced in their entry and in their integration into American life, but this may be because of the popular audience for which it was intended.

The CBS television production of "To America" in 1976 showed three families escaping from eastern Europe for the United States. In this film, Allen Arkin plays an old man on Ellis Island. It emphasizes the refugee aspect of Jewish history. The "America" series, narrated by Alistair Cooke, shows in Episode 9, "The Huddled Masses," scenes of Ellis Island, ships and the lower east side.

The NBC Special "Life, Liberty and the Pursuit of Happiness," and the Public Broadcasting System series, "Connection," narrated by E. G. Marshall, addressed the inteconnections between isolated events in history. In one segment, Marshall related the connection between the use of punch cards and computers and the processing system on Ellis Island.

The National Archives sponsored several series of films that reflect the difficulties and the successes of America's immigrants. Between June 1 and July 21, 1978, there were films shown on "Changing Images: Ethnic Americans on Film." Of particular importance in this series is "The Journey: Old World, New World." This 52-minute film tells the story of 35 million Europeans who left their troubled homelands for the promise of freedom and opportunity, and it shows the hardships of the trans-atlantic voyage they endured to reach America. It was part of the "Destination America Series" produced by Thames Television in 1977. Another film in the same series was called "The Italians: A Place in the Sun," a 52-minute film on the struggles of the five million Italians who immigrated to the United States. While many were poorly-paid laborers, some found America the land of opportunity, particularly in California. Another film in this series is "The Poles: City of the Big Shoulders," a 52-minute film focusing on Polish immigrants who were the driving force behind Chicago's industrial growth. There are currently 1 million Polish-Americans living in Chicago and they make up one-third of the city's population. This film discusses their social and economic contributions to America.

Between September 5 and December 28, 1975, the National Park Service presented a series of films in the Statue of Liberty Auditorium on "Portraits of Immigrant Life, 1902-1975."

There have been countless movies which have shown scenes of Ellis Island, including "Godfather II." An AFL Film, "The Inheritance," tells the story of labor history in the twentieth century; it contains scenes of Ellis Island and of immigration. A PBS special of March 7, 1986, "Irving Berlin's America," showed scenes of Ellis Island and the Lower East Side of Manhattan, where Berlin lived after he landed from Ellis Island.

"Journey to America"--a part of the PBS series, "The American Experience," contained much about the journey to America and the processing at Ellis Island. It was broadcast on December 12, 1989.

Some films were produced as part of the Ethnic Heritage Studies Program. One such project was the television series, "The Immigrant--Journey to America," produced by the State Univeristy of New York at Albany from September 1979 to December 1980. The series documents (through first person, narrative accounts) the experiences of a selected number of Eastern, Central and Southern Europeans who immigrated to this nation early in the century. To give the series additional scope, the experiences of relatively-recent immigrants have been included as well.

Each of the three parts is approximately one half hour in length and treats individual themes and issues. Part One, "First Contact," documents the motives for immigrating to the United States, the hardships and difficulties initially faced by the newcomers. Documents, personal photographs, film footage and location footage were incorporated into the series.[1]

Lubomyr R. Wynar and Lois Buttelar produced a companion volume to their 1977 "Building Ethnic Collections" that is the most comprehensive guide to films and film strips. Their *Ethnic Films and Filmstrip Guide for Libraries and Media Centers: A Selective Filmography*" (Littleton Libraries Unlimited, 1983) represents 46 individual ethnic groups and annotates 1,400 titles. Their survey includes film producers, distributors, editors and organizations.

OTHER VISUALS

Photos, Slides and Cassettes

The National Archives and Records Administration has a "Still Pictures Division," which has some photographs of the public health service and hospital activities on Ellis Island (Record Group 90). Considering the volume of traffic that went through the inspection process, these holdings are rather small.

There is a very large collection of photos of Ellis Island at the Statue of Liberty Museum, which were taken by chief clerk Augustus E. Sherman from 1902 to 1925. These photos are excellent and not found elsewhere; they number about 1,000 photos. The International Museum of Photography at the George Eastman House in Rochester New York, includes 500,000 photographs, including photos of Ellis Island immigrants from the 1920's to the 1940's. Another good source of Ellis Island photographs is the Lewis W. Hine collection. He is best remembered for his very powerful photographs of immigrants arriving at Ellis Island in the early decades of this century

---

[1] This information was provided by Professor Frank Femminella, the project director.

and their lives in the New York tenements. These photographs resulted from his work with the National Child Labor Committee from 1908 to 1930. This explains his emphasis on child labor, dangerous machines, and impoverished families.

Other locations in New York City contain Ellis Island photographs. One is the "Calendar of William Williams collection of photographs of Ellis Island" prepared by Joseph Halpern for the New York Public Library. The library also includes duplicates of some of the Hine photos, especially in Unit 1 "Immigration, 1905-1939." The Museum of the City of New 1ork has the Jacob Riis Papers of 1910, which includes photographs and slides of immigrants. Also in New York, the UPl and AP have archives that include early photos, especialiy "Wide World Photos" of the Associated Press.

The New York Historical Society, Central Park West and 7th St., has a collection of photos in its Print Department. which were purchased from Alexander Alland, The North Salem Galley, North Salem, New York. The prints are predominantly of the early twentieth century. *The New York Times* sells old photos from past issues, if proper credit is given. Many of its pictures were taken from the AP and UP Wire Services. The Times imposes a $25 search fee in addition to the cost of the photograph.

Francis J. Duffy, who teaches an immigration course at the New School of Social Research, has an extensive collection of contemporary photos of Ellis Island, most taken since 1913. He also has a slide presentation, including some of the photos of the Augustus E. Sherman collection.

The Terence V. Powderly collection of negatives at the Catholic Univeristy of America is excellent. They were developed by Professor Thad Jones of the School of Music. under a grant from the National Historic Publications and Records Commission. and they are available to the public for a modest charge.

Powderly was a very talented amateur photographer. He produced several thousand glass and nitrate-based negatives and glass lantern slides. The Catholic University Archives, under a grant from the

National Endowment for the Humanities, transferred the images to safety film. A card index gives ready access to the collection. Powderly, a meticulous record keeper recorded the camera type, shutter speed, and f-stops on many of his negative jackets, and he usually gave some information on the subjects of his photographs. One expert stated that, "Powderly was a photographer of uncommon skill and professionalism." Powderly's immigration photographs record his trips through Europe, immigrants on ships, Ellis Island structures, and persons landing on the Island.

Brown Brothers, of Sterling, Pennsylvania, has one of the best collections of still photographs of immigration history. These include the buildings on the Island, the physical examination, the intelligence test, the waiting room and various nationality costumes. According to a representative of the company, "they have so many photos that they can't catalogue them."[2]

Albert Carcieri, of Cranston, Rhode Island has a collection of slides dating from 1880-1910. They include Russian, Jewish, Polish, Irish, Italian, German and Greek immigrants, mostly in the New York City area. His collection also includes 3" x 4" glass plate negatives of Ellis Island buildings and ships from many countries. These slides and photographs were produced by Dewitt C. Wheeler, 51 West 28th St., New York; Walter L. Isaacs Co., 36 East 23rd St., New York; and Charles Beseler, Lantern Slide Co., Inc., 131 East 23rd St., New York. Thomas Bernadin, of New York City, who served as a National Park Service Ranger for three years, also has a slide-lecture program of Ellis Island that has been presented on the Island and in the New York City region.

Prentice-Hall Media has available filmstrips, cassettes and recordings of immigrants. In particular, it has produced "The Immigrants, 1870-1917," and "Immigration: The Dream and the Reality." These deal with the flight of Europeans to the U.S., the

---

[2]Telephone conversation with the author, August 7, 1981.

disparities in life slyles and the constant hardship.

In a related source, Prof. John Appell of Michigan State University, and his wife, are collectors of cartoons and caricatures dealing with emigrants and immigration. The Appels have put together a 60-slide casette, including detailed lecture notes, called "The Distorted Image" concerning the stereotypes of the immigrants and ethnics. These may be obtained from the Anti-Defamation League of B'nai B'rith in New York City. Professor Louis Giansante, of the New York School for Social Research, produced a 3/4" videocasette, "Return to Ellis Island," to celebrate the centennial of St. Finbar's Church in Brooklyn. Men, women and children of the parish played the roles of immigrants, officials, medical personnel and social workers. The tape includes intewiews of persons who recalled their experiences of sixty years earlier.

Microfilms and Reprints

There are several hundred volumes on immigration now available from the Arno Press and the R & E Research Associates, of San Fransisco. Arno also has reprints Irish-American, Italian-American, Scandinavian-American, and Jewish-American books. In addition, Xerox University Microfilms has catalogues of unpublished masters and doctoral dissertations concerning immigration. There is a guide to these microfilms: *National Register of Microfilm Masters*, Library of Congress, 1965-.

Ellis Island Drawings

The Denver Service Center of the National Park Service has a computerized Drawings Index System which includes all types of architectural and engineering drawings (and related textual records) pertaining to the construction of buildings on Ellis Island. These documents were stored in one of the buildings on Ellis Island and had been abandoned with the structure. This collection includes renderings, tracings and prints; bound volumes of records and construction catalogs. The original drawings have been put on microfilm by the National Park Service and they are catalogued.

Mr. Set Momjian, a director of the Ellis Island Restoration Commission, collected some paintings done by a woman in the 1920's, who was with the Metropolitan Opera Company and who had some association with Ellis Island. She returned to the Island and did the paintings, some of which were exhibited in the nation's Capital and in the Balch Institute in Philadelphia.

The WPA Murals

One important result of the Ellis Island beautification process during the era of the New Deal was the approval in March, 1935, of a series of murals to be painted on the walls of the Administration Building's dining hall. The murals were painted by Edward Laning with the assistance of Doria Kravis, Herman Rose, Louis Nisonoff and Joseph Soloman. The twenty-four panels, together measuring twenty-five hundred square feet, depicted the immigrant's role in America's industrial development.

They were given to Ellis Island by Audrey McMahon, Director of the WPA project in New York. These Federal Arts Project murals portrayed immigrants at work in coal mines, steel mills, lumber camps, and railroad manufacture. (Some of the surviving panels are presented in Figure 31.)[3]

Through the efforts of the General Services Administration this long-neglected prize was restored in the early 1970's. GSA administrator, Robert L. Kunzig directed the work on the art collection containing over one hundred thousand pieces. He assigned Karel Yasko the project of locating the treasures and Hiram H. Hoelze; a New York restorer, the task of restoring the only remaining Ellis Island mural. The mural was covered with rice paper and removed

---

[3]New York Times, February 25, 1938, p. 13

Figure 31   The Láning Mural

from the wall for restoration.[4] It now hangs in the Federal Courthouse on Cadman Plaza in Brooklyn, New York.

The entire restoration process was filmed by John Korty Film Co., of Mill Valley, California. Korty received a grant from the National Endowment for the Arts to make a 15 minute, 35-mm film of the restoration, and he also conducted a lengthy oral interview with Edward Laning during the process.[5]

Sketches and Sculptures

Phillip Ratner, the Washington D.C. Sculptor, whose grandparents came to Ellis Island from Kiev. interpreted Ellis Island history through three sets of statues: he created eight four-foot sculptures, thirty-two eighteen inch pieces and five life-like statues.

Ratner began his Ellis Island fascination by drawing immigrant scenes from old photos, but he did not become officially involved in the Ellis Island project until he described these sketches to Eleanor Sreb, of the American Folklife Center of the Library of Congress. Sreb mentioned them to Ross Holland, formerly of the National Park Service, and in short time all three were meeting with David Moffitt. Superintendent of the Statue of Liberty National Monument, which includes Ellis Island.

Holland supported the idea of a traveling exhibit of small sculptures that would heighten interest in the restoration of the Statue of Liberty and Ellis Island. To keep traveling expenses to a minimum, Ratner created vinyl statues on steel frames that were coated with bronze powder--very lightweight and nearly indistinguishable from bronze metal. Figure 32 illustrates the size of the small sculptures.

---

[4]"WPA Art: Rescue of a U.S. Treasure," U. S. News and World Report June 21, 1971, pp. 75-8.

[5]Korty donated this film to the Ellis Island Restoration Commission in 1983.

At this point, the project grew larger. Moffitt suggested a permanent exhibit for the Statue of Liberty garden on a site that had been designated "Founders Park" in 1935. They agreed on five larger-than-life Statues of Frederic Bartholdi, the sculptor of the Statue of Liberty; Gustav Eiffel, the engineer on the project; Joseph Pulitzer, the man behind the finding process for the statue; and Emma Lazarus, whose poem gave us the famous lines "Give us your tired, your poor / your huddled masses yearning to be free." A fifth statue was added to honor the man who conceived the idea. Ratner says that "he dashed off about a thousand skeches" of immigrants for his statues, and he used 39 to make up his suites of sketches. One set was presented to President Reagan.[6]

Figure 32 Washington Sculptor Phillip Ratner, left, and August C. Bolino, With Ratner's Ellis Island statues.

---

[6]One of these sketches is on the dust jacket of this book--a sketch which represents Ratner's grandparents.

PART IV

CHAPTER X:

THE FAMOUS AND NOT SO FAMOUS ALUMNI

The story of Ellis Island can best be understood by reviewing the lives of those who went through there. Some were well known--"They made it big." Others were "lesser-known" alumni. The first part of this chapter offers brief biographical sketches of a few famous immigrants who came to that New York port. We stress the successes, because immigrants still believe that they can "make It big" in the United States. And many do. By doing this, we do not diminish the stature of the millions of "lesser-known" individuals who first encountered America at this place.

The biographies that follow are grouped by fields of achievement, which are given alphabetically.[1]

ART AND ARCHITECTURE

Arshile Gorky (1904-1948)

Ellis Island alumni are well represented in the visual arts. Gorky, the "lyrical Armenian," arrived at Ellis Island in 1920 after watching his mother starve to death after their village was overrun by the Turks. He captured the love and mourning of these episodes in his painting "Portrait of the Artist and his Mother" completed in 1926 after ten years work.

Gorky was born Vosdanig Manoog Adoian in Khorkom Vari, in Turkish Armenia on October 25, 1904. After a period of study at the Polytechnic Institute in Tblisi (Now in the USSR), he emigrated to the Unites States, and settled in Providence, Rhode Island, where he continued his studies in the Rhode Island School of Design and the New School in Boston. He also studied and taught in New York

---

[1]Biographical sketches are taken from the Dictionary of American Biography, unless otherwise noted.

City. Gorky's first show In 1932 marked him as a leading abstract expressionist in the United States. His art was influenced at first by cubism, but his later works showed a more surrealist approach. During the 1940's, he was influenced also by Vasili Kandinsky and Willem de Kooning, with whom he shared a studio. During the New Deal, he was part of the Federal Arts Project, for which he completed murals for the Newark, New Jersey airport and for the Aviation Building at the New York World's Fair in 1939.

Gorky's story did not end happily. In 1944, his studio was destroyed by fire, and in that same year he learned that he had cancer. In rapid succession he broke his neck and was paralyzed in an automobile accident, his wife left him, and he committed Suicide on July 21, 1948.[2]

Walter Gropius (1883-1967)[3]

Gropius, the founder and director of Germany's *Bauhaus* was born In Berlin, on May 18, 1883. His father, Walter, Sr., was a surveyor in a Berlin suburb. But it was his mother who often told young Walter of the long tradition of architecture and painting in the Gropius family. And so at an early age the boy decided on architecture as an occupation. After his graduation from the gymnasium, or secondary school, in 1903, he enrolled in a technical school in Munich, but he had to leave school for his required military training. When he was able to return to school, he attended the *Berlin Technische Hochschule,* an advanced technical school, from 1905 to 1907. During this period the young student designed his first buildings, In Pomerania. Upon graduating, Gropius spent some time visiting Spain, Italy, and England, and when he returned to Berlin he was appointed chief assistant to Professor Peter Behrens, his former

---

[2]H. Rosenberg, Arshile Gorky--The Man, The Time, The Idea (New York: Horizon, 1962).

[3]See Annie E. S. Beard, Our Foreign Citizens (New York: Thomas Crowell, 1968).

teacher at the *Hochschule.*

In 1910, Gropius temporarily abandoned teaching to practice architecture. He soon won several commissions. But his first fame came in the use of new building materials, including concrete, aluminum, stainless steel, and polished glass. He let these new materials speak for themselves and they spoke so well that other architects began to use the same materials and methods. This technique came to be known as the International Style. Its early exponents were Le Corbusier, Mies Van der Rohe and J. J. Oud.

Their activities were soon interrupted by World War I. Gropius was called by the German Army, and he was commissioned as a lieutenant. During the war, he was wounded and received the Mark of Distinction. In 1919, after his discharge, he was made director of the *Staatliches Bauhaus,* aimed at introducing new methods in teaching art. He set out to destroy the artist's prejudice against the use of practical objects in art. The *Bauhaus* fostered a new respect for the machine and its products. Under Gropius' direction, the *Bauhaus* attracted the foremost artists and the best craftsmen of the time. Mies Van der Rohe joined Gropius in training young architects. Internationally famous painters like Paul Klee and Vasili Kandinsky worked there, and Max Breuer, the father of modern furniture design, was on the staff.

Gropius was concerned with the human condition, so when the *Bauhaus* was taken over by the Nazis in 1934 he went into exile. He went to England first, but in 1937 he established permanent residence in the United States. He settled in Lincoln, Massachusetts and joined the Harvard University faculty as Senior Professor. He and Marcel Breuer designed a number of residences, and he also designed the Pennsylvania exhibit at the New York World's Fair of 1939. In 1947 he served as consultant to General Lucius Clay on a plan for the reconstruction of Germany. In 1953 at the age of seventy Gropius retired from the Harvard faculty, when in a new burst of creativity he designed the new University of Bagdad, the U. S. Embassy in Athens and a new housing project in West Berlin. Gropius always fought against ugliness; he railed against developers who cut down trees.

Jacques Lipchitz (1891-1973)

Jacques Lipchitz was born Chaim Jacob Lipchitz to Abraham and Rachael Lipchitz in the Lithuanian town of Druskieniki on August 2, 1891. Chaim was an indifferent student in the schoolhouse in Bialystok, but he spent much time making and painting small figures in red Clay. His father, who was a prosperous building contractor, wanted Chaim to study mechanical engineering, but despite family opposition, he was determined to be a sculptor. He set out for Paris, and there his name was changed by a French policeman, who issued him an identification card. From that time he was Jacques.

He arrived in Paris in October 1909, and he enrolled as a free student in the Ecole des Beau-arts. By this time, his father was convinced that Jacques was serious so Abraham sent him an allowance, which permitted him to enroll at the Academie Julian. He traveled all over Paris meeting other art students and teachers, but in his second year, after his father was ruined financially, Jacques moved to cheaper lodgings and supported himself by carrying vegetables at night at railroad stations. His health and financial conditions were not good, but in this period he produced his first important works ("Woman and Gazelles," (1912) and "The Encounter," (1913). When he met Modigliani, Picasso, Rivera and Gris, Jacques began to experiment with cubism. He went to Spain and produced "Girl With the Braid" (1914) and "Sailor with Guitar" (1914).

When Lipchitz returned to Paris, he spent a year doing Cubist pieces, but after 1925, he turned to his "transparents." He developed a process that allowed him to represent the luminous, using ribbons and melted wax. Two results were "The Harpist" (1930) and "The Song of the Vowels (also 1930). Lipchitz said, "I soar with this thing heavier than air."

When the Nazis were about to occupy Paris, Lipchitz fled to the south, and in 1941, he boarded the *Nyassa* for the United States. He carried a few things and one sculpture, "Flight" (1940), which was a symbol of the tragedies of war. In New York, He was forced to do portraits to survive, but in 1942, he had his first show, which established him in his new country. He accepted a unique commission for the Church of Assy in the French Alps. The statue bore the following inscription: "Jacob Lipchitz, Jew, faithful to the religion of his ancestors, has made this Virgin to foster understanding between men on earth, that the life of the spirit may prevail."

Lipchitz' style continued to change in cycles. He made semiautomatics by dipping hot wax in water and he made a number of bronzes. In 1961, he gave 300 plaster models to the American- Israel Cultural Foundation to commemorate his seventieth birthday.

BUSINESS

John W. Kluge (1914-)

John W. Kluge was born in 1914 in Chemnitz, Germany. He came to the United States with his family in 1922 and settled in Detroit. He worked briefly until he earned a scholarship to study economics at Columbia University, where he graduated in 1937.

During World War II, he became a captain in the U. S. Army, specializing in intelligence. During his military service, Kluge learned communications, so when the war ended, he started a radio station in Silver Spring, Maryland. By 1959, he and his partners had gained control of the Metropolitan Broadcasting Co., which he built into a vast communications empire. In 1960, they purchased Foster & Kleiser, a giant in the billboard industry, and in the next 20 years the company evolved into Metromedia, Inc, with Kluge as Chairman.

In 1984 Kluge celebrated his $1.2 billion leveraged buyout of Metromedia Inc. that raised his personal wealth to more than $2.5 billion. He accomplished this by selling off major components of Metromedia. The sales included Metromedia's seven television stations, eleven radio stations, the Harlem Globetrotters basketball team, the the Ice Capades, the Chalet and Foster & Kleiser. The sale of Metromedia's cellular telephone operation to Southwestern Bell

Corporation surprised everyone, because it came shortly after a Federal court decision which allowed the Bell companes to buy cellular companies outside of their regions. But Kluge cited "timing" and the right price for his decision. It was this type of bold action that made him the second richest man in the United States.

Kluge didn't retire for long. In April 1987, he began Metromedia Technologies--a company that promised to provide a computerized billboard painting system, based on a process developed after years of research by Gerber Scientific Company. The system can paint a billboard-sized sheet of coated canvas with greater clarity and color than conventional methods.

A final note on John W. Kluge: When President Reagan was searching for a Chairman of the Statue of Liberty/Ellis Island Centennial Commission, he found only two chief executive officers of major American corporations who had a connection with Ellis Island: Lee Iacocca and John Kluge.

William S. Knudsen (1879-1948)

William S. Knudsen rose to the top of the business world as President of General Motors Corporation in 1937. He had come a long way from his home in Copenhagen, Denmark, He was born Signius Wilhelm Paul Knudsen on March 5, 1879 to Knud and Augusta Knudsen and attended grammar, high and technical schools in Copenhagen. After a short apprenticeship in a bicycle shop, he emigrated to the United States in 1899.

He started at the Gas Engine & Power and Company, moved on to the Erie Railroad and finally to the John R. Klein Bicycle Manufacturing Company in Buffalo, New York, where he started as a clerk. When the Klein Company became a part of the Ford Motor Company in 1911, Knudsen became a factory manager. Two years later, he transferred to Detroit to manage Ford's twenty seven assembly plants. In 1922, General Motors employed him as a consultant and a short time later, he became Vice President of the Chevrolet Motor Company's operations, then a subsidiary of General

Motors. Under his leadership, Chevrolet surpassed Ford's production in the late nineteen twenties. As a result he was appointed Executive Vice President of General Motors, and he finally succeeded Alfred P. Sloan as President. During World War II, Roosevelt appointed him Director General of the Office of Production Management (OPM). He was responsible for the production of all war materials, and his direction encouraged many factories to set production records, which brought the war to a speedier end.

Spyros P. Skouras (1893-1971)

Spyros Skouras was born in a small village, Skourahorian, on shore of the Ionian Sea in Greece on March 28, 1893. He was one of five boys and five girls, the children of Panagiotes Skouras, a shepherd. When Spyro was 15 years old, he began to study for the priesthood and he worked as a journalist. In the evenings, he attended the school of theology, where he studied English and accounting, The five brothers pooled all of their savings to send the oldest, Charles, to the United States. He sailed in 1907. In three years, Spyros joined him in Saint Louis. Spyros worked at the old Planter's Hotel, and he spent his evenings studying English, business and law at the Jones Commercial College.

In 1914, the brothers, believing that there was growing future in the motion picture industry purchased their first theatre with their $4,000 savings. They interrupted their profitable venture to serve in the United States Air Force from 1917 to 1919, when they returned to Saint Louis to expand their theatre interests. By 1926, Spyros controled 37 theatres, and his small empire was purchased by Warner Brothers. From there, he and his brothers joined Paramount. Spyros was President of a subsidiary of Fox Theatres, and in a series of mergers involving Chase National Bank and on the death of Sidney Kent, Spyros was named President of Twentieth Century Fox, and Wendell L. Wilkie was made Chairman of the Board.

But whatever his fame as a business executive, Spyros Skouras made his mark as an international humanitarian. In the summer of 1941, the American Ambassador to Greece wrote that the food situation was appalling. Famine, disease, looting and pillaging were rampant. Spyros negotiated with the German, Italian and British governments and received a promise that none would intecept the food shipments. By 1973, more than 110,000 tons in food and supplies of medicine were shipped. Spyros Skouras was the Greek angel.

ENTERTAINMENT

Samuel Goldwyn (1882-1974)

Samuel Goldwyn was one of the founders of Hollywood's motion picture industry. Born Samuel Goldfish in Warsaw, Poland on August 7, 1882 to Abraham and Hannah Goldfish. When he was orphaned at ten years of age, he went tn London. Two Years later (1895), he landed in the United States. He started in a glove factory in Gloversville, New York, and at 30 he owned his own wholesale glove business. After moving to the top of his sales career, he joined his brother-in-law, producer Jesse L. Lasky, and playright Cecil B. DeMille in founding the Jesse L. Lasky Feature Play Company. Goldwyn had seen a nickelodeon and was very impressed with its potential for mass entertainment.

The new entrepreneurs made their first film in 1913 and it was a large success. They next merged with Adolph Zukor's Famous Players to form Famous players--Lasky, with Goldwyn becoming a director and Chairman of the Board. In 1918, he left the Lasky organization to form his own company, and in 1925, he joined with Louis B Mayer to form Metro-Goldwyn-Mayer. Within a year, he sold out and produced pictures independently until 1941, which were distributed by United Artists.

Goldwyn produced a long line of hits, including "All Quiet on the Western Front" (1930), "The Pride of the Yankees" (1942), "The Best Years of Our Lives" (1946) and "Gigi" (1958). He launched the careers of Eddie Cantor, Danny Kaye, Ronald Coleman, Joan Bennett and countless others. He is also famous for his Goldwynisms: (the fracturing of the English lanquaqe). One of his best known is, "Include me out." For all of his activities he was given the

Presidential Medal of Freedom.

Leslie Townes (Bob) Hope (1906-)

Bob Hope came to Ellis Island with his mother, Avis, and six brothers from Southampton on March 21, 1908. Hope turned early to a performing career as a boxer and a softshoe dancer. In the 1930's, he won several roles on Broadway musicals, and in 1941, he made his first "Road" picture with Dorothy Lamour and Bing Crosby. It was at this time that Hope developed his irreverent, rapid fire, topical style of delivery that became his stage and screen trademark. He became what one man called, "the fastest tongue in town."

Bob Hope's humanitarian service commenced when he did his first radio show for servicemen on May 6, 1941 at March Field, California. From that date until the end of World War II, he travelled all over the United States, Europe and Asia doing shows for the troops. But it was Secretary of the Air Force Stuart Symington who started Hope on his annual treks to visit troops during Christmas time, These journeys continued through the Berlin Airlift, the Korean War and in Viet Nam. They made Bob Hope an American institution.

Bob Hope has been married to former nightclub singer Dolores Reade for over 50 years. They have four adopted children. Next to his family and his career, Hope spends most time with golf. He belongs to 18 country clubs and has played golf on 1,500 courses throughout the world.

John Houseman (1902-1988)

John Houseman was born Jacques Haussmann in Bucharest, Romania on September 2, 1902 to a Jewish-Alsatian father and a British mother. He attended prep school in England, after which he went to Argentina as a representative of his father's grain business.

In 1925, Houseman was processed at Ellis Island and he continued his work as a grain dealer, but he began writing and translating plays from German and French. He lived in high style in New York and he married an Hungarian actress, Zita Johann. When the stock market crashed, they were bankrupted, and it was at this time that Houseman decided to devote his life to the stage. In the 1930's, he directed Virgil Thompson's "Four Saints in Three Acts," he worked for the WPA Negro Theatre in Harlem, and he founded the Mercury Theatre with Orson Welles. He and Welles produced the famous radio production of H.G. Wells's "War of the Worlds," a production that was so real that many persons clogged the highways to escape the invaders from another planet.

In 1941, Houseman severed his collaborative effort with Welles and joined Selznick Production as Vice President, but he left to become head of the oveas division of the Office of War Information. He returned to Hollywood after World War II and produced several distinguished films at the same time he was producing for the New York Staqe.

Among his many MGM credits we find: "Julius Caesar" (1952), "Executive Suite" (1954), "Lust for Life" (1956), and "Seven Days in May" (1964).[4] An extremely productive person, Houseman nearly always had two or more jobs at one time. He rescued the American Shakespeare Festival Theatre when it was near bankruptcy; he was artistic director of the UCLA Professionial Theatre Group; his career took another turn in 1973 when he was awarded an Academy Award for his role of Professor Kingsfield in "Paper Chase." Until then he had only appeared in a bit part in "Seven Days in May." John Houseman died on October 30, 1988 at Malibu, California of spinal cancer.

Sol Hurok (1888-1974)

Theatrical impresario Solomon Hurok was born on April 9, 1888 in Pogar, Russia, the son of Israel and Anna Hurok. When he was in his early teens, his parents gave him 1,500 rubles to go to a big city to learn the hardware business, Instead, he ran away to the

---

[4]John Houseman, Run Through (New York: Simon and Schuster, 1972.)

United States, arriving with just three rubles and knowing no English. He decided to go to Philadephia, because it was the home of Benjamin Franklin and it was there the Declaration of Independence was signed.

At first, he tried to sell needles door to door, but the housewives did not understand him, so ran a streetcar. But he failed at this too, because he let people off at the wrong corners. After other failures, he left for New York, where his first job was in a hardware store. In all this time, he took every opportunity to listen to musical events, and he began to see himself with a career in that field.

In 1906, he formed the Van Hugo Musical Society and he started arranging concerts for clubs and labor unions. By 1909, he was renting Madison Square Garden, but by 1925 he was bankrupt. Hurok began again, however, and in the Depression he opened the Continental Varieties. This put him in the big time. By 1941, he was sponsoring Auturo Rubenstein, the Don Cossack Chorus, and Marian Anderson.

In 60 years of managing artists, he presented Isadora Duncan, Chaliapin, Richard Strauss, the Comedie Francaise, Fonteyn, Nureyev, the Old Vic, the D'Oyly Carte, Stern and Cliburn. On May 13, 1973, the *New York Times* called Hurok the "Last of the Redhot Showmen." Hurok was married twice. He divorced his first wife, Tamara, in the late 1920's. They had one daughter. He married Emma Rifkin, but they had no children.

Bela Lugosi (1884-1956)

Born in Lugos, Hungary, now a part of Romania, on October 29, 1884, Bela Lugosi made his debut as actor in 1900. By 1913, he was playing leading roles at the Roqal Hungarian National Theatre. His acting career was interrupted by his service as an officer in the Hungarian army in World War I. Because of the political turmoil in the postwar, he fled Hungary. Arriving at Ellis Island in 1921, he soon formed a company of Hungarian actors. He played several good roles, but he did not become a star until his appearance as the vampire in Dracula in 1927.

His success led him to Broadway, and in 1930, he started his career in the new sound films. By 1950, he had made over sixty motion pictures, including a recreation of Dracula in 1931. He usually portrayed sinister figures and monsters. His credits include, "Murders in the Rue Morgue," (1932), "The Black Cat," (1934) , Murder by Television," (1935), "The Wolf Man," (1941) and "Night Monster. (1942)

Lugosi returned to the New York stage in 1944 as Brewster in "Arsenic and Old Lace." In the next ten years, he fought a drug addiction that consumed him and his fortune. He died on August 16, 1956, and he was buried in the cape he used in his dracula role.

Lee Strasberg (1902-1982)

Lee Strasberg was born in Budzanov, Austria-Hungary in 1902, and he was processed through Ellis Island in 1909. When one of his brothers died in the flu epidemic of 1918, Lee was compelled to go to work in the garment industry of New York City. While working at odd jobs, he began his acting career in a Lower East Side settlement house. By 1925, he was acting for the Theatre Guild. His initial success was his directinn of Sidney Kingsley's Pulitzer prize-winning "Men in White." In 1948, a year after the Actors Studio was organized, he was asked to replace one of its founders, and this began a twenty-eight year associatian as director.

In more than 50 years in the American theatre, Lee Strasberg worked with four generations of actors, and he became a legendary acting coach and a major influence in the theatre. He directed and taught hundreds of young actors in his two Institutes in New York and Hollywood. Many of his acting students have won Oscars, Emmys and Tonys. He was a perfectionist in the studio, where he propounded his "Method" approach to acting. His students pay especial tribute to his genius. When Al Pacino won a British best-acting award in 1976, he gave the prize to Strasberg.

Rudolph Valentino (1895-1926)

Rudolph Valentino, "The Great lover," was born on May 6, 1895 in the inland town of Castellaneta, just under Italy's heel. His father was Italian and his mother French. From them he received his many names: Rodolpho Guglielmi di Valentina d'Antonguolla. Athough he attended an agricultural college, he went into the restaurant business, from which he received his facility with language. His father died when he was very young, and this may account for his lack of attention to his studies, although he was particularly attracted to dancing and gymnastics. His facilities with languages, acrobatics and dancing became the mainstays of his Hollywood career.

Valentino sailed to the United States on the *S. S. Cleveland* in December 1913. Although he dreamed of an acting career, his first job was as a gardener in New York City. His love of dancing took him to the dance floors, where he acted out his role of gigolo, and soon he had full-time employment as a partner with flirtatious females around the dance floor for a fee. The payment was always made discreetly. His dancing prowess came to the attention of Bonnie Glass, who was looklng for a man to replace Clifton Webb in a Tango scene. From this beginning, he traveled across the United States with a touring musical company, and he settled in Los Angeles.

His first appearance in films was in 1917 as an extra, but his "dandy" figure, his skill on the dance floor, and his attractive looks projected him as a "Latin ladykiller." He won a part as Julio in "The Four Horseman of the Apocalypse," which made his an instant success because of its tango scene. But it was "The Sheik" that gave him life-long title of the "Great Lover." The theme of the movie appealed to the liberated woman of the 1920's, who wore short skirts and bobbed hair. There followed a succession of parts as a dancer, an American Indian, a Chinese and as a matador.

Valentino was not as successful in marriage. His marriage to Jean Acker, for reasons not known, did not survive the first evening. She shut her door to him on the first night and so they were divorced. His second marriage, to Natacha Rambova in May 1922, also ended in divorce, but not until 1925. She was born Winnifred Shaughnessy, was educated in England and came to Hollywood by way of Russia and the Imperial ballet.

On August 15, 1926, Valentino was rushed to the Polyclinic Hospital in New York for surgery on his gastric ulcer and a ruptured appendix. He died on August 23, and there followed one of the most bizarre funerals in American history. The crowds became a mob, and they were beaten back by mounted police. Over 100,000 persons filed by the casket.[5] . For many years after his death, a mysterious "Lady in Black" appeared in the.burial crypt to place roses at the tomb.

LABOR

David Dubinsky (1892-1982)

David Dubinsky was born David Dobnievski in Nemirov, Russia on February 22, 1892. At age 10, he was apprenticed in his father's bakery, and he began early to work for a union, for which he was banished to Siberia. But he escaped and made his way to the United States, landing at Ellis Island on January 2, 1911. In New York, he joined the cutters Local 10 of the International Ladies Garment Workers Union (ILGWU). In a short time, he was chosen head of the local and then vice president of the international in 1922, general secretary in 1929 and president In 1932.

When Dubinsky took over the union, it was $1 milllon in debt, and its membership was down to 45,000. In two years, the debt was liquidated and the membership had swelled to 200,000. In time, the union became rich, and Dubinsky invested in a number of ventures that benefited the members. These included cooperative housing on the East Side, low cost housing in Puerto Rico, and an 850-acre resort.

---

[5]I. Shulman, Valentino (New York: Trident, 1967)

Dubinsky quit the Socialist Party in 1936 and he became a staunch supporter of Franklin Roosevelt. He fought corruption in the labor movement and he fought for his members' welfare. He negotiated the first 35-hour week, the first employer-financed fund for workers vacations and the first health and welfare program for the union. At the same time, he always accepted a lower salary than other presidents of other unions.

Dubinsky was a strong supporter of the merger of the AFL and the CIO, and he became a member of the new executive council. He retired in 1966 and he was awarded the Presidential Medal of Freedom in 1969.

Joe Hill (1879-1915)

The promise of political freedom brought many radicals to Ellis Island and Joe Hill was among them. Born Joel Hagglund in Sweden in 1879, he emigrated in 1902 and became an itinerant laborer and balladeer. He worked in mines, on farms, in factories, and on the waterfronts. In 1910, Hill joined the International Workers of the World (IWW) in California. While moving eastward in 1913, he stopped in Salt Lake City to earn travel money and became involved in a murder of a grocery store Owner, John G. Morrison and his 17-year-old son Arling. Hill was indicted because he reported to a physician with a bullet in his chest on the night of the murder. Hill who was many miles from the murder scene claimed that he received his wound in a lover's quarrel. But it was a poor time to preach a radical gospel in the United States, because the IWW (the Wobblies) had led a successful strike by 25,000 persons in a mill at Lawrence, Massachusetts. It turned to violence; many were hurt, as police forced the strikers to take trains out of Lawrence.

In the trial, which followed, he refused to testify. When the Mormon-owned *Deseret Evening News* sought his conviction, Hill was doomed. Many people, including President Wilson, called for a new trial, but Hill was executed by a firing squad on November 19, 1915. One of his last statements was, "Don"t waste any time in mourning--organize." The labor song, "I Dreamed I Saw Joe Hill Last Night," memorializes Hill's story.

In his will, Hill ordered that his ashes be scattered across the United States, Some ashes were mailed to followers in many states, but the remains were seized by the U. S. government and they are now stored in the National Archives.

Sidney Hillman (1888-1946)

Joe Hill's story is spectacular, but not typical of American labor. Most immigrant labor leaders held conservative political views, although some, like Samuel Gompers and David Dubinsky, originally had socialist leanings. Sidney Hillman was one of the many Russian Jews who fled oppression and he too entered the garment industry. A rabbinical student, he went through Ellis Island and began working in a New York sweatshop. Seven years later, he organized the International Ladies Garment Workers Union (ILGWU), and he began to press for social changes, including unemployment insurance, health care and pension benefits. He became a close ally of President Roosevelt and his New Deal program.

After Hillman died in 1946, his followers continued his work. The union, which originally attempted to end sweatshops, now controls health and pension plans, cooperative housing, a union-run bank and a college-scholarship program. As the number of garment jobs declined in the United States from foreign competition, the union has tried to sing its way back to health with its Slogan "Look for the Union Label."

LAW

Felix Frankfurter (1888-1965)

Felix Frankfurter may be the most distinguished alumnus of Ellis Island. Born on November 15, 1882 in Vienna, Austria to Leopold and Emma Frankfurter, he came to to the United States in 1894 aboard the *Marsala*, "a typical immigration tub," having come steerage.[6] His father became a merchant in New York, where Felix attended the College of the City of New York (now CUNY) in 1902 and Harvard Law School in 1906. Upon graduating from law school, he became the assistant to Henry L. Stimson, the U. S. Attorney for the Southern District of New York State.

Later Frankfurter worked in the War Department, but he resigned to accept the Byrne Chair of Administrative Law at Harvard, which he held until 1939, when President Roosevelt appointed him Associate Justice of the U. S. Supreme Court to succeed Benjamin N. Cardozo, to what was considered to be the "Jewish Seat" of the court. Frankfurter established a reputation for his attempt to interpret the law while taking social and economic conditions into consideration. He urged a "more continuous awareness of the role of the Court in the dynamic process American society."[7]

Louis Nizer (1902-)

A very popular alumnus of Ellis Island, Louis Nizer claims that he still remembers what he wore on his arrival with his mother in 1905.[8] After putting himself through college teaching English to foreigners, he entered Columbia University Law School. He came to know many government officials through his lucrative practice in New York. Among his more famous clients and cases as he recounts them in his book, *My Day in Court,* are Richard M. Nixon, whom he defended during the latter's impeachment proceedings, the producer of the movie "Carnal Knowledge", whom he defended before the U. S Supreme Court, and the libel case of Quentin Reynolds vs Westbrook Pegler. Nizer's reputation rests on his extraordinary facility in libel cases.

---

[6]Liva Baker, Felix Frankfurter (New York: Coward-McCann, 1969, p. 18.)

[7]H. B. Phillips, Felix Frankfurter Reminisces (New York: Reynal, 1960).

[8]Louis Nizer, Reflections Without Mirrors: An Autobiography of the Mind (New York: Doubleday, 1978).

MUSIC

Irving Berlin (1888-1989)

Irving Berlin was born Israel Baline on May 11, 1888 to Moses and Leah Baline in Mologne, Russia. Irving adopted his new name when his family came to Ellis Island on the *Brynland* from Antwerp on September 14, 1893. They lived in a tenement on Cherry Street, in the heart of the Lower East Side.

Irving went to school for two years, but when he was eight years old, his father died and he was forced to help support his mother, brothers and sisters (two were left behind in Russia). From 1905-1907, Berlin worked as a singing waiter in Chinatown, where he wrote his first song, "Marie from Sunny Italy." It was a typical American event: an Italian song written by a Russian Jew in a Chinese Restaurant. The song was not a sensation, but it got him a job as a lyricist for a publishing house. It was not until 1911 that he wrote his first "sensational hit" with the publication of "Alexander's Ragtime Band."

Berlin performed in several vaudeville shows before World War I, but he preferred writing songs. When he was drafted in the Army as a private in 1917, he was commissioned to write songs. One song from that experience has become a classic. His rendition of "Oh How I Hate to Get up in the Morning" showed his lifelong preference for sleeping late (probably because of his insomnia).

In the period between the two world wars, Berlin started his own musical company, built his own theatre, and wrote some haunting melodies. The list includes "Remember," "Always," "Russian Lullaby," "Blue Skies," and "How Deep is the Ocean." In the Great Depression, his songs lost their frivolity, as he wrote tunes about corruption, lynchings, and hunger. But at the same time, he also wrote "Easter Parade," and in 1935, be started his long list of hits for motion pictures. He produced the music for "Top Hat," "Cheek to Cheek," "On the Avenue," and "Holiday Inn." The last show, produced in 1942, gave the world "White Christmas," which he wrote in 1939.

Like many immigrants, Berlin was very patriotic. When World War II began in Europe, he revived a tune he had written for a World War I musical. On Armistice Day, 1939, Kate Smith introduced "God Bless America." This song, which made him millions of dollars, was considered several times as a second national anthem. In 1942, Berlin produced "This is the Army," which raised $10 million for the Army Relief Fund. For this he was given the Medal of Merit by the U. S. Army. He was given many other honors. President Eisenhower presented him with a gold medal on February 18, 1955 for his many patriotic contributions, and he was awarded a special Tony for his "distinquished contributions to the musical theater."

Berlin was married twice. His first wife, Dorothy Goetz, died in 1917 of typhoid fever. His second marriage was widely reported, because his new wife was Ellin Mackay, the daughter of a leading Catholic layman. They had three daughters. Berlin died in 1989, at age 101, after living a reclusive life for many years.

Jule Styne (1905-)

Jule Styne was born in London on December 31, 1905 to Isadore and Anna Stein, both orphans, who had emigrated from the Russian Ukraine in 1900. Anna Stein tried to enroll Jule in the London Conservatory of Music at age six, but failing this she arranged for Jule to have music lessons on a rented piano.

With war more likely in Europe and with Anna pregnant again, the Steins boarded a Cunard liner in steerage and made their way to Ellis Island in 1912. The family chose to go to Chicago, where Jule resumed his piano lessons. At the age of ten, he played with the Chicago, Detroit and Saint Louis Symphonies, but at age eleven, his teacher told him that his fingers were too small for him ever to become a great pianist, so he turned to jazz. He was in the right place, because Chicago was a jazz Mecca. In the 1920's, one could find Benny Goodman, Glenn Miller, Louis Armstrong, Jack Teagarden, Bix Beiderbecke, Harry James, Gene Krupa, Eddie Condon, and David Rose in the various "dives and dance halls." As Jule Styne said, "God, it was a feast." When the gang wars got too hot in Chicago, Styne went to New York City, where he became a vocal coach and where he could join the jazz greats around Fifty-Second Street. His success took him to Hollywood, where he coached Shirley Temple and Alice Faye. His next stop was Republic Studios, where he wrote songs for Gene Autry and Roy Rogers and where he teamed up with Frank Loesser and Sammy Cahn.

After writing more successful movie songs than any one else in history, Styne returned to New York to start composing Broadway shows. His first big hit "High Button Shoes" was drawn from his own experience. Shortly after, he did "Gentlemen Prefer Blondes," and "Gypsy." Although he made a fortune, he was always in financial trouble because of his obsession for gambling. At one time he was in debt over one-half million dollars to the U. S. government, to his former wife, and to bookies. Styne's answer was "Funny Girl," which was a huge hit, but the Internal Revenue Service put a lien on him earnings.

Jule Styne married Margaret Ann Bissett Brown, a budding actress from Devonshire, England on June 4, 1962. She miscarried during her first pregnancy, but a daughter, Katherine, was born on July 23, 1968. Styne had three sons by his first wife, Ethyl, who died in 1963.[9] .

Arturo Toscanini (1867-1957)

Toscanini was born on March 25, 1867, and he attended the Parma Conservatory of Music, intending to become a cellist. He graduated at age 18, and he became first cellist with Claudio Rossini's

---

[9]Theodore Taylor, Jule Styne: The Story of Composer Jule Styne (Random House, 1979

opera company. During an appearance in Rio de Janeiro, he was called on to substitute for the conductor. So successful was his performance of "Aida," that he was engaged to conduct for the remainer of the season and he was launched on his successful career.

For 12 seasons, he conducted operas in Bologna, Milan, and Turin, and in 1898, he became chief conductor and artistic director of the La Scala in Milan. He remained at this post until 1908, when he left to assume the job as conductor of the Metropolitan Opera. In 1915, however, he returned to Milan to conduct benefit concerts during World War I.

Following the war, he organized his own orchestra and toured the United States. He was registered at Ellis Island, but in 1921, he resumed his post at La Scala. He made several visits to the United States, appearing in 1926 and 1927 with the New York Philharmonic as guest conductor. In 1928, he was appointed conductor of the newly-merged New York Philharmonic-Symphony orchestra. He made several very successful European tours, and in 1937, at the age of seventy, he became conductor of the NBC Symphony in New York City--a group created for him by the National Broadcasting Company. By then, Toscanini was considered by many to be one of the world's greatest conductors. His drive, his pursuit of excellence, his gestures made his performances memorable, particularly when conducting Beethoven.

RELIGION

Edward Joseph Flanagan (1886-1948)

Monsignor Flanagan, who was widely known for his rehabilitation of boys was born in Roscommon, Ireland on July 13, 1886. He came to the United States with his parents, John and Nora Flanagan in 1904. Two years later, he graduated from Mount Saint Mary's College, Emmitsburg, Maryland. After a year at St. Joseph's Seminary, Dunwoodie, New York, and another at the Gregorian University in Rome, and three more at the Jesuit University in

Innsbruck, Austria, he was ordained a priest in the Roman Catholic Church in 1912.

Fr. Flanagan was assigned to the archdiocese of Omaha, Nebraska, where he started immediately to help the poor. His first effort was the Workingman's Hotel, a place of refuge for derelicts. It was there that he was convinced that poverty should be attacked at its roots, that is in childhood. In 1917, he rented an old house and with five boys, three of them delinquents, he started his Home for Homeless Boys. The next year tbey moved to a tract of land outside of the city and built the first Boys Town. In 1922, it was incorporated as a town, with the town government run by the boys themselves.

Thousands of boys (and now girls) passed to adulthood under the guiding hand of Fr. Flanagan, which gave truth to his deeply-held belief that, "There is no such thing as a bad boy." The fame of Boys Town reached all over the world when in 1938 Spencer Tracy won an Academy Award for his role as the priest. After World War II, Fr. Flanagan was given a post as an adviser to the United States Government on youth in occupied nations, and it was while serving in this capacity in Berlin that he died on May 15, 1948.

SPORTS

Knute Kenneth Rockne (1888-1931)

In 1951, an Associated Press poll of sportcasters voted Knute Rockne the "all-time coach." Born in Norway he emigrated to the United States at the turn of the century and attended Chicago's public schools. Despite his status as a high school dropout, he graduated magna cum laude in chemistry from Notre Dame University and began coaching track there in 1916. Two years later, he started to compile his amazing record in football: five undefeated, untied seasons in 13 years, finishing with 150 victories, 12 losses and 5 ties (an .897 percentage).

Rockne's undergraduate achievements illustrate the drive and excellence of the immigrants who shaped America's future. Throughout his student life, he played the flute in the symphony orchestra, participated in every dramatic production, wrote for the school newspaper, fought in semi-professional matches, set a school record for the pole vault and was selected third-string all-American end in football, while working as a janitor and a lab assistant in chemistry.

Rockne was the first celebrity to die in a plane erash. On March 3, 1931, he took a train from Chicago to Kansas city in order to board a Transcontintal-Western 599, trimotor Fokker plane for Los Angeles. The plane flew into a storm, ice piled up on the wings and it crashed in a Kansas wheat field.

SCIENCE

Simon Kuznets (1901-1985)

Simon Kuznets was born in Kharkov, in the Ukraine, and he came to the United States in 1922. He earned his bachelor's, master's and doctoral degrees in economics from Columbia University and then went to work for the National Bureau of Economic research, a private, non-profit agency, with which he was affiliated until 1960.

It was at this agency that he commenced his pioneering work on the national product. He responded to a request from the U. S. Senate, which, in the early 1930's, had no real measure of the performance of the economy. The measure that Kuznets developed was the gross national product (GNP)--the value of all goods and services produced in a given year.

Dr. Kuznets' work in incomes accounting not only illustrated the chief problems of national economic growth, but it also transformed economics into a science. He used statistical methods to determine the sources of a nation's wealth, and he analyzed population changes, technology and the structure of industry to measure changes in economic growth.

Kuznets joined the faculty at the University of Pennsylvania in 1930, and it was there that he published his two-volume classic *National Income and its Composition, 1919-1938.* He also taught at Johns Hopkins University from 1954 to 1960, and then he moved to Harvard University, where he was made professor emeritus in 1971. In the same year he was awarded the Nobel Prize in economics. The citation accompanying the award emphasized his "empirically founded interpretation of economic growth which has led to new and deepened insight into the economic and social structure."

His fellow economists heeped praise upon him. Paul Samuelson, also a Nobel Laureate, said, "Kuznets was the founder of national income measurement," and John Kenneth Gallbraith, said "When we speak of gross national product, national income, their components and the policies pertaining thereto, it is the structure created by Kuznets that we address." Galbraith called the gross national product "One of the greatest discoveries of all time."

Kuznets was associate director of the Bureau of Planning and Statistics at the War Production Board during World War II, he was a past president of both the American Economic Association and the American Statistical Association. He died on July 9, 1985 at his home at Cambridge, Massachusetts.

Hyman G. Rickover (1898-1986)[10]

Hyman Rickover was born on August 24, 1898, the son of a tailor, in Makow, about 50 miles from Warsaw, in Czarist Russia. He came to the United States in 1904 with his sister and mother to

---

[10]Rickover's official Navy biography states that he was born in 1900, but his biographers claim that his actual birth year was 1898. see Norman Polmar and Thomas B. Allen, Rickover: Controversy and Genius (Simon and Schuster, 1982).

join their father in New York.[11] Following a bad investment in the Panic of 1907, his family moved to Chicago, which he always considered to be his home town.

As a high school student, he worked part time delivering telegrams for Western Union. One of the offices he visited regularly was that of Adolph J. Sabath, a Congressman from Chicago, who was also a Jewish immigrant. It was Sabath who recommended Rickover for appointment to the Naval Academy at Annapolis in 1918. Since Rickover was one of a few Jewish midshipmen at the Academy, he and they suffered from anti-Semitism, a fact that he often recounted later. Rickover stated on CBS television's "6O Minutes" that he received more than his share of hazing "because I as Jewish." In a class of 539, Rickover graduated l06th, and he entered a peacetime Navy that was cutting budgets. After five years of sea duty aboard a destroyer he returned to Annapolis in 1927 for a year of advanced study in electrical engineering, and then he spent another year of post-graduate study at Columbia University. There he met and later married (in 1931) Ruth Masers, a native Washingtonian. In 1937, Rickover received his only sea command--on th Battleships California and New Mexico.

During most of World War II, he was ashore as director of the the electrical section of the Bureau of Ships. Following the war, the Navy began to investigate the possibility of using nuclear power for submarines and other ships. In 1946, Admiral Rickover received orders to join a team of naval officers and civilians that was assigned to observe the work being done on nuclear reactors at Oak Ridge, Tennessee. Two years later, he was named to head a joint Navy-Atomic Energy Commission program to develop the first Naval nuclear propulsion system. In 1953, the prototype model ran at full power continuously for 66 days, long enough to carry a ship twice around the world without refueling. The Nautilus was launched in 1954 and put out to sea for the first time in 1957. It became the first

---

[11]He discussed his Ellis Island recollections on the Johnny Carson show.

submarine to pass under the North Pole in 1958, and in 1960 another nuclear submarine, the Triton, became the first ship to circumnavigate the globe onder water. It was during this period that Congress rescued then Captain Rickover from retirement. When in 1953 he was passed over a second time for promotion to rear admiral, a congressional investigation ensued. Soon after, Rickover was promoted to rear admiral, in 1958 to vice admiral and in 1973 to admiral.

In developing his nuclear ships, Admiral Rickover concluded that many persons under his direction had heen poorly educated.[12] Thus, he began a twenty-five year crusade against the American education system. He wrote three books critical of professional educators. He thought they were too "progressive." But Rickover fought not only educators but Navy regulations, which he considered to be stupid. He recommended that 40 percent of all jobs at the Pentagon be eliminated.

Hyman Rickover died on July 8, 1986. In life and in death he was much honored. He received the Congressional Gold Medal twice; he was praised by three living Presidents. Although he was a harsh taskmaster, he received respect and popular acclaim. The respect was deserved. Witness this statement eulogizing Rickover by Navy Secretary John F. Lehman: "More than 150 U. S. naval ships [are] under nuclear power, with a record of 3,000 ship years of accident-free operations. All Americans owe him a debt of gratitude."

Some Undistinguished Americans

Much has been written about famous Americans who came to the United States through Ellis Island. But we need to celebrate also those whom Hamilton Holt called "undistinguished Americans." The following stories, gleaned from oral histories and personal accounts, demonstrate the variety of ways the millions who came to the United

---

[12]President Jimmy Carter's book, Why Not the Best? is a quotation from the admiral. Carter, who was an engineer, worked with Rickover and was a great admirer of the admiral.

Immigrants leaving barges at Ellis Island (1913) Photo from Terence V. Powderly Collection

States adjusted to life here. [13]

Nicholas B. (Italian)

Nicholas B. was born in Montemarano, Italy, a typical small Italian town, with a central business district where the bus now stops. He began his journey to the United States by taking a horse and carriage from Montemarano to Naples, where he stayed for three months while he worked to earn his passage money. He left Naples on the *Duca degli Abruzzi* on June 8, 1910. His ship landed at Ellis Island on June 21, 1910. According to the ship manifest, he entered the United States with $19 and went to stay with an "uncle" in Brooklyn, New York.

Nicolo's "uncle" Vicenze, also from Montemarano, had arrived in New York a year earlier with his two brothers, John and Rosario. Vicenze, who was a shoemaker in Italy stayed in Brooklyn and carried on his trade there; his brothers settled in Iynn, Massachusetts, where Rosario ran a tailor shop and John was a musician. While in Brooklyn, Nicolo (now Nicholas) worked for a marble craftsman for four dollars per week and paid three dollars per week for room and board, an arrangement that lasted about a year and a half. However, he left suddenly when Vicenze wanted to marry him to a doctor's daughter whom he did not choose to marry. Venturing to Bridgeport, Connecticut, Nicholas took up residence with another "uncle." While there, he worked in a silver factory inspecting spoons. Nicholas eventually settled in Boston where he held a variety of jobs: first as a mixer at the United Drug Company, then from cook's helper to chef at hotels. He used some of his hotel earnings to help bring his mother and brother to Massachusetts.

William B. (Russian)

He came from Kreisk, Russia, in Vilna Gubernia, One of eleven children. William was the first to come to

---

[13]These stories are taken from August C. Bolino, "Isles of Tears, Isle of Hope," Michigan Alumnus, July/August 1986, pp.23-24.

the United States and would eventually help the others get here, one by one.

His early memories were of long, cold walks to the Jewish school and that last long walk out of Russia, in which he walked most of the way to Hamburg. He missed the boat that was to take him to America, but was able to catch the next one. Conditions aboard the boat were so bad he could not talk about it.

William arrived in New York with fifty cents in his pocket. For a time he sewed collars in a sweatshop during the day and slept on a table in the factory at night, after going to school. Every extra penny that he did not spend for his daily apple (which is all he remembers having to eat) went back to Russia. His recollections of later years when he arrived in the Midwest and became a peddler were happier. Remembering his wagon and his horses, he used to say, "I had the finest team in the vest." But he returned to the East and opened a clothing store in Brooklyn.

C.A.W. (Swedish) The day after graduating from the university town of Uppsala on June 4, 1924, he moved to Stockholm to obtain a visa from the American consulate. To his consternation he was told that no visas were being issued, for that was the summer that Congress changed the immigration laws to the quota systen . Not until the middle of October did he read in the paper that visas could be had. The first available ship was the *Drottningholm*, which sailed from Gothenberg on October 25, 1924.

When the *Drottingholm* arrived in New York on November 3, 1924, a large German liner had also docked so the main building at Ellis Island was a bedlam. A large label with his name and destination was attached to his suit coat. He admired the speed and efficiency with which he was processe His physical examination consisted of one medical doctor looking into hius eyes and asking him to lower his trousers. He next headed for a large room where all the Swedish immigrants where waiting. After he left Ellis Island, he was taken to a one-story building on the very tip of Battery Park where he joined seven other Swedes and one German, all going to Boston.

His parents, who had preceded him by a few years, had sent a telegram to the ship saying that they would meet him in Fall River. He had no idea where Fall River was, but an elderly man befriended him on the ferry pulling out a map and explaining he would leave for Fall River by boat that evening, to arrive the next morning and be met by his parents.

Mary and James O. (Scots) Agnes O. was thirteen years old when she arrived with her family at a very unwelcoming Ellis Island. While her eyesight is fading, momeries of that awful place are hauntingly vivid. The date of arrival was May 8, 1921.

Mary and James O., along with their five sons and three daughters, left Flantyre, Scotland, behind and on April 29, 1921 sailed for the United States aboard the *H.M.S. Coronia.* Their hope was to find a better, healthier way of of life in this country. Ellis Island was a very traumatic experience for Agnes and her family. Upon arrival, they were separated by sex, with the men and boys channeled one way and the women and very young children directed another. Each entrant was issued three blankets--one to place over bedsprings, one to fold and serve as a pillow, and one to use as a cover. One small bar of soap and one paper towel were the daily bathing supply.

They were awakened each morning by the not-so-dulcet tone of an employee, shouting, "Get up and get dressed." People from many countries were crowded together; some would grab food from the tables before others were seated.

PART V

CHAPTER XI:

APPENDICES

A. ELLIS ISLAND CHRONOLOGY[1]

Ellis Island as an Immigration Station

1798	--Unsuccessful Irish rebellion; rebels immigrated to U.S. along with distressed artisans and farmers depressed by bad harvests and low prices.
	--Alien and Sedition Acts gave President arbitrary powers to seize and expel resident aliens suspected of engaging in subversive activities. Though never invoked, Acts induced several shiploads of Frenchmen to return to France and Santo Domingo.
1803	--Resumption of war between England and France. Disruption of trade; immigration from continental Europe practically impossible.
	--British Passenger Act limits numbers to be carried by immigrant ships, which effectively checked Irish immigration.
1807	--Congress prohibited importing Negro slaves into the U.S 1812.
	--War of 1812 brought immigration to complete halt.
1814	--Treaty of Ghent ended War of 1812. First great wave of immigration began, with 5,000,000 immigrants between 1815 and 1860.
1818	--Black Ball Line of sailing packets began regular Liverpool-New York service; Liverpool became main

---

[1]This chronology is taken <u>verbatim</u> from Tedd McCann, el al, <u>Ellis Island Study</u> (Washington National Park Service, May 1978) pp. C-1 to C-18; D 1-2; E-1 to E-3. It has been updated to 1990.

port of departure for Irish and British along with considerable numbers of Germans and Norwegians.

1825 --Great Britain repealed prohibition of immigration, an official endorsement of view that England had become overpopulated.

--U.S. arrival of first group of Norwegian immigrants, consisting of freeholders leaving an overpopulated country and shrunken farms; followed by colters, laborers and servants.

1830 --Polish revolution spurred refuge to the U.S.; Congress allocated thirty-six sections of public land in Illinois to Polish refugees.

1837 --Financial panic led to nativist complaints that immigration lowers wage levels, contributes to the decline of the apprenticeship system and generally depresses the condition of labor.

1840 --Cunard Line founded, beginning the era of steamship lines especially designed for passenger transportation between Europe and the United States.

1846 --Crop failures in Germany and Holland set tens of thousands of dispossessed immigrating to U.S.

1846-47 --Irish potato famine caused large-scale immigration to U.S. All classes of Irish population, not only cotters and laborers, but even substantial farmers.

1848 --Revolution in Germany failed, resulting in immigration of political refugees to America.

1850 --Imigration through the New York harbor reached proportions demanding a centralized receiving station. Disembarking from 1,912 ships, 212,736 newcomers arrived.

1855, Aug. 1 --Castle Garden on the Bay at the tip of Manhattan officially opened as first U.S. receiving station for immigrants arriving through the national principal port of entry at New York City. Site of the former Castle Clinton of the War of 1812, Castle Garden had just five years previously been a theatre housing a record turnout for singer Jenny Lind's triumphant American debut.

1881   --Over 455,600 immigrants passed through Castle Garden, more than double the past average annual rate, and increasing to 476,000 the following years.

1882   --First Federal immigration law enacted, barring lunatics, convicts and those likely to become public charges.

--Chinese Exclusion Act denies entry to Chinese laborers.

--Outbreak of anti-semitism in Russia spurred sharp rise in Jewish immigration to the U.S.

1885   --Foran Act prohibited importing contract labor but not skilled labor for new industries, artists, actors, lecturers, domestic servants; individuals in U.S. not to be prohibited from assisting immigration of relatives and friends.

1886   --Statue of Liberty dedicated, just when resistance to unrestricted Immigration was accelerating.

1887   --Investigations by Congress and the Department of Treasury found Castle Garden's facilities hopelessly inadequate for daily flow of immigration.

1890   --Federal government assumed full control of immigration for previous state-contracted management of New York Port.

--Ellis Island chosen as new site for Federal immigration station in New York harbor. Simultaneously, Congress responded to recent public pressure to remove Navy explosives from the site.

--Temporary immigration processing established at the Barge Office (Custom Station) as construction underway at Ellis Island.

1891   --New legislation placed all national immigration under full Federal control, creating the Bureau of Immigration under the Department of the Treasury. Office of Commissioner of Immigration established at New York Port, with Colonel John Weber the first appointee.

--Legislation added health requirements to immigration restrictions.

--Russian pogroms spurred large volume of Jewish immigration.

--Immigration through the Barge Office totaled 405,664, eighty percent of the national total.

1892, Jan. 1 --Ellis Island Immigration Center formally opened to process steerage passenger; first and second cabin passenger processed on board and directly disembarked in Manhattan.

--At a cost of $500,000. The new immigration station consisted of a large two-story processing building, separate hospital facilities, a boiler house, laundry and utility plant, all constructed wholly of wood. In addition, the old brick and stone Fort Gibson and Navy magazines were converted for detainees' dormitories and other purposes. Added landfill approximately doubled the original 3.3 acre island.

--Immigration through the New York port totaled 445,987, with a shift from northern and western Europeans to southern and eastern Europeans becoming evident.

1893 --Dr. Joseph Senner an educated German Austrian who had been with leading German language newspapers in the U.S., named new Commissioner of Immigration under President Cleveland.

--Legislation enacted requiring ship owners to prepare manifests carrying detailed information on individual immigrant passengers.

--U.S. Supreme Court upheld Board of Inquiry rather than courts of law to rule on deportation of alleged illegal entries, under regulations established by the Secretary of the Treasury authorized by the law of 1882.

--Cholera epidemic and national economic depression resulted in immigration decrease, to continue for several years.

1894   --Immigration Restriction League organized, to be the spearhead of restrictionist movement for the next twenty-five years favoring the "old" (northern and western European) over the "new" (southern and eastern European) immigrants.

1896   --Italian immigration sharply increased, accompanied by public disfavor previously vented against the Italian influx during the 1840's.

1897   --Literacy test for immigrants, aimed at restricting Italian influx, vetoed by President Cleveland.

--Fire destroyed Ellis Island's wooden buildings, along with immigration records from 1855-1890 used in old Navy magazine. All, immigrants and staff safely evacuated. Immigration processing temporarily transferred back to Barge Office.

--Commissioner Senner replaced by Thomas Fitchie, and Terence Powderly, former chief of Knights of Labor; named Commissioner-General of Immigration in Washington. Both strong supporters of President McKinley, but a feud evolved, and Powderly influenced Congress to legislate tightened contract labor restrictions.

1898   --Congress authorized funds for new fire-proof facilities at Ellis Island, awarding the contract to Boring and Tilton, the first important Government architecture to be designed by private architects under competition mandated by the Tarnsey Act of 1875.

--U.S. immigration reached low point of 229,299, with New York port's share only 178,748, the result of years of national economic depression.

--Immigration officials mistakenly estimate that no

more than 500,000 immigrants would ever again arrive in New York in one year and architects proceed under that miscalculated projection.

1899 --Serious scandals of graft and brutality among immigration inspectors spurred Federal investigation revealing these practices at the Barge Office. Only minimal corrective measures taken in anticipation that Ellis Island reopening would rectify conditions.

1900, Dec. 17 --New Ellis Island Immigration Station opened, with a total of 2,251 immigrants received for inspection that day. At a cost of some $1.5 million the new complex, unlike the former station, was situated to retain some green space and show the best advantage to approaching ships.

1901-2 --Theodore Roosevelt, on assuming the presidency immediately focused on "cleaning house" at Ellis Island following exposure of several scandals under the Powderly-Fitchie-McSweeney administration.

1902 --William Williams, respected young lawyer; named new Commissioner of Immigration at New York Port and immediately instituted procedures to ensure efficient, honest and sanitary treatment of immigrants.

--Hospital Building and auxiliary laundry other facilities opened.

--Commissioner Williams appeals to Congress for funds to expand the critically overcrowded facilities, inadequate to handle the immigrants since the opening of the new station.

1903 --Immigration control transferred to newly established Department of Commerce and Labor; immigration having become considered an addition to the labor force rather than a species of import when control had originally been placed under Treasury Department.

--New legislation denied entry to anarchists and

prostitutes; required examination of discharged alien seamen to be brought to Ellis Island; and imposed a $100 fine on steamship companies bringing in immigrants with loathsome or contagious diseases.

--Iron and glass canopy constructed over walkway from dock to main hall.

--On one day, 12,600 immigrants arrived at New York Port, with nearly half required to remain in steerage for several days due to inadequate facilities to process all in a day or provide overnight quarters at Ellis Island. This came to be a common occurrence over the next several years.

1904

--New 160-foot "Ellis Island" ferry completed, with a capacity for 600. Steerage immigrants transported to Ellis from docks at the Battery by barges and tugs provided by steamship companies; when cleared for admission, new ferry ran them hourly to their "new land" at N.Y.

--Sanitary immigrants' dining room installed at a site previously used for detainees.

--Portion of roof garden on main hall converted to play area for detained children.

--Question of title to Ellis Island settled when New Jersey Riparian Commission favorably ruled on Federal application to enlarge Ellis Island and conveyed to the U.S. by deed approximately 48 acres surrounding and including the original Island and area already landfilled.

1905

--Commissioner Williams resigned to return to law practice, replaced by Robert Watchorn, a career Immigration Service official. While Williams shared the common growing attitude that immigration should be restricted in quantity and quality, Watchorn favored admitting all immigrants meeting legal requirements.

--821,169 immigrants processed at Ellis Island, with

many logistical problems regarding numerous detainees frequently required to remain for several days.

--Japanese and Korean Exclusion League formed by organized labor in protest against influx of coolie labor and fear of threat to living standards of American working class.

1906   --Island No. 3 landfill of approximately four acres completed for construction of contagious disease hospital group.

--Changes initiated for more efficient medical examinations, including separate mental ward provided in hospital.

1907   --Climax of immigration, with 1,004,756 received at Ellis Island. On April 12 alone, 11,747 immigrants passed through the station, an all-time high. Detained immigrants totaled 195,540. Facilities proven inadequate since original construction in 1900 now critically under required capacity.

--New immigration law not only excluded prostitutes, but made them deportable for three years after arrival.

1907-8   --Gentlemen's Agreement established, with Japanese Government denying passports to labor immigrating to U.S. failed to satisfy West Coast exclusionists.

1908   --Baggage and dormitory building of Island No. 1 completed.

--Twelve buildings of contagious disease hospital group completed, with construction of five others underway on Island No. 3.

--New hospital and administration buildings on Island No. 2 completed.

--Kitchen and laundry building on island No. 1 remodeled: entire upper floor converted to large dining room accommodating 1,000 at one sitting, with tile installed on walls and floors for better sanitay conditions; first floor laid with sanitary cement and improved laundry machinery installed.

--Main building altered: former two large dormitories divided into small rooms each with a 5O-person capacity and new system of beds installed; sanitary plumbing installed and ventilating appratus allowing continuous air circulation in each room; additional dormitories constructed at ends of balcony; corridors on both second and third floors tiled; skylights installed for improved lighting and ventilation.

1909   --William Williams returned for second term as Commissioner at urging of President Taft.

--Following a sharp falloff in 1908, immigration again rising.

1910   --Contributions of the immigrants to date to the American working force clearly were significant during the era of the industrializing, urbanizing nation.

1911   --Greatest number of exclusions to date, 13,000 immigrants of the 650,000 arrivals at Ellis Island deported.

--Contagious disease hospital group opened for use, having been delayed for two years due to lack of furnishings and lighting facilities. For the first time, all sick immigrants could be cared for on Ellis Island.

--Third story to the west (north) wing of main building completed, providing day quarters for detainees and administrative space.

--Medical offices moved from main floor to larger space on lower floor of main building; entire main floor now used for inspection of immigrants.

--Old stairway through large opening in middle of main floor removed and replaced with one beneath gallery, increasing capacity of floor space for inspection.

--Iron railways dividing main floor into passageways removed and replaced with simple, comfortable benches.

--Information office space quadrupled by combining several small rooms; new area tiled and wainscoted; new stairway construction from office to immigrants' dining room, reducing distance travelled by several hundred immigrants three times daily by four-fifths.

--Unsightly temporary wooden barrack and debris removed from Island No. 1's north side and ground graded.

1913   --California legislature passed Alien Land Law, effectively barring Japanese, as "aliens ineligible for citizenship," from owning agricultural land in the state.

1913-14   --Third story added to baggage and dormitory building, providing more and better ventilated dormitory space, separate day rooms, and large open-air porches.

--Connecting corridor in contagious disease hospital group enclosed in glass and copper. Additional electric tie lines connecting the Island No. 3 complex with main power plant installed.

--Old hospital building on Island No. 2 renovated, with new floors and modern sanitary plumbing installed.

--Construction of new fireproof carpenter and bakery shop underway.

--Third story on east (south) wing of main building completed, providing needed space for medical inspection.

--First section of new concrete, granite-faced seawall completed, replacing a portion of rapidly decaying old cribwork.

1914-18	--World War I ended period of mass migration to the U.S.
	1914: 1,218,480 total U.S. immigration; 878,052 through New York Port.
	1915: 326,700 admitted, 178,416 through New York Port (75% decrease) .
	1918: Only 28,867 immigrants entered New York Port.
1914	--Frederic C. Howe, well-known municipal reformer, named new Commissioner of Immigration at New York Port just after war erupted.
July 30,	--Explosions by German saboteurs at nearby Black Tom Wharf.
1916	severely damaged Ellis Island Station. Safe evacuation of all 600 occupants on the island accomplished. Extensive repairs required.
1917	--Literacy test for immigrants adopted, after being defeated in seven previous proposals from 1896 through 1915. Passed over veto of President Wilson, it repealed all prior legislation inconsistent with it, codified previous provisions for exclusions and added new categories now totalling thirty-three; also mandated medical examination by Ellis Island staff on board all arriving vessels of alien members of ship crews.
	--U.S. entered war. German merchant ship crews in New York Harbor held at Ellis Island in baggage and dormitory building. Numerous suspected enemy aliens throughout the U.S. brought to Ellis under custody.
1918	--Repairs of Black Tom explosion damage and other improvements accomplished: New ceiling over main registry floor constructed in form and a Gustavino arch and augmented by red-tile floor replacing old worn asphalt; concrete walk laid back of granite-faced seawall, eliminating hazard of badly-rotted

plankwalk; second section of new seawall completed on ferry basin's south side; metal-covered concrete pipe tunnel installed between power plant and baggage/dormitory building; water pipes replaced in main hall and several other facilities; new boiler for power plant installed.

1918-19 --Suspected enemy alien detainees transferred to other locations and U.S. Army Medical Department and U.S. Navy take over main hall, baggage/dormitory building and hospital complex for duration of war. Regular inspection of arriving aliens conducted on board ship or at docks.

--Covered way between Islands 2 and 3 constructed by U,S, Army.

1919 --Close of war accompanied by "Big Red Scare," with anti-foreign fears and hatreds transferred from German Americans to suspected alien anarchists.

--Thousands of suspected alien radicals interned at Ellis Island; hundreds deported under new legislation based on principal of guilt by association with any organization advocating revolt.

--Commissioner Howe resigned, following his thwarted efforts to mitigate internment and deportion of often innocent suspected alien radicals.

1920 --Ellis Island Station reopened for immigration inspection, while continuing to function as a deportation center.

--Immigration took a noticeable upturn, with 225,206 aliens admitted through New York.

--Facilities at Ellis in disrepair, following hard use during war.

--Frederick Wallis appointed Commissioner of Immigration at Ellis Island; his proposal for a rehabilitation program was ignored by Congress.

--The only improvements were accomplishment of much of the concrete and granite seawall, with professional praise attributed its unique engineering. Landfill between Islands 2 and 3 had begun. However, substantial portions of old cribbing seawall remained in steady decay until work was renewed and completed in 1933.

1921 --Immigration rose to nearly pre-war proportions; 560,971 immigrants passed through the New York Port of a national total of 805,228.

--Emergency immigration restriction law introduced the quota system, heavily weighted in favor of natives of Northern and Western Europe. The act provided that the number of any given European nation's immigrants to the U.S. annually could not exceed three percent of foreign-born persons from that nation living in the U.S. in 1910. An annual total of admissible immigrants was set at 358,000, with not more than twenty percent of the quota to be received in any given month.

--Steamship companies rushed to land each month's quota of immiglants in keen competition, overloading the processing capacities of Ellis Island.

--Commissioner Wallis resigned in despair over the quota restrictions, replaced by Robert Tod, a banker and philanthropist.

1921-23 --Commissioner Tod managed some improvements with very limited funds, but resigned in frustration; replaced by Henry Curran, long experienced in New York City Republican politics.

--Steamship companies found steerage no longer profitable and new liners were designed in each with comfortable third class cabins, marking the passage of the steerage era.

1924 --National Origins Act (or the Second Quota Law) further restricted immigration, changing the quota basis from the census of 1910 to that of 1890, and reducing annual quota immigration to 164,000.

--Act further required selection and qualification of quota immigrants at countries of origin, with inspections conducted by staff of U.S. consuls in Europe.

--Ellis Island no longer used for primary inspection of immigrants.

1929   --National Origins Act amended, with new quotas based on 1920 census, and the maximum number of admissions annually lowered to 150,000. Act increased bias against Southern and Eastern Europeans.

1930   --Principal function of Ellis Island changed to detention station.

--Immigration sharply reduced during economic depression following stock market crash. Much of this was voluntary; also, President Hoover in attempt to keep any available employment in hands of Americans, ordered American consuls to strictly enforce prohibition against admission of persons liable to become public charges.

1931   --Secretary of Labor Doak, following President Hoover's policy, led a national roundup of illegal aliens for prospective deportation and transferred to Ellis Island.

--Many aliens also voluntarily sought deportation to escape economic depression. Any alien in the U.S. less than three years who could prove himself destitute could be deported at Federal expense.

--Deportations totaled 18,142, the greatest number to date in history of the Bureau.

--Edward Corsi, former immigrant through Ellis Island and long a social service worker with New York City immigrants, appointed new Commissioner of Immigration at New York Port.

--In addition to repairs of facilities at Ellis Island accomplished by funds appropriated before Corsi took office, old marquee fronting the main building torn down and replaced by plaza laid with flower beds.

1933 --In contrast to only 4,488 incoming aliens through Ellis Island, there were 7,037 outgoing aliens. Immigrants returning home were often detained for long periods while European consuls prepared passports for them or slowly investigated their right to return.

--Hitler became German Chancellor, initiating anti-semitic campaign; Jewish refugees came to U.S., but quota system barriers not lifted to admit large numbers in jeopardy in Germany.

--Immigration and Naturalization Bureaus merged, Ellis Island became No. 3 of 22 districts nationwide, with Ellis covering southern New York and northern New Jersey.

1934 --Philippines Independence Act restricts Filipino immigration to annual quota of fifty.

--Funds from the New Deal's Public Works Administration allocated for landfill, making room for recreational grounds on Manhattan side of Main building. Landscaping of new playgrounds and gardens continued for several years with WPA labor including the area between Islands 2 and 3.

1934-35 --Under recommendations of a committee established under President Franklin Roosevelt, last major construction accomplished on Ellis Island.

--Baggage and dormitory building remodeled to allow better segregation of different classes of deportees.

--Recreation hall and shelter constructed on filled in area belween Islands 2 and 3.

--Sun porches added to several contagious wards on Island 3 for tuberculosis patients.

--Improved quarters for medical staff on Island 2

reconstructed.

--New fireproof ferry house built at end of boat slip, containing waiting rooms, lunch counter, guard room and repair shop.

--New immigration building constructed on recently landfilled 100-acre wide area behind new ferry house, intended as a place for immigrants to be segregated from "criminal or undesirable" deportees. Extensions on both sides of building, well-fenced in, was to provide recreation space. (Once this new facility was completed, immigration flow was so minimal that maintenance funds were not provided for its use and it remained closed for several years, never to be used to its original purpose. New immigrants continued to be received in the main building.)

--New fireproof passageways constructed to connect ferry house and new immigration building with Island 1.

--Commissioner Corsi resigned to accept appointment under Mayor Fiorello LaGuardia, having become confident that operations at Ellis Island were well established and not requiring intensive direction.

1938   --Investigating committee appointed by Secretary of Labor examined immigration and naturalization records over previous nine years, revealing altered manifests, missing official documents and the theft of entire files. Investigation led to successful prosecution of over 250 racketeers, employees, aliens and steamship companies.

1939   --World War II erupts. New, never-used immigration station and ground floor of baggage and dormitory building occupied by Coast Guard to train and house recruits to patrol the area's waters to enforce the Neutrality Act of 1935.

1940   --Commissioner Reimer, Corsi's successor, observed

the fiftieth anniversary of the Ellis Island Immigration Station, with Governor's Island firing an 11-gun salute and the Coast Guard on Ellis responding by cannon.

--Alien Registration Act required not only registration of all aliens but also added to the list of deportable classes and called for finger printing arriving aliens.

--Immigration and Naturalization Service transferred to Department of Justice because immigrants had come to be considered primarily in the aspects of potential threats to national security.

1941   --U.S. entered World War II. Ellis Island again used for detention of suspected alien immigrants.

1942   --Japanese Americans evacuated from West Coast to detention camps.

1943   --Numerous detainees held at Ellis Island required all available facilities. Administrative functions transferred to WPA Headquarters Building in Manhattan, with Ellis kept solely as a detention station for aliens.

1945   --Large-scale Puerto Rican migration to escape poverty occurred, with many settling in New York.

1946   --Coast Guard station on Ellis Island decommissioned, leaving entire new immigration building, half the ferry house and much of the baggage and dormitory building untenanted.

--War Brides Act provided for admission of foreign-born wives of American servicemen.

1948   --Displaced Persons Act provided for admission of 400,000 refugees during a four-year period three-quarters regular displaced persons from countries with low quotas; and one quarter German, special groups of Greek, Polish and Italian refugees, orphans and European refugees stranded in the Far East.

1946-49	--Excessive operating costs of little-used station prompted Federal consideration of the Immigration and Naturalization Service vacating Ellis Island.
1950	--Internal Security Act, passed over President Truman's veto, excluded arriving aliens who had ever been members of Communist and Fascist organizations.
	--Brief flurry of activity at Ellis Island as incoming aliens had to be carefully screened for membership in the proscribed organizations.
1951	--Rearrangement of space and extensive repairs accomplished to accommodate detained aliens rounded up throughout the country as suspected illegal residents.
	--Public Health Service, unable to obtain funds, closed the hospital group on the island; Island No. 2 complex temporarily taken over by the Coast Guard.
1952	--Immigration and Naturalization Act, codifying existing legislation, made the quota system even more rigid and repressive.
1953-56	--Refugee Relief Act granted visas to some 5,000 Hungarians afer 1956 revolution; President Eisenhower invited 30,000 more on parole.
1954	--New detention policy enacted under which only those aliens "likely to abscond and those whose release would be inimical to the national security" were to be detained, while those with purely technical difficulties were allowed to proceed under parole. New policy resulted, within ten days, of a drop to 25 detained aliens at Ellis Island, compared to the previous several hundred.

Ellis Island Officially Closed

1954, Nov. 3   --Ellis Island officially closed and declared excess Federal property.

1955, Mar. 15   --In accordance with standing procedures, a screening of Federal agencies surfaced no need for the site, and the General Services Administration (GSA) declared Ellis Island surplus property

1955-56   --States, local governments and qualified non-profit institutions had next chance at the property and many varied proposals were submitted to GSA, e.g., New York City interest in site as home for aged and homeless; New York State introduced bill for site's use as alcoholic clinic; New Jersey State favored its use as an ethnic museum. Problems including required 50% cost by purchaser and revival of traditional boundary disputes between New York and New Jersey along with proposals for ineligible uses mitigated approval of any of these alternatives.

1956, Sept.   --GSA advertised Ellis Island for private sale by sealed bid, with response of 21 bids. Widespread public opposition to private sale developed, prompting GSA to again, unsuccessfully, canvass for public uses.

1957   --Special legislation enacted to admit Hungarian refugees.

1958-59   --GSA made three attempts to sell the island by sealed bids, but all were rejected as not being commensurate with the property's value. Among numerous proposals were a self contained city designed by Frank Lloyd Wright, a large resort complex, drug addiction rehabililation center, religious center, etc.

1960   --Interest in educational use of the Island led GSA to authorize HEW to review proposals and make the island available without charge for suitable applicant.

--Cuban immigration began, following Castro revolution.

1961   --HEW advised GSA that none of the proposals met requirements for a health or educational transfer of the property.

1962   --Subcommittee on Intergovernmental Relations reviewed 5 bills introduced in The 87th Congress: S. 2596 (Ellis Island for Higher Education, Inc.); S. 2852 (The Training School at Vineland, N.J.); and S. 867, S. 1118, and S. 1198, slightly different versions for health, education, and housing for the elderly. Action withheld pending further review.

--A final offer of $2.1 million to GSA was turned down.

Sept. 4   --Senator Muskie called Executive Meeting of the Subcommittee. Legislation enacted to allow admission of Hong Kong refugees.

1963   --Congress urged by President Kennedy to pass new legislation eliminating national origins quota system.

Ellis Island as a National Park

1963   --With New York and New Jersey state and local officials along with involved Federal agency representatives. New Jersey presented Liberty Park proposal, which prompted Sen. Muskie to request Dept. of Interior to review proposal for Ellis Island as a national park, monument, or recreational area in conjunction with the New Jersey sholeline."

--Dec. 3 meeting held at Federal Hall with 28 people representing Senate Subcommittee, NPS, BOR, GSA, Housing and Home Finance Agency, States of New York and New Jersey, New York City and Jersey City, to review the problem. NPS northeast Regional Director Lee designated coordinator of Ellis Island study in cooperation with BOR.

--Dec. 20, Study team met with New Jersey State officials to discuss technical aspects.

1964, May-June --Draft report reviewed with New Jersey and New York state and local officials.

--June 24, Study Report on Ellis Island forwarded to Senate Subcommittee, recommending Ellis Island be designated a National Historic Site.

1965 --Ellis Island declared part of the Statue of Liberty National Monument on May 11. President Johnson issued Proclamation 3656 adding Ellis Island to the Statue of Liberty National Monument.

--President Johnson signed into law liberalized immigration abolishing national origins quotas.

--August 17, P.L. 89-192 authorized appropriations of not more than $6 million for development of Ellis Island, with not more than $3 million to be appropriated during first five years.

--200-enrollee Job Corps Conservation Center was established on the New Jersey Waterfront and corpsmen worked on clean-up of Ellis Island as well as on Liberty Island and the Liberty State Park.

--Secretary of Interior Udall designated Philip Johnson to prepare a plan for Ellis Island.

1966   --Philip Johnson's design plan unveiled with some ceremony at Federal Hall, NY. It was met with mixed reactions. Subsequent NPS appraisal concluded that exhorbitant required costs necessitated shelving the plan.

--July, Cooperative Agreement between the Secretary of the Interior and the National Ellis Island Association, Inc. This cooperating association, an offshoot of the former U.S. Committee for Refugees (now the American Immigration and Citizenship Conference) was short lived, with no activity after 1967.

1968, Feb.   --NPS/Ellis Island Master Plan Team and guidelines established.

--June, Master Plan completed. Development concept focused on retention of the main building and removal of other structures except the ferryboat, covered walkways, three fairly modern buildings and possibly the older hospital group. Three physical units were recognized: the north unit, containing the main immigration building would communicate the park story; the south unit to be cleared would serve as a park activity area and for special ethnic events; the filled area joining these units would serve as a transition between them. Access would be a boat shuttle between Ellis and Liberty Islands and Ellis and Manhattan, with later access to Liberty Park when developed; careful study of a monorail or footbridge connection to New Jersey was recommended. The plan calls for interpretive development of the main building, for interpretive and administrative facilities in its west wing, and for a maintenance and residential area; facilities needed for ethnic events and a concession food service on the south unit; and space for a restaurant and evening program seating if either proves feasible.

--Nov., Master Plan approved.

1970, April   --Estimate for Master Plan implementation set by DSC as $3,950,600 for Phase 1 minimal requirements and $609,400 for Phase 11.

--Sept. 1, Special use permit issued to Dr. Thomas Matthew of the National Economic Growth and Reconstruction Organization, Inc. (NEGRO) for Sept. 21, the south side of the island. The group vacated the island in 1971. Health and safety considerations resulted in termination of the permit in April, 1973.

1972, Aug.   --During his dedication of the American Museum of Immigration, President Nixon expressed interest in completing development of Ellis Island by the Bicentennial celebration in July, 1976.

1973   --Nixon apparently became interested in possible private donations to rehabilitate Ellis Island. At the request of the Department, the region prepared five alternative options including private and joint Federal/private projects and returning Ellis Island to GSA. Costs ranged from $21 million to $77 million. During the same period, Secretary Morton expressed the view that Ellis should be divested due to rehabilitation cost burdens.

1974, Nov.   --A meeting was organized at Ellis Island with ethnic groups and NPS representatives for possible organization of private donation efforts. Outcome:

Most felt that government funding was essential as a demonstration of good faith and interest, and subsequent donations could be sought from the private sector. Dr. Peter Sammartino, Chancellor of Fairleigh Dickinson University. then with the New Jersey Bicentennial Commission and looking for a "pet project," was designated temporary chairman of an ad hoc committee--The Restore Ellis Island Committee.

1975   --Supplemental appropriations proposed to initiate a visitor use program at Ellis Island ($1.5 million: $550,000 development; $950,000 operating funds).

--Congressional party toured Ellis in May (Congressmen Sidney Yates, Frank E. Evans, and K. Gunn McKay). NARO had costed four options for actions required to allow visitors on Ellis, from $416,000 to $1,556,600.

--Two development options prepared by NARO for Assistant Secretary: a) $10 million for stabilization; b) $24 million for restoration.

--Old Master Plan recognized as out of date. Required revisions identification of buildings to be retained and appropride presenation action; land use classification of entire property as historic zone due to its status on National Register.

--Congress approved only $1 million for restoration: directed NPS to find $450,000 for operations.

1976   --Action plan implemented to open Ellis Island including dredging ferry basin, new dock, seawall study, limited rehabilitation of main building, installation of utilities, and employee housing. Interpretation plan developed by Ed Kallop, Regional Curator.

1976, May 30   --Ellis Island opened to visitation.

1977   --Ellis Island Subcommittee of the NAR Advisory Committee submits reporton review of 1968 Master Plan with their views on current issues regarding the future of Ellis Island.

--Meeting at north Atlantic Regional office with key regional and WASO staff; Regional Director recommended to Director that Phase 1 development of Ellis concentrate on keeping it open to limited visitation; stabilization of main building, other structures of high priority and seawall; development of utility systems.

--Omnibus legislation (H.R. 96-31) introduced by Congressman Skubitz on 10/18/77 included proposed ceiling authorization increase for Ellis from $6 million to $18.6 million. House subcommittee hearings in November; no NPS testimony. NPS justification for increase construction of sewage disposal system; rehabilitation of seawall and docking facilities.

--H.J. Resolution 651 to increase ceiling authorization to $50 million introduced by Congressmen Koch and Bingham, on Nov. 11. Rep. Koch inserted in Cong. Record NPS breakdown of obligated funds to date by project ($2.221 million of $6 million ceiling) and estimated remaining rehabilitation costs ($31 million).

1978   --Director called for study of Ellis Island to be conducted under lead of Tedd McCann.

--New York City Council passed resolution calling upon U.S. Congress to appropriate additional funds for Ellis Island rehabilitation.

--Congressman Bingham testified before Interior

Subcommittee on H.J, Rs. 651. Professor August C. Bolino accompanied him.

--Philip Lax elected President of the Restore Ellis Island Committee. He recommends that its name be changed to the Ellis Island Restoration Commission.

1980. Dec. 12 --Memorandum of Agreement signed between the Ellis Island Restoration Commission and the Department of the Interior, designating the Commission as the primary private fund raising organization.

1981 --After the election of Ronald Reagan as President, Garnet Chapin was appointed by Secretary James Watt to serve as liaison with the Ellis Island Restoration Commision.

--Dec. 14, Secretary Watt releases RFP WASO 82-11 for proposals for leasing Islands 2 and 3 with the private sector.

1982, May 18 --President Reagan announces the formation of the Statue of Liberty-Ellis Island Centennial Commission, with Lee Iacocca as Chairman. The Commission was charged with responsibility of raising money for restoring the two monuments in time for their centennials (1986 and 1992).

--The New York architectural firm of Beyer Blinder and Belle was appointed to restore the two landmarks, in association with Notter Finegold of Boston.

1984 -- Philip Lax appointed Chairman of the Subcommittee on Restoration, Architecture and Engineering of the Centennial Commission.

1986 --William N. Hubbard, President of the Center for Housing Partnerships of New York, was selected to build a conference center on the south end of Ellis

Island (the 17 acres of abandoned buildings).

--When the SI-EI Commission dropped plans for a genealogy room on Ellis Island, the Ellis Island Restoration Commission voted to raise funds for this purpose.

1987   --   INS proposes to donate microfilm records of ship manifests to establish an Immigration Archives and Genealogy Center on Ellis Island.

1988, June 9   --The Ellis Island Restoration announced plans to raise $25 million for the Ellis Island Family History Center. The first donation for the Center came from Mrs. Margaret O'Connell Middleton, granddaughter of the first person to be processed at Ellis Island in 1892.

--The SL-EI Foundation invited persons to place the name of an immigrant ancestor on the "Wall of Honor." Each tag on the wall will indicate the name and the country of origin.

--The U. S. Navy offered to raise the sunken ferryboat *Ellis Island* as part of a training exercise for Navy divers. When recovered, the boat will be placed on display next to the slip.

1990   --The Ellis Island Museum opens.

B. PERSONS WITH ELLIS ISLAND INTERVIEWS

Anderson, Prof. R Wayne,
   Dept. of History, Northeastern University, Boston, MA 02115

Archives, University of Missouri - St. Louis, 8001 Natural Bridge Rd., St. Louis, MO 63121 (314) 453-5143

Bernard, Prof. Richard
Dept of History, Marquette University, Milwaukee, WI 53201

Balmori, Prof. Diana
Dept. of History, SUNY - Oswego, Oswego, NY 13126

Barton, Prof. Joseph
Dept. of History, Northwestern University, Chicago, IL 60201

Bodnar, Dr. John
Pennsylvania Museum and Historical Commission, Box 1026, Harrisburg, PA, 17202

Candeloro, Prof. Domenic
Dept. of History, Governors State University, Chicago, IL 60606

Caroli, Prof. Betty Boyd
Kingsborough Community College, Brooklyn, NY 11235

Dixon, Dr. Harvey
Historian, American Museum of Immigration, New York, NY

Donnelly, Judith Tierney
Kings College, Wilkes Barre, PA 18711

Fox, Prof. John J.
Dept. of History, Salem State College, Salem, MA 01970

Greater Cleveland Ethnographic Museum,
137 Arcade, Cleveland, OH 44114

Giovinco, Prof. Joseph
Dept, of History, Sonoma State College, Santa Rosa, CA 95404

Jacobson, Charlolte
Archivist, Norwegian American Historical Association, St. Olaf College, Northfield, MN 55057

Kalcik, Susan
Folklife Program, Smithsonian Institution, Washington, D.C. 20560

Krog, Bronwyn
National Historical Park, Lowell, MA

La Gumina, Prof. Salvatore J.
Nassau Community College, Garden City, NY 11530

Langlois, Prof. Janet
Folklore Archives, Dept. of English, Wayne State University, Detroit, MI 48202

Lamppa, Barbara
Gilbert City Hall, Gilbert, MN 55741

Luther College
Decorah, Iowa 52101

Multicultural History Society of Ontario, Toronto, Ontario M552C3

New Jersey Historical Commission, Trenton, NJ 08625

Pane, Prof. Remigio
Rutgers University, New Brunswick, NJ 08902

Rippianen, Ellen M.
The Finnish American Historical Archives, Suomi College, Hancock, MI 49930

Santoro, Dr. Carmella
Rhode Island College, Providence, RI 02903

Simon, Prof. Roger D.
Dept. of History, Maginnes No. 9, Lehigh University, Bethlehem, PA 18015

Smemo, Prof. Kenneth
History Department, Moorhead State University, Moorhead, MN 56560

Stolarik, Dr. M. Mark
Balch Institute, Philadelpha, PA 19106

Sundberg, Prof. Edward F.
c/o Luther College, Decorah, Iowa 52101

Weinberg, Prof. Daniel
San Diego State University, San Diego, CA 92115

Wynar, Prof. Lubomyr R.
Dept. of Library Science, Kent State University, Kent, OH 44242

YIVO Institute for Jewish Culture
1048 5th Ave., New York, NY 10028

C. PERSONS AND PLACES WITH DOCUMENTS Of ELLIS ISLAND

Anderson, Harry
Milwaukee County Historical Society, Milwaukee, WI 53233

Blouin, Dr. Francis X.
Bentley Historical Library, University of Michigan, 1150 Beal Ave., Ann Arbor, MI 48109

Bentivegna, Prof. Joseph
26 College Heights, Loretta, PA 15940

Bockman, Eugene
Commissioner, Department of Records and Information Services, New New York City Archives, NY 10013

Cadzow, Dr. John Director, Ethnic Heritage Program, Kent State University, Kent, OH 44243

Caroli, Prof. Betty Boyd
Kimbrough Community College, Brooklyn, NY 11235

Chlobot, Fr. Leonard
St. Mary's College, Orchard Lake, MI 48033

Cubelic, Prof. Charles
Robert Morris College, 610 5th Ave., Pittsburgh, PA 15219

Douet, Madeline
Archivist, New York City YWCA, 610 Lexington Ave., NYC 10022

Drobniak, Vincent
Jednota Museum and Archive Institute, 10 Rosedale Ave., Middleton, PA 17057

Genealogical Society of Utah
Salt Lake City, Utah 84115

Glazier, Prof. Ira
National Immigration Archives, Temple University, Philadephia, FA 19122

Grabowski, Dr. John
Western Reserve Historical Society, Cleveland, OH 44113

Harris, Joan
Brooklyn YWCA, 30 3rd Ave., Brooklyn, NY 11217

Hefner, Loretta L.
Utah State Historical Archives, Salt Lake City, Utah 84115

Hines Collection
International Museum of Photography, George Eastman House, Rochester, NY

Hruban, Dr. Zbemek
Prof. of Pathology, University of Chicago, Chicago, IL 60637

Jacobson, Charlotte
Archivist, Norwegian American Historical Association, St. Olaf College, Northfield, MN 55057

Johnson, Dr. Mary Ann
Jane Addams Hull House, 750 S. Halstead, Chicago, IL 60607

Kemble, Harold
Rhode Island Historical Society, Providence, RI 02903

Kindberg, Dr. Youngie
New York International Bible Society, 144 Tices Lane, East Brunswick, New Jersey, 08816

Kovach, Kenneth J.
The Ohio Historical Society, 140 Arcade, Cleveland, OH 44114

Laurano, Michael
East Boston Historical Society 73 Meridian Street, East Boston, MA 02128

Lundeen, Rev. Joel
Archivist, Lutheran Church of America, 1100 E. 55th St., Chicago, IL 60615

Montalto, Dr. Nicholas
International Institute, Jersey City, NJ 07306

Moore, Milton C.
Slavic-American Collection, Lovejoy Library, S. Ilinois Univ., Edwardsville, IL 62026

Multicultural Historical Society of Ontario, 43 Queens Park Crescent E., Ontario M552C3

National Personnel Records Center
111 Winnebago St., St. Louis, MO 63118

New York City Historical Society
170 Central Park West, New York, NY 10024

Norris, Elizabeth
National Board of the YWCA of the USA, 600 Lexington Ave, New York, NY 10022

Parker, Peter
Historical Society of Pennsylvania, 1300 Locust St., Philadelphia, PA 19107

Richardson, Prof. James
Dept. of History, University of Akron, Akron, OH 44325

Rischin, Prof. Moses
Dept. of History, San Francisco State University, San Francisco, CA 94132

Siegel, Stephen W.
155 E. 93rd, Apt. C, New York, NY 10028

Svoboda, Dr. Joseph

Archivist, University of Nebraska, Lincoln, Nebraska 68588

Society of American Archivists S. Wells, Chicago, IL 60606

Stolarik, Dr. M. Mark
Balch Institute, 18 S. 7th, Philadelphia, PA 19106

Thompson, Katherine
Wisconsin State Historical Society, 816 State St., Madison, WI 53702

Tegeder, Fr. Vincent
Archivist, St. Johns College, Collegeville, MN 56321

Tomasi, Fr. Lydio F.
Center for Migration Studies, 209 Flagg Place, Staten Island, NY 10304

U.S. Catholic Conference
Migration and Refugee Service, 1312 Massachusetts Ave., NW, Washington, D.C. 20005

Vecoli, Prof. Rudolph J.
Immigration History Research Center, 826 Berrry St., St. Paul, MN 55114

Vinyard, Prof. Jo Ellen
History Department, Marygrove College, Detroit, MI 48221

Wax, Dr. Bernard
American Jewish Historical Society, Thornton Rd., Waltham, MA 02154

Weldon, Edward
Archivist, New York State Archives, Albany, NY 12224

Yans-McGloughlin, Prof. Virginia
61 Jane St,, New York, NY 10014

YIVO Institute for Jewish Culture
1048 5th Ave., New York, NY 10028

Zabrosky, Dr., Frank

Archivist, Archives of Industrial Society, Univ. of Pittsburgh, Pittsburgh, PA 15260

D. AMERICAN COUNCIL FOR NATIONALITIES SERVICE

Member Agencies

AKRON - International Institute, 207 East Tallmadge Ave., Akron, OH 44310, Exec. Dir: Maxine Floreani (216) 376-5106

ALBANY - International Center, West Mall Office Plaza, 875 Central Ave., Albany, NY 12206 Exec. Dir. Helene Smith (518) 459-8812

BINGHAMTON - American Civic Association, 131 Front St., Binghamton, NY 13905, Exec. Dir: Irene Krome (607) 723-9419

BOSTON - International Institute of Boston, 287 Commonwealth Ave., Boston, MA 02115, Exec. Dir: James Aldrich (617) 536-1081

BRIDGEPORT - Internalional Institute of Connecticut, 670 Clinton Ave. Bridgeport, Connecticut 06608, Exec. Dir: Myra M. Oliver (203) 336-0141

BUFFALO - International Institute of Buffalo, 864 Delaware Ave., Buffalo, NY 14209, Exec. Dir: Hinke Boot (716) 883-1900

CHICAGO - Travelers & Immigrants Aid of Chicago, 327 S. LaSalle St., Chicago, IL 60604, Exec. Dir: Sid Mohn (312) 435-4500. Dir., Prog. Operations: Steve Voss

CINCINNATI - Traveler's Aid-International Inst. of Cincinnati, 632 Vine St. Suite 505, Cincinnati, OH 45202, Exec. Dir: Dr. Ernest Barbeau (513) 721-7660

CLEVELAND - The Nationalities Service Center, The Price Bldg., 1715 Euclid ave. Cleveland, OH 44115, Exec. Dir: Algis Ruksenas (216) 781-4560

DETROIT - International Institute of Metropolilan Detroit, 111 E. Kirby Ave., Detroit, MI 48202, Exec. Dir: Mary Ball (313) 871-8600

ERIE - International Institute of Erie Pennsylvania, 330 Holland St., Erie, PA 16507 Exec. Dir: Paul Jericho (814) 452-3935

FLINT - International Institute, 515 Stevens St., Flint, MI 48502, Exec. Dir: Mary E. Schultz (313) 767-0720

GARY - International Institute of Northwest Indiana, Inc., 4433 Broadway, Gary, IN 46409, Exec. Dir: Larry Sharp (219) 980-4636

HOUSTON - YMCA International Services, 3635 W. Dallas St., Houston, TX 77019 Exec. Dir. Nancy Falgout (713) 527-8690

JERSEY CITY - International Institute of New Jersey, 880 Bergen Avenue, Jersey City, NJ 07306, Exec. Dir: Nicholas Montalto (201) 653-3888

KANSAS CITY - Don Bosco Cummunity Center, 529 Campbell St., Kansas City, MO 64106 Exec. Dir. Lou Rose (816) 421-0546

LAREDO - Asociacion Pro Servicios Sociales, Centro Aztlan, 406 Scott St., Laredo, TX 78040 Exec. Dir. Albrerto Luera (512) 724-6244

LAWRENCE - International Institute of Greater Lawrence, Inc., 454 Canal St., Lawrence, MA 01840, Exec. Dir: Gregory Miller (508) 687-0981

LOS ANGELES - International Institute of Los Angeles, 435 S. Boyle

Ave., Los Angeles, CA 90033, Exec. Dir: Lavinia Limon (213) 264-4623

LOWELL - International Institute of Lowell, 79 High St., Lowell, MA 01852, Exec. Dir: Lydia A. Mattei (617) 459-9031

MANCHESTER - International Center, Inc., 102 N. Main St., Manchester, NH 03102, Program Dir: Jackie Whatmough (603) 668-8602

MILWAUKEE - International Institute of Wisconsin 2810 West Highland Blvd., Milwaukee, WI 53208, Exec. Dir: Alexander P. Durtka (414) 933-2538

NEW YORK - Travelers Aid Services, 2 Lafayette St., New York, NY 10007 Exec. Dir. Helene Lauffer (212) 385-0331

OAKLAND - International Institute of East Bay, 297 Lee St., Oakland, CA 94610, Exec. Dir: Zoe Borkowski (415) 451-2846

PHILADELPHIA - Nationalities Service Center of Philadelphia, 1300 Spruce St., Philadelphia PA 19107 Exec. Dir: Michael D. Blum (215) 893-8400

PROVIDENCE - International Institute of Rhode Island, Inc, 421 Elmwood Ave., Providence, RI 02907, Exec. Dir: William B. Shuey (401) 461-5940

ST. LOUIS - International Institute of Metropolitan St. Louis, 3800 Park Ave., St. Louis, MO 63110, Exec. Dir: Anna Crosslin (314) 773-9O9O

ST. PAUL - International Institute of Minnesota, 1694 Como Ave., St. Paul, MN 55108, Exec. Dir: Robert J. Hoyle (612) 647-0191

SAN FRANCISCO - International Institute of San Francisco, 2209

Van Ness Ave., San Francisco, CA 94109, Exec. Dir: Don Eiten (415) 673-1720

TOLEDO - International Institute of Toledo, 2040 Scottwood Ave., Toledo, OH 43620, Exec. Dir: Janice Clark (419) 241-9178

WASHINGTON, D. C. - Travelers Aid Society of Washington, D. C. 1015 12th St. N. W. 20005 Exec. Dir. Pauline Dunn (202) 347-0101

E. MAJOR AMERICAN ETHNIC ORGANIZATIONS[2]

B'nai B'rith, 1640 Rhode Island Ave., N.W., Washington, D.C 20036, 500,000 members

Polish National Alliance of U.S., 1520 W. Division Street, Chicago, IL 60622, 306,022 members

Lithuanian Roman Catholic Federation of America, 4545 W 63rd Sl., Chicago, IL 60629, 300,000 members

Ancient Order of Hibernians in America, 27 Mada Ave., Staten Island, NY 10310, 191,000 members

Patriarchal Parishes of the Moscow Patriarchate in America, St. Nicholas Cathedral, 15 E. 9th St., New York, NY 10029, 150,000 members

Polish Roman American Catholic Union of America, 984 Mllwaukee Ave, Chicago, IL 60622, 140,000 members

National Slavic Convention, 16 South Peterson Ave., Baltimore, MD 21231, 120,000 members

American Hungarian Federation, 3216 N. Mexico Ave., N.W.,

---

[2]Lubumyr R. Wynar, Encyclopedic Directory of Ethnic Organizations in the Unied States (Littleton: Libraries Unlimited, 1975); Encyclopedia of Associations, 1985 (Detroit: Gale Research, 1985).

Washington, D.C, 20016, 120,000 members

Croatian Fraternal Union of America, 100 Delaney Dr., Pittsburgh, PA 15235, 112,000 members

Sons of Norway, 1455 W. Lake St., Minneapolis, MN 55408, 105,000 members

National Council of Columbia Associations in Civil Service (Italian), 299 Broadway, Room 1500, New York, NY 1OOO7, 105,000 members

First Catholic Slovak Union of the U.S. and Canada, 3289 E. 55th St., Cleveland, OH 44127, 96,800 members

Croatian Fraternal Union of America, 100 Delaney Dr., Pittsburgh, PA 15235, 90,000 members

Ukranian National Association, 30 Montgomery St., Jersey City, NJ 07302, 85,000 members

First Slavic Union of the U.S.A. and Canada, 3289 E, 55th St., Cleveland, OH 44127,

Williarn Penn Association (Hungarian), 100 Wood St., Pittsburgh, PA 15222, 63,078 members

Greek Catholic Union of the U.S.A., 502 E. Eighth Ave., Munhall, FA 15120, 52,000 members

Slovene National Benefit Society, 166 Shore Dr., Burr Ridge, IL 605:21, 50,310 members

Order of Ahepa (Heilenic), 1422 K St., NW, Washington, D.C. 20005, 49,000 members

Czechoslovak Society of America, 2137 S. Lombard Ave., Cicero, IL 60650, 46,000 members

American Slovenian Catholic Union, 351-53 N. Chicago St., Joliet, IL 60431, 44,000 members

English Speaking Union of The United SIates, 16 E. 69th St., New York City, NY 10021, 37,000 members

VASA Order of America, 32 Temple Place, Boston, MA 02111, 36,000 members

United Societies of the United States of America (Greek), 613 Sinclair St., McKeesport, PA 15132, 34,000 members

American Committee on Italian Migration, 9 E. 35th St., New York, NY 10016, 30,000 members

Serbian National Defense Council, 3909 West North, Chicago, IL 60647, 30,000 members

Polish National Union of America, 1002 Pittman Ave., Scranton, PA 18505, 30,000 members

Polish Falcons of America, 97 S. 18th St., Pittsburgh, PA 15203, 29,686 members

Hungarian Reformed Federation of America, P.O. Box 3491; Bethesda, MD 20817; 25,000 members

National Slavic Society of the United States, 2325 E. Carson St., Pittsburgh, PA 15203, 23,000 members

German American National Congress, 4740 N. Western Ave., Chicago, IL 60625, 20,000 members

Alliance of Poles of America, 6966 Broadway, Cleveland, OH 44105, 20,000 members

Federation of French Alliances in the United States, 22 E. 60th St., New York City, NY 19,000 members

Providence Association of Ukranian Catholics in America, 817 N. Franklin St., Philadelphia, PA 19123, 19,089 members

Selfreliance Association of American Ukranians, 98 Second Ave., New York, NY 10003, 14,520 members

Croatian Catholic Union of the U.S.A., One W. Old Ridge Rd., Hobart, IN 46342, 13,000 members

Russian Brotherhood Organization of the U.S.A., 1733 Spring Garden St., Philadelphia, PA 19130, 12,000 members

Danish Brotherhood in America, P.O. Box 31748, 3717 Harney St., Omaha, NE 68131, 12,000 members

Polish Union of America, Box 79, 761 Filmore Ave., Buffalo, NY 14212, 12,000 members

Polish National Alliance of Brooklyn, U.S.A., 155 Noble St., Brooklyn, NY 11222, 11,135 members

Lithuanian Alliance of America, 307 W 30th St., New York, NY 10001, 10,000 members

F. MEMORANDUM OF AGREEMENT BETWEEN THE NATIONAL PARK SERVICE AND ELLIS ISLAND RESTORATION COMMISSION, INC.

THIS MEMORANDUM OF AGREEMENT is hereby entered into this 5th day of June, 1987, by and between the Ellis Island Restoration Commission, Inc. a corporation organized and doing business under the laws of the State of New Jersey, hereinafter referred to as the CORPORATION and the NATIONAL PARK SERVICS, U.S. Department of the Interior, covering certain fundraising and philanthropic activities which are intended to benefit the National Park System.

WHEREAS, Ellis Island, part of the Statue of Liberty National Monument, a unit of the National Park System, and a national symbol of United States immigration policies that for more than a century played a pivotal role in the growth and settlement of the Nation, requires large scale rehabilitation, preservation and development to serve public programs in education, recreation, and study;

WHEREAS, the NATIONAL PARK SERVICE supports the development of, and has reserved space for, an Immigration Data Center on the second floor of the west wing of the Main building on Ellis Island which would enable visitors to: supplement their knowledge and understanding of the immigration experience; conduct a computerized search of historical records of individuals who passed through Ellis Island; obtain data from the ship's manifest for the vessel which carried specific individuals.

WHEREAS, the NATIONAL PARK SERVICE through the Secretary of the Interior has authority to accept donations for the purposes embraced by this MEMORANDUM of AGREEMENT (see 41 Stat. 917, 16 U.S.C. 6); and

WHEREAS, nothing in this MEMORANDUM OF AGREEMENT shall affect or interfere with fulfilling of the obligations or exercise of the authority of the NATIONAL PARK SERVICE or any other Federal agency; and

WHEREAS the NATIONAL PARK SERVICE wishes to recognize and encourage the Ellis Island Restoration Commission, Inc. as the organization which will plan, fund and operate an Immigration Data Center subject to the guidance and approval of the the NATIONAL PARK SERVICE; and

WHEREAS, the NATIONAL PARK SERVICE and the Statue of Liberty/Ellis Island Foundation, Inc. have agreed that the Foundatlon will undertake a supplemental fundraising campaign to provide an additional $14 million to support the the Ellis Island restoratlon efforts.

NOW THEREFORE, the parties agree as follows:

1. The NATIONAL PARK SERVICE recognizes the CORPORATION as an organization suited to raise funds for the benefit of the PARK;

2. The NATIONAL PARK SERVICE will not provide funds for the development or the operation of the Immigration Data Center; the Center will be operated by an independent organization.

3. The CORPORATION, in recognition of the supplementary fundraising campaign to be conducted by the Statue of Liberty/Ellis Island Foundation, Inc. will not publicly seek funds or promote the fundraising effort for the Immigration Data Center through the public media for a period of one year from the date of this agreement;

4. After one year, the CORPORATION will coordinate efforts closely With the NATIONAL PARK SERVICE and the Statue of

Liberty/Ellis Island Foundation, Inc, to ensure that the CORPORATION'S fundraising activities do not compromise those of the Foundation;

5. The CORPORATION Will donate to the NATIONAL PARK SERVICE funds, materials and/or services to develop an Immigration Data Center under the following terms and conditions:

A. Fundraising Activities

1. The CORPORATION shall be fully qualified under State and Federal law to engage in fundraising and receive philanthropic contributions for the purposes enumerated herein, and will provide an opinion of counsel to that effect.

2. The CORPORATION is authorized to solicit donations only by methods approved by the NATIONAL PARK SERVICE as appropriate to the mission of the NATIONAL PARK SERVICE and only for purposes within the legal authority of the NATIONAL PARK SERVICE to undertake.

3. Within 120 days and prior to any fundraising solicitations pursuant to this MEMORANDUM OF AGREEMENT, the CORPORATION shall furnish to the NATIONAL PARK SERVICE for approval a project plan indicating the specific scope of the Immigration Data center project (including concepts, objectives, revenues operational requirements, development timetables and costs) and a plan of operations which will clearly identify the roles and responsibilities of both the NATIONAL PARK SERVICE and the CORPORATION and will also indicate the overral strategy for fundraising, the fundraising techniques to be used, timetables covering the length of time required for the fundraising effort, administrative and support structures, projected costs, and estimated results. These plans shall be updated as conditions change, and, in any event, on at least an annual basis. Any materials prepared for public consumption, such as individual promotional activi+ies, brochures, or any other form of publicity will be submitted to the NATIONAL PARK SERVICE for formal review and approval prior to its release. In addition, any agreements the CORPORATION proposes to enter into

with third parties in furtherance of its activities hereunder shall be subject to approval by the NATIONAL PARK SERVICE.

4. Within 90 days from the approval of the operatlons plan and quarterly thereafter, the CORPORATION shall submit status reports to the National Park Service setting forth the progress of the fundraising effort, any present or anticipated problems, and financial projections for remaining work and the progress of the fundraising programs. The report shall set forth quarterly goals for the fundraising efforts and shall compare the performance during the prior quarter to the goals set forth for that quarter. The reports following the first shall be submitted by the 15th day of the month following the end of each calendar quarter.

5. All costs of the fundraising campaign shall be borne by the CORPORATION.

6. Funds received and expended by the corporation from whatever source shall be expended only in furtherance of the purposes of this MEMORANDUM OF AGREEMENT and shall be accounted for under a system of accounts and financial controls meeting accepted professional standards for non-profit charitable organizations; the CORPORATION shall engage an annual audit by a qualified audit firm and shall publish an annual report of its activities and finances. All such accounts shall be subject to audit by the NATIONAL PARK SERVICE or its authorized representative.

7. Funds donated to the NATIONAL PARK SERVICE by the CORPORATION will be placed in a special donations account and shall be used solely on behalf of and for benefit of the projects and activities set forth above unless otherwise provided by law. In the event that insufficient funds are collected to accomplish the project specified herein, however,

the NATIONAL PARK SERVICE reserves the right to utilize such funsa as collected for other worthy projects ln the park.

8. The NATIONAL PARK SERVICE will make available to the CORPORATION such information and data as may reasonably be

required and is generally available to inform potential donors and others about the status of plans for the projects and activities to benefit.

9.   The CORPORATION is recognized as a fundraiser of donations for the purposes and projects enumerated in this MEMORANDUM OF AGREEMENT. The NATIONAL PARK SERVICE may choose to enter into similar arrangements with others.

10.   The CORPORATION agrees to assure that it's financial efforts and purpose will be explicitly identified to the public so as not to be confused with other fundraising efforts for the Statue of Liberty National Monument (Liberty Island and Ellis Island) also approved by the NATIONAL PARK SERVICE. All advertising, fundraislng materials, and other information made available to the public must receive prior written approval of the NATIONAL PARK SERVICE before release or dissemination to ensure that there is no confusion associated with the various fundraising activities.

11.   The CORPORATION agrees that all materials (printed, audio, video) and capital improvements developed through this fundraising effort shall be the exclusive property of the NATIONAL PARK SERVICE unless at such time the NATIONAL PARK SERVICE specifically declines to accept such materials orcapital improvements.

B. In-park Activities:

1.   The NATIONAL PARK SERVICE to the extent practicable agrees to arrange for and conduct tours, interpretive events and inspections for individuals and groups at the request of the CORPORATION provided that such activities shall not, in the judgment of the NATIONAL PARK SERVICE, unduly infringe upon or detract from normal visitor activities and services of the PARK. The CORPORATION shall request such tours and other events through the park Superintendent (hereinafter referred to as the SUPERINTENDENT) in advance. The SUPERINTENDENT shall have final decision making responsiblllty as to such arrangements, depending upon park workloads and staff availability.

2. The CORPORATION shall apply for and abide by the terms and conditions, of a special events permit for each such event it proposes to conduct. The SUPERINTENDENT shall have the final authority over the granting of such permits.

3. The CORPORATION may not undertake any activities or operations, construct any structures or buildings on park land or otherwlse make alterations to park land without further written permission from the NATIONAL PARK SERVICE.

C. Key Officials

National Park Service: Herbert S. Cables, Jr.
Regional Director
North Atlantic Region
National Park Service
15 State Street Boston,
Massachusetts 02109-3572

Ellis Island Restoration
Commission, Inc.:   Philip Lax, President
830 Morris Turnpike
Short Hills, New Jersey 07078
201-467-1333

D. Insurance

1. The CORPORATION shall procure public and employee liability insurance from responsible companies with a minimum limitation of $250,000 per person for any one claim and an aggregate limit of $1,000,000 for any number of claims arising from any one Incident. The United States of America shall be named as an additlonal insured on all such policies. All such policies shall specify that the insurer shall have no right of subrogation against the United States for payments of any premiums or deductibles thereunder and such insurance policies shall be assumed by, credited to the account of, and undertaken at the CORPORATION's sole risk.

2. The CORPORATION shall indemnify, save and hold

harmless and defend the United States against all fines, claims, damages, losses, judgments, and expenses arising out of or from any omission or activity in connection with activities under this Agreement.

E. General Provisions

1. All activities performed under this MEMORANDOM OF AGREEMENT will be accomplished in conformance with the formal fundraising policies of theNATIONAL PARK SERVICE which are made a part of this MEMORANDUM OF AGREEMENT (See Appendix 1).

2. The NATIONAL PARK SERVICE may terminate this MEMORANDUM OF AGREEMENT for the convenience of the Government at any time.

3. Subject to Section D-2 above, this MEMORANDUM OF AGREEMENT effective when signed by both parties, and shall remain in effect as needed for up to three years from that date, subject to renewal by mutual agreement for a further period not to exceed three years.

4. All obligations of the NATIONAL PARK SERVICE hereunder are subject to the availability of funds, and to such direction and instructions as may have been or are provided by Congress.

5. During performance under this MEMORANDUM OF AGREEMENT, the CORPORATION agrees to abide by the terms of Executive Order 11246 (Apendix 2) on nondiscrimination and will not discriminate against any person because of race, color, religion, sex or national origin. The CORPORATION will take positive action to ensure that applicants are employeh without regard to their race, color, religion, sex or national origin.

6. No member of, or delegate to, Congress, or resident commissioner shall be admitted to any share or part of this MEMORANDUM OF AGREEMENT, or to any benefit that may arise therefrom; but this provision shall not be construed to extend to this MEMORANDUM OF AGREEMENT if made with a CORPORATION

for its general benefit.

Dated the 5th day June 1987.

AGREED TO BY:

Herbert S. Cables, ,Jr.
Regional Director
National Park Service

Philip Lax
President
Ellis Island Restoration
Commission, Inc.

ADDITIONAL BIBLIOGRAPHY [1]

BOOKS

Allen, Leslie. Liberty: The Statue and the American Dream. Statue of Liberty/Ellis Island Foundation, 1986.

Arendi, Bruno A. Italian Americana. Buffalo: State University, 1974.

Arnason, H. H. Jacques Lipchitz. Sketches In Bronze. New York: Prraeger, 1969.

Arnold Elliot. Deep in My Heart. New York: Duell, Sloan and Pearce, 1949.

Baxter, Angus. In Search of Your German Roots. Baltimore: Genealogical Publishing, 1987.

----------. In Search of Your British and Irish Roots. Baltimore: Genealogical Publishing, 1989.

Beard, Annie E.S. Our Foreign Born Citizens. New York: Thomas Crowell, 1969.

Blair, Clay. Atomic Submarine and Admiral Rlckover. Holt, Rinehart and Winston, 1954.

Bodnar, John. The Transplanted. Bloomington: Indiana University Press, 1985.

---

[1] The first edition of this Source Book presented a 112-page bibliography. Although the first edition is out of print, it is available in many libraries. In this edition, we offer additional references, most of which were published after 1984 or which deal with chapters that are new to the Second Edition.

Cateura, Linda Brandi. Growing Up Italian. New York: William Morrow, 1987.

Chasims, Abram. Leopold Stokowski. New York: Hawthorn, 1979.

Cordasco, Francesco and Michael Vaughn Cordasco. The Italian Emigration to the United States, 1880-1930. Fairview: Junius-Vaughn Press, 1989.

Cremer, Robert. The Man Behind the Cape. New York: Regnery, 1976.

Crimi, Alfred D. My Life Story. Staten Island: Center for Migration Studies, 1988.

Daley Arthur. Knute Rockne. 1906.

Diner, Hasia. Erin's Daughters in America. Johns Hopkins University Press, 1983.

Directory of German-American Resources and Organizations. U. S. Information Agency, 1987.

Dolan, Ray, The Immigrant Church. Johns Hopkins University Press, 1975.

Dollarhide, William. Managing a Genealogical Project. Baltimore: Genealogical Publishing, 1988.

Dubinsky David and A. H. Raskin, David Dubinsky: A Life of Labor. New York: Simon and Schuster, 1977.

Dwyer, Joseph D. (Comp.) Slovenes in the United States and Canada: A Bibliography. Saint Paul, 1981.

Erickson, Charlotte. English Immigration to America. New York: Holmes and Meier, 1988.

Freedland M. Irving Berlin. New York: Stein and Day, 1974.

Fucilla, Joseph G. Our Italian Surnames. (Revised edition; Baltimore: Genealogical Publishing, 1987.

Furman, Bess. A Profile of the United States Public Health Service, 1798-1948. Washington: Department of Health, Education and Welfare, 1950.

Glazier, Ira A. and Luigi de Rosa (eds.) Migration Across Time and Nations. New York: Holmes and Meier, 1986.

Gordon, Milton. Assimilation in American Life: The Role of Race, Religion and National Origins. Oxford University Press, 1964.

Higham, John. Strangers In The Land. Atheneum Press, 1963.

Hoerder, Dirk (ed.). The Immigrant Labor Press in North America. Vol. II: Migrants from Eastern and Southeastern Europe. Greenwood Press, 1987.

Hoogland, Eric J. (ed.). Crossing the Waters: Arabic-Speaking Immigrants to the United States before 1940. Washington: Smithsonian Institution, 1987.

Hope, B. Have Tux, Wlll Travel. New York. Simon and Schuster, 1954.

Hope, B. and B. Thomas. My 40-Year Love Affair With the Movies. New York: Doubleday, 1977.

Houseman J. Run Through, A Memoir. New York: Simon and Schuster, 1972.

Houseman, J. Front and Center. New York,: Simon and Schuster, 1979.

Jerome, Harry. Migration and Business Cycles. New York: National Bureau of Economic Research, 1926.

Kazan, E. Kazan on Kazan. New York: Viking, 1974.

Klayman, Richard. The First Jew. Malden: Old Suffolk Square Press, 1985.

Kobler, J. Capone, The Life and World of Al Capone. New York, 1971.

Kraser, Jerome and William Egelman (eds.). The Melting Pot and Beyond: Italian Americans in the Year 2000. Staten Island: Center for Migration Studies, 1985.

Kraut, Alan. The Huddled Masses. Harlan Davidson, Inc., 1982.

Kuznets, Simon and Ernest Rubin. Immigration and the Foreign Born. New York: National Bureau of Economic Research, 1954.

LaGumina, Salvatore J. From Steerage to Suburb: Long Island Italians. Staten Island: Center for Migration Studies, 1988.

Lash, Joseph P., From the Diaries of Felix Frankfurter. New York: W. W. Norton, 1974.

Lennig, Arthur. Count: The Life and Films of Bela "Dracula" Lugosi. New York: Putnam, 1974.

Light, Ivan. Ethnic Enterprise in America. University of California Press, 1972.

Lovoll, Odd S. A Century of Urban Life: The Norwegians in Chicago Before 1930. Northfield: Norwegian-American Historical Association, 1988.

Magocsi, Paul Robert. Our People. Fairview: Carpatho-Rusyn Research Center, 1985.

----------. Carpatho-Rusyn Studies. Fairview: Carpatho-Rusyn Research Center, 1988.

----------. The Carpatho-Rusyn Americans. Fairview: Carpatho-Rusyn Research Center, 1989.

Miller, Wayne C. Minorities in America. University Park: Pennsylvania State University Press, 1987.

Moody, Suzanna and Joel Wurl (Comps.). The Immigration History Research Center: A Guide to Collections. Greenwood Press, 1989.

Mormino, Gary Ross. Immigrants on the Hill: Italian-Americans in Saint Louis, 1882-1982. Hagerstown: University of Illinois Press, 1986.

Mormino, Gary Ross and George E.Pozzetta. The Immigrant World of Ybor City. Hagerstown: University of Illinois Press, 1987.

Morrison, Joan and Charlotte Fox Zabusky, American Mosaic. Meridian, 1989.

Naff, Alixa. Becoming American: The Early Arab Experience. Carbondale: Southern Illinois University Press, 1985.

Nash, Gary. Red, White and Black. Harvard University Press, 1982.

National Center for Urban Ethnic Affairs. 1987 Report. Washington, D.C.

Ness, E. Untouchables. New York: Messner, 1957.

Nizer, L. Reflections Without Mirrors. New York; Doubleday, 1978.

Patai, Irene. Encounters--Life of Jacques Lipchitz. New York: Funk and Wagnall, 1961.

Phillips Harlan B. Felix Frankfurter Reminisces. New York: Reynal, 1960.

Piore, Michael. Birds of Passage. Cambridge University Press, 1979.

Polmar, Norman and Thomas B. Allen. Rickover: Controversy and Genius. New York: Simon and Schuster, 1982.

Rosenberg H. Arshile Gorky--The Man, The Time, The Idea. New York: Horizon, 1962.

Saarinen, E. Eero Saarinen. New York.: Simon and Schuster, 1971.

Scourby, Alice. The Greek Americans. Boston: Twayne Publishers, 1984.

Seller, Maxine. Immigrant Women. Temple University Press, 1980.

Shulman, Irving. Valentino. New York: Trident, 1967.

Simons, Howard, Jewish Times: Voices of the American Jewish Experience. Houghton Mifflin, 1988.

Smithsonian Institution. The New Immigration. 1983.

Sowell, Thomas. Race and Economics. David McKay, 1975.

Swierenga, Robert P. The Dutch in America: Immigration, Settlement, and Cultural Change. New Brunswick: Rutgers University Press, 1985.

Taylor, Theodore. Jule: The Story of Jule Styne. New York: Random House, 1979.

Temko, Allan. Eero Saarinen. Braziller, 1962.

Tezla, Albert. Valahol tul, Meseorszagban: Az amerikas magyarok, 1895-1920. (Somewhere in a Distant Fabled Land: American-Hungarians, 1895-1920) Budapest: Europa Publishing, 1987. Voices from Ellis Island: An Oral History of American Immigration. University Publications.

Vardy, Steven Bela. The Hungarian-Americans. Boston: Twayne, 1985.

Walker, Alexander. Rudolph Valentino. New York: Stein and Day, 1976.

Wallace, The Notre Dame Story. 1949.

West, Herbert F. The Autobiography of Robert Watchorn. Oklahoma City: Watchorn Charities, 1958.

Wielenski, Bernard. Doctoral Dissertations, Master Thesis and Bachelor Honor Essays Regarding Polish Subjects: 1900-1985. Pennsylvania Commission on History and Archives, 1988.

Woolcott, The Story of Irving Berlin. 1925.

Wyman, Mark. DP: Europe's Displaced Persons, 1945-1951. Philadelphia: Balch Institute Press, 1989.

Wynar, Lubomyr R. Guide to American Ethnic Press: Slavic and Eastern European Newspapers and Periodicals. Kent: Kent State University, 1986.

ARTICLES

Barkai, Avraham. "German-Jewish Migration in the 19th Century, 1830-1910," Paper delivered at the 8th International Economic History Congress, Budapest, 1982.

Berrol, Selma, "A Bibliography for the Study of German Jews in the United States," The Immigration History Newsletter. June 1989.

Bolino, August C. "Isle of Tears, Isle of Hope," Michigan Alumnus. July/August 1986.

Breen, Joseph I. "Our Immigrants, What they Need and How We are Helping Them," NCWC Bulletin. March 1923, 3-5.

Cerase, Francesco P. "A Case Study of Italian Migrants Returning from the U.S.A.." International Migration Review. Summer 1967, 67-74.

Cordasco, Francesco. "The Bolletino del'Emigrazione (1902-1927) as a Guide to the Chronicles of Italian Mass Emigration," Ethnic Forum. (1987), 57-68.

DiComiti, Luigi and Ira A. Glazier. "Socio-Demographic Characteristics of Italian Emigration to the United States from Ship Passenger Lists: 1880-1914," Ethnic Forum. Spring 1984.

Dobbins, Elizabeth V. "Assisting the Newly Arrived Immigrant," NCWC Bulletin. January 1921, 8-10.

"Ellis Island," Engineering News-Record. May 31, 1984.

"Ellis Island," New York Times. June 15, 1989.

Finkelstein, Monte S. "The Johnson Act, Mussolini and Fascist Emigrant Policy, 1921-1930," Journal of American Ethnic History. VIII (Fall 1988), 38-55.

Ford Foundation. Letter. August 1988.

Gould, J. D. "European Intercontinental Emigration: The Role of 'Diffusion' and 'Feedback,' The Journal of European Economic History. IX (Fall 1980).

Immigration and Naturalization Service. "Ellis Island: A Proposal for a National Center," 1987.

Lintelman, Joy K. "America is the Woman's Promised Land: Swedish Immigrant Women and American Domestic Service," Journal of American Ethnic History. VIII (Spring 1989), 9-23.

Marzolf, Marion T. "A Vital Link: The Ethnic Press in the United States, Michigan Alumnus. July/August 1986.

Matteson, Edith M. "State of the Art: The Historiography of Danish Immigration to North America,' The Immigration History Newsletter. November 1987.

Militello, Thomas E. "POINT," (Pursuing Our Italian Names Together," Rancho Verdes, California.

Nelson, Alan C. "INS Proposal for Ellis Island," INS Reporter. Spring 1986, 15-16.

Petersen, Peter L. The Danes in America. Minneapolis: Lerner Publications, 1987.

Pithcaithly, Dwight T. and Michael H. Frisch, "Audience Expectation as Resource and Challenge: Ellis Island as Case Study," in Jo Blatti. (ed.). Past Meets Present. Smithsonian Institution, 1987.

Rich, J. C. "David Dubinsky: The Young Years," Labor History. Spring 1968, 5-13.

Senn, Alfred Erick and Alfonsas Edintas. "Lithuanian Immigrants in America and the Lithuanian National Movement Before 1914," Journal of American Ethnic History. Spring 1987.

"The Arab Immigrants," Aramco World Magazine. September-October 1986.

Weadick, Sarah. "With the NCWC at Ellis Island," NCWC Bulletin. Marchh 1922.

White, Jerry C. "A Statistical History of Immigration," I and N reporter. Summer 1976.

U. S. DEPARTMENT OF LABOR

List 63

LIST OR MA[NIFEST]

ALIENS arriving at a port of continental United States from a foreign port or a part of [...]

S. S. CASERTA — 3-4 Passeng[ers]

No. on List	HEAD-TAX STATUS (This column for use of Government officials only.)	NAME IN FULL — Family name	NAME IN FULL — Given name	Age — Yrs. Mos.	Sex	Married or Single	Calling or occupation	Able to read	
	P-1205-81 6/24/38	3:5938 10/27							
1		Testi...ano	Grazia	35	f	M	H/wife	yes	Itali...
2	USCit son	"	Paolo	8	m	S	none	no	"
3	USCit "	"	Turo	8	m	S	"	"	"
4	USCit "	"	Dario	10	m	S	"	"	"
5		Di Stefano	Desiderio	41	m	M	labeure	yes	4 4
6	wife		Nataliana	48	f	M	H.Wife	"	4 6
7	UNDER 16 daughter		Iolanda	15	f	S	"	"	
8	UNDER 16 "		Fernanda	12	f	S	none	no	"
9	UNDER 1 son		Fausto	9	m	S	"	"	"
10	UNDER 1 "		Alfredo	6	m	S	"	"	"
11	UNDER 16 "		Aldo	8	m	S	"	"	"
12		Santoro	Orsola	32	f	M	H.Wife	"	
13	UNDER 16 daughter		Anella	6	f	S	none	"	"
14		Capezzi	Rosa	18	f	S	H.Wife	"	
15	UNDER 16 sister		Lucia	14	f	S	"	"	
16	UNDER 16 brother		Pietro	9	m	S	none	no	"
17	sister		Anna	6	f	S	"	"	"
	brother		Giuseppe	17	m	S	labeure		